Naturalizations
of
Washington County Maryland

Prior to 1880

Marsha Lynne Fuller, CGRS

HERITAGE BOOKS
2010

HERITAGE BOOKS
AN IMPRINT OF HERITAGE BOOKS, INC.

Books, CDs, and more—Worldwide

For our listing of thousands of titles see our website
at
www.HeritageBooks.com

Published 2010 by
HERITAGE BOOKS, INC.
Publishing Division
100 Railroad Ave. #104
Westminster, Maryland 21157

Copyright © 1997 Marsha Lynne Fuller

Originally published in 1998 by Desert Sheik Press

Other Heritage Books by the author:

African American Manumissions of Washington County, Maryland

Family Bible Records in the Washington County Free Library, Hagerstown, Maryland

St. Mary's Catholic Church Records: 1818–1900, Hagerstown, Washington County, Maryland

All rights reserved. No part of this book may be reproduced or transmitted in any form or by any means, electronic or mechanical, including photocopying, recording or by any information storage and retrieval system without written permission from the author, except for the inclusion of brief quotations in a review.

International Standard Book Numbers
Paperbound: 978-1-58549-740-9
Clothbound: 978-0-7884-8412-4

*This book is dedicated to
my brother,*

   *Clayton Scott Fuller*

- the kindest person I have ever known

Acknowledgments

My grateful thanks to the following people who helped to make this book possible:

Nedra Dickman Brill, Certified Genealogist, Portland, Oregon

Kevin N. Dye, Technical Consultant, San Jose, California

John Frye, Director, Western Maryland Room, Washington County Free Library, Hagerstown, Maryland

Rick L. Hemphill, Administrative Officer/Deputy Clerk of the Circuit Court of Washington County, Maryland

Patricia Nowell Holland, Sharpsburg, Maryland

Kathleen Mary O'Connell, Assistant Director, Washington County Free Library, Hagerstown, Maryland

Ramona Powers, Hagerstown, Maryland

Table of Contents

I. Citizens by Ceremony: The Naturalization Process

II. How to Use This Book

III. Appendix

    A - Washington County Court Minutes

    B - Naturalization Laws

    C - Existing Washington County Court Records

    D - Hagerstown Newspaper Articles

IV. Naturalization Records of Washington County

V. Index of Witnesses and Report Locations

Citizens by Ceremony:
The Naturalization Process

Coming to America...how joyous and frightening that thought must have been for Europeans in the 18th and 19th centuries. To start a new life...in a land where everyone was free and everyone was equal. To believe in a dream!

The Germans fleeing despotic rulers, the French fleeing the Napoleonic wars, the Scotch fleeing the land clearances, and the Irish fleeing British rule and the potato famine...all were coming to America to believe in a dream. All of them were searching for a new way of life and for land of their own. Some were bringing their families, some were coming alone, but all, no doubt, were coming with the prayers of the friends they left behind.

They worked long and hard, saving and selling everything they owned for passage money. Some couldn't manage the fare and had to indenture themselves to work for a number of years after their arrival. Many of them died on the voyage. Sometimes it seems a miracle that anyone at all was left alive to land on American soil. But some did survive, and they prospered!

Unless you are a Native American Indian, you are descended from immigrants who came into this country sometime in the last three centuries. We are a nation of immigrants - the melting pot of the world. Never in history has there been such a heterogeneous people as ours. To use the term "All-American" is to embrace the concept of "a little bit of everything works quite well."

In countries with homogeneous populations, such as China, there is much less strife; people are in agreement because they look at things the same way. Our strength is in our variety. While other "purebred" countries may snub their nose at our feisty, argumentative style in resolving difficulties and in determining policy, *this is our strength.* We know that someone, somewhere, has faced the problem before and has

Naturalizations of Washington County

developed a solution to it. This is what has made America the greatest country on earth: our ability to bring a hundred different viewpoints and insights to a situation; to keep working on a problem until the *majority* of people are satisfied with it; to resolve the conflict until we are stronger than we were before it happened.

Yes, we fight. We fought to wrest this country away from King George III of England. And, later, thousands of English poured into America to make it their new home.

Yes, we fight. We fought the Civil War against our brothers to provide freedom for African immigrants who came to these shores unwillingly, and we were enriched by their diversity.

Yes, we fight. We fought World War II to save a people from extinction, and were rewarded when thousands of Germans and Jews flooded into this country and provided America with the know-how to push into space and land the first man on the moon.

We have fought long and hard to preserve the contributions of all of our citizens. Is it any wonder that we cherish our diversity? It has expanded our borders from sea to shining sea, and embraced all those within. On the following pages, you will find the stories of people who started out in many different parts of the world, but came together to form the United States of America.

The Naturalization Process

At the time of the Revolutionary War, everyone was considered, *de facto*, an American citizen. In 1790, the relatively new American government, wishing to bind her new people to her, decided that some form of oath and loyalty was necessary. On March 26, 1790, it enacted the first naturalization law, "An act to establish an uniform rule of naturalization." The first naturalization in Washington County occurred three years later

Maryland, Prior to 1880

when Dennis Cahill went through the naturalization process, including the professing of his belief in the Christian religion. Becoming an American citizen was highly desirable for a new immigrant. It gave him, among other things, a sense of belonging, a standing in the community, a strong claim to his property, and the right to vote. In addition, for Civil War veterans, naturalization provided access to pensions.

The naturalization ceremony was not only important to the immigrant, but was also considered prestigious for the Clerk of the Court who performed it. Even in the 1900's, I am told, the honor of conducting the naturalization process was not given to the Deputy Clerks, but was reserved for the Clerk of the Court.

The naturalization process worked like this: an immigrant appeared in court and gave his "Report;" where he would tell the Court about his nation of birth and former allegiance to the government of his homeland. Other information was generally asked, such as birth date and birth place, departure place and date, port of arrival and date of arrival. Every immigrant was asked to take an oath on "The Holy Evangely of Almighty God" that it was his true intention to become an American citizen and to serve his new country well. If someone had arrived in America as a minor child, he would be naturalized on the spot. Those arriving as adults, as most immigrants had, would have to appear in court to give the Report and then wait several years before returning for a second court appearance to be officially naturalized as a citizen of the United States.

Naturalizations in the 1790's listed the profession of the immigrant. There were weavers, taylors and millwrights moving into the county. And, surprisingly, people in the 19th century moved around a great deal more than we suppose. William Thompson originally immigrated to York, Pennsylvania with his parents. He subsequently lived in Frederick, Maryland for four years and Washington, DC for three years, before being naturalized in Hagerstown. Patrick Murphy, naturalized in 1874, made his report in northern California before coming to Washington County.

Naturalizations of Washington County

As a professional genealogist, I know how important these naturalization records can be to the family researcher. These treasured records contain facts about our immigrant ancestors such as age, place of birth and ports of departure and arrival. We can also learn the names of friends who stood up as witnesses for them during the naturalization proceedings, attesting to their good character and earnest desire to become loyal citizens of the United States.

Methodology

To copy these naturalization records, I worked long hours in the cold, dank basement of the Washington County Courthouse. The records are very dusty and the high stools uncomfortable. I doubt that anyone has touched these old books in years.

It did awe me to know that I was actually holding 200-year-old records. They are made of beautiful old paper and written in faded brown ink. One early book is actually covered in a newspaper that was printed in 1779.

To obtain the information listed here, I read through all the Washington County Court Minutes and Proceedings that were available at the courthouse, page by page. I did not depend on the card index, prepared in 1994, that is located in a metal box near the court books in the basement.

Due to the Washington County Courthouse fire of 1871, some court records are missing. In such cases, I turned to the *Naturalization Book 1798-1860*, a chronological list of all who were naturalized in Washington County. The listings in it give each immigrant's name, the date of the Report and the date of the Naturalization. If such information came solely from the *Naturalization Book 1798-1860*, I have added the abbreviation "IN" in the Page Number column. (Please note: there are two indexes in the basement of the courthouse - *Naturalization Book 1798-1860*, a chronological index, and *Index to Naturalization Book 1798-1860*, an alphabetical index. The book I used for this was the chronological index.)

German Bibles.

P. BLOOD respectfully informs the public, that he has received an invoice of most *Splendid GERMAN FAMILY BIBLES*, superior to any edition ever before offered for sale in the United States. As he has had so many applications for them, and has hitherto been unable to supply them, he particularly invites the attention of all who are yet in need of a copy, to embrace this opportunity of procuring them, as another so favorable may not soon occur. Immediate application will be absolutely necessary to obtain Bibles of this invoice. Also, received

Ship Hersteller from Amsterdam.

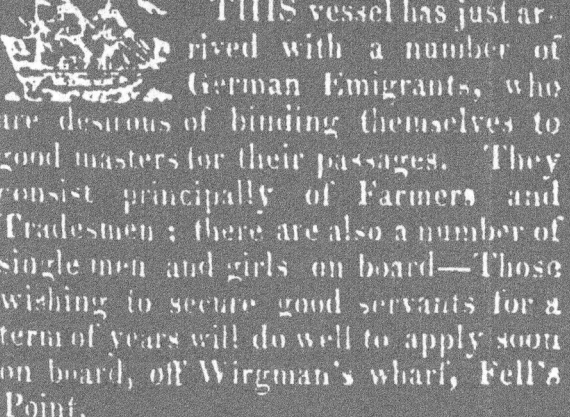

THIS vessel has just arrived with a number of German Emigrants, who are desirous of binding themselves to good masters for their passages. They consist principally of Farmers and Tradesmen; there are also a number of single men and girls on board—Those wishing to secure good servants for a term of years will do well to apply soon on board, off Wirgman's wharf, Fell's Point.

Baltimore, October 2.

According to the several enumerations of the inhabitants of various districts of the United States, the population of this country exceeds all the estimates heretofore published on the subject. Some persons may say the amazing increase in particular places, is owing in a great degree to emigrations. Grant this to be the case, where is the spot in those states which have furnished the largest number of emigrants, that has not made advances in its population. The fact is, that this country is advancing to the sovereignty of the globe with a rapidity that baffles all calculation.

There is a profession, which it has become a good deal fashionable to rail against, to whom civil society is under no small obligations, both on account of their public spirit, and as assertors of the rights of freemen—I mean lawyers. It is said the present glorious revolution of France owes its rise in a great measure to the gentlemen of the bar—and in our own country they have always borne a conspicuous part in the council, and in the field. (*Penns. Mercury.*)

Maryland, Prior to 1880

In cases where the court records no longer survive, the indexes are the only records which are now in existence. Thus, even though they provide nothing more than the immigrant's name and dates of Report and Naturalization, they at least place the immigrant ancestor in a certain place at a certain time.

You will notice that the Clerks of the Court made many misspellings of the names of places throughout the records. I have reproduced them exactly as they are written in the court records. It may take some effort on the researcher's part to discern the true place of birth for the immigrant.

I would encourage everyone to check *every possible* spelling of their ancestor's names in this book, particularly the first letter of the last name. In many cases, it was truly impossible for me to tell how the name was spelled. The handwriting of the clerk was often difficult to read, and the spelling prowess of the clerks was not legendary, in any event. In some cases, the immigrant's name was actually spelled differently two or more times *in the same report*. If the immigrant signed his report, and if his signature was legible, I used his spelling. If not, I used the clerk's spelling.

It is important to remember that many European names were changed to American ones (Anglicized) either by the family or by the Clerk of the Court and thus, may have been spelled any number of ways. Also, an immigrant may have changed the spelling of his name some years after his naturalization, so that the name being used by this family in 1997 may not be the same as the one being used in 1797.

The only information that I did not copy from the naturalization records was the name of the king or ruler that the immigrant formerly owed allegiance to, unless it seemed somewhat unusual. There did not seem to be any use for this information. In addition, I did not list oaths given at a third court appearance. This happened infrequently and, as far as I can tell, did not appear to offer any additional information.

Naturalizations of Washington County

Please note: I have copied all the available information from the Washington County Court records. When a column for any listing in this book is empty, it means that there was no information for this column in the original court records.

The Index appearing at the back of this book uses names of immigrants instead of page numbers. This will enable the reader to immediately locate a name instead of scanning an entire page for it. I did not use middle initials or middle names in the index entries; if the person you are searching for was named "John Peter Weber," you should check the listings under "Weber, John."

I hope that this book proves useful to everyone. If you do find a mistake in this book, please notify me by writing to the publisher; I will not be offended. I know well that no work is perfect. My only wish is to make this as correct and complete a record as possible of the naturalizations of Washington County, Maryland. Your help will make future editions more accurate and will assist others who are doing similar research.

Researching Your Ancestor

I would encourage anyone who is researching an ancestor listed in this book to send for a photocopy of his or her report record and naturalization record. (Prior to 1853, the original signatures of your ancestor may appear in the court record.) I suggest that you do this because you may interpret the spellings of the names differently than I did, or you may find that I inadvertently omitted information. As with all things in life, perfection is not possible.

When requesting photocopies, specify the month and year of the court session you are requesting, along with the page number listed with each name. Photocopies are 50¢ per page, with a $2.50 minimum for processing an order. The address is:

> Clerk of the Circuit Court
> Washington County Courthouse
> Hagerstown, MD 21740

and ——————
order has put the whole kingdom into a g———
The Commanders in chief of the army and navy at New-York, it is said, do not draw well together, which is the reason of Admiral Arbuthnot going over to relieve the latter.

A letter from Paris says, that 17 men of war are put on cruises from Brest alone, 11 of them frigates, and six of the line.

Dr. Franklin is appointed by Congress sole Minister Plenipotentiary to the Court of France from the United States of America, and the Commission is arrived with the despatch which supersedes the two Commissions of Adams and Lee, neither of whom are well pleased at this event.

Letters from Lisbon bring advice, that several Portuguese men of war have orders to put to sea the 18th inst. in order to clear their coasts of the American privateers, which have greatly obstructed their trade.

This afternoon was brought in here by the Active privateer, Capt. Boom, of this port,————————

many others, for all our vessels are taken. In spite of our withes to depart, we can't fix a time from the fear of being taken, the great scarcity of money, the impossibility of selling our sugars, &c. &c. The war occasions here a dismal cloud. The court seems to have totally abandoned this noble colony, for there arrives here not one vessel; they are all taken by the English. We conclude for want of convoy. We are on the point of wanting flour; no flight affair. Wine one may do without, but bread hardly. It now sells 30 sous (ten-pence) a pound; in two days it will be at 54, and in less than a fortnight there will be none to be had—unless possibly by force of money, from some barrel which has been concealed; as last war, when a loaf of two pounds cost 15 livres (8s. 6d.) and so detestable, one ——— It begins already to be bad, which occasions ———————— We have no news from ——————— will easily believe, as no vessels arrive, ——— which prizes no, which would excite

The SECOND BATTALION *of* MARYLAND MILITIA, *met at the Head of Elk, on Monday the 21st day of June,* 1779. *agreeable to Law —*

BEING deeply impressed with the growing Evils that threaten not only this State, but the United States in general, from the exorbitant prices of every necessary of life, the venal practices of monopoly, engrossing, and forestalling, which have depreciated our Currency, and counteracted every virtuous measure adopted by our most worthy citizens, in direct violation of the laws of the State—wishing, as much as possible, to coincide with our brethren in the neighbouring States, in restoring the Credit of our Currency, &c.

And as we trust the constitution and the laws of the State are very sufficient (if properly executed) or if not, we look on it as the only safe way of remedy to remonstrate and petition to our Legislature, in a constitutional way, for such amendments as from time to time may be thought necessary.

We therefore bind ourselves to each other, under the strictest ties of virtue and honour, that we will invariably support the Civil Authority in the execution of the laws, that they may be duly executed by the proper Officers, as appointed by law; nor shall any man, or set of men, usurp the power of legislation, or presume to execute the laws, but such as have authority by the Constitution, and from the Legislature of the State; that we will use our utmost endeavours to prevent all monopolizing, engrossing, and forestalling, of every sort whatsoever, and will present all persons guilty of any of them to the executive power. We earnestly recommend it to the Magistrates, Grand Jurors, and all other persons in authority, to exert themselves, at this crisis, informing against, and prosecuting all such persons as may be so lost to virtue as to attempt to prey on their brethren, the honest citizens; and we pledge ourselves that we will, by the strict ties aforesaid, support them in the same. And we earnestly entreat all traders, merchants, farmers, mechanics, and others, to conform to the laws of the State; to sympathize with and contribute to the relief and necessities of their distressed brethren; and we do caution all traders in goods of every sort, to conform to the regulations as directed by the acts of Assembly, as we hold ourselves bound, they must answer for the contrary to the penal Laws of the State.

The above being unanimously agreed to by the Battalion, was ordered immediately to be made public, that all persons concerned may govern themselves accordingly.

Signed, by desire of the Battalion,
H. HOLLINGSWORTH, Col.

IT ordered, that all absent Officers that join their respective corps immediately, Major-General Baron De Kalb, therefore, most seriously recommends the strictest and speediest compliance with his Excellency's Order, to all Officers belonging to the Maryland line, who are absent on furlough, or on their own private business; those only excepted who are on the recruiting or any other actual public service.

By Command of Maj. Gen. BARON DE KALB,
SAM KING, A-d-d-Camp.

THREE HUNDRED DOLLARS REWARD.
Baltimore-Town, June 28, 1779.

STRAYED, or stolen, last Thursday night, out of the pasture of the Subscriber, a likely Bay GELDING, 14 hands 3 inches high, 10 years old, paces, trots, and canters well, has a small star in his forehead, and one hind foot white.—Whoever takes up said Gelding, and secures him, so that I may get him again, shall have One Hundred Dollars Reward; and if stolen, the above Reward for the Thief and Horse.
GEORGE M'CANDLESS.

Maryland, Prior to 1880

For those of you who are fortunate enough to visit the courthouse in Hagerstown yourself on a research trip: to find the Report and Naturalization records, you need to look in the small (8 1/2 x 11") books entitled "Court Minutes and Proceedings" which are stored inside the larger, tan, clothbound books with the month and years of the court term printed on the front, up until the end of 1844. From 1845 onward, such records are in the hardbound main court record books and both sessions for that year are in the same book. Thus, there may be several pages labeled "Page 1" within each book because the two or three court sessions held in that year are numbered as if they were in separate books.

Naturalization records are available in the Washington County Courthouse for dates after 1880. I hope to abstract them at a later date.

The Washington County Historical Society Library has a list of Washington County immigrants who took the Oath of Allegiance and Fidelity to the State of Maryland in 1778. The same list is also published in *Revolutionary Records of Maryland* by Gaius Marcus Brumbaugh and Margaret Roberts Hodges (1967, Genealogical Publishing Company, Baltimore), available at the Washington County Free Library.

Washington County Court

Washington County was originally formed on July 1, 1776 as part of the Royal Colony of Maryland. The first Washington County Court session was held on that day. This was prior to the signing of the Declaration of Independence, on July 4th, when Maryland was made a state. Several months later, on September 6, 1776, Washington County was officially formed from Frederick County.

The Circuit Court is the direct descendant of the British Admiralty Court. It is the oldest governmental agency in Washington County and was formed on the day of the founding of the county. Washington County was on the 5th Judicial

Naturalizations of Washington County

Circuit and court sessions were conducted by a judge who traveled from town to town, known as a circuit rider.

The first term of court (longer than a one-day session) in Washington County was held in March 1777. It would appear from the records that Washington County Court terms were held three times per year in the 1700's and twice per year during the 1800's.

Elie Williams was the first Clerk of the Court from 1777 to 1800. He was the brother of Revolutionary War General Otho Holland Williams, who founded Williamsport. Elie's son, Otho Holland Williams, II, was Clerk from 1800 - 1845. Then Isaac Nesbitt took over at the beginning of 1845 and continued until 1865. He was followed by Lewis B. Nyman, 1865-67, William Kepler, 1867-1873, and George B. Oswald, 1873-1908.

Originally, under the Constitution of Maryland, the Clerk was the only one empowered to collect fees. He retained the fees himself and used them for the operation of the office. The Clerk could also appoint such deputies as he saw fit, paying their salaries out of the fee monies. In 1851, there was a change in the Maryland Constitution, and the Clerk no longer kept the money; the fees collected were now used specifically to run the office and to pay personnel. This continued until 1986, when tax dollars were used for the first time to run the office.

Immigrants at Work in Washington County

Immigrants from all countries have poured into Washington County, and we are the richer for it. If you open up a Washington County telephone directory of 1997, you will find many of the same names that you find in the following pages of this book - descendants of the immigrants who braved the rigors of an ocean voyage and the loss of their family and friends in Europe. These new immigrants quickly became prominent members of Washington County society and business.

Der Volksfreund und Hägerstauner Calender,

Auf das Jahr unsers Heilandes Jesu Christi

1832,

John Gruber

Welches ein Schalt-Jahr von 366 Tagen ist.

Darinnen, nebst richtiger Festrechnung, die Sonn- und Monds-Finsternisse, des Monds Gestalt und Viertel, Monds Auf- und Untergang, Monds Zeichen, Aspecten der Planeten und Witterung, Sonnen Auf- und Untergang, des Siebengestirns Aufgang, Südplatz und Untergang, Venus Auf- und Untergang, Jupiters Auf- und Untergang, Sirius Auf- und Untergang, Uhr-Tafel, hoch Wasser zu Philadelphia, Courten, und andere zu einem Calender gehörige Sachen zu finden.

Nach dem Maryländischen Horizont mit Fleiß berechnet, von Carl F. Egelmann, jedoch in den angrenzenden und übrigen Staaten ohne merklichen Unterschied zu gebrauchen.

Zum fünf und dreyßigstenmal herausgegeben.

Hägerstaun, (Maryland), gedruckt und zu haben bey Johann Gruber.
Wo auch Englische Calender (nach dem deutschen Plan) zu haben sind.

The American Farmers' Almanac, Hagerstown, Maryland

GRUBER AND MAY'S
BY INDUSTRY WE THRIVE

American Farmers' ALMANAC,

FOR THE YEAR OF OUR LORD
1828.

HAGERS-TOWN, Md.
PRINTED BY GRUBER AND MAY.

The American Farmers' Almanac, Hagerstown, Maryland

Maryland, Prior to 1880

As the descendant of German and Scotch-Irish immigrants, I feel great pride at the accomplishments and contributions they made to Western Maryland. Among other things, they created publications of note, and built an important trade route, the Chesapeake and Ohio Canal, which connected Washington, DC with Cumberland, Maryland.

Due to the tremendous influx of Germans into Washington County, there were many publications printed in German. Among these was John Gruber's "The Farmer's Almanac," published in German and in English, the first farmer's almanac ever printed in the United States

Without immigrants, the C & O Canal could never have been built. Western Maryland was primarily a farming area, with little skilled labor. Stone cutters, masons, carpenters and laborers were solicited from Europe and brought in as indentured labor to construct the canal. The advertisements circulated in Europe promised meat three times a day, plenty of bread, vegetables and liquor, and ten or twelve dollars a month in wages. [MS. Letter Book, Chesapeake and Ohio Canal Company, 1828-1832, 39]

The Civil War

The Battle of Antietam at Sharpsburg, in Washington County, on September 17, 1862, was the defining moment of the Civil War. It was the bloodiest single day of battle of the war, with over 23,000 soldiers lying dead or wounded at day's end. This event changed the entire course of the war. From this point on, the Union was clearly in a winning position. Issuance of the Emancipation Proclamation paved the way for European countries to provide aid and support to the North. (Europe did not believe in slavery and would not support the South in its pro-slavery stance.)

Several of the immigrants listed in this book fought in the Civil War and were, no doubt, in the Battle of Antietam. See the Index under "Civil War" to view these listings.

Naturalizations of Washington County

Washington County, Maryland

Washington County, formed in 1776, sits on the crossroads of two major travel routes, the National Road (present-day U.S. Rt. 40) running east- west, and the route from Pennsylvania to the Shenandoah Valley, Virginia running north-south. There is no doubt that John Gruber's *Farmers Almanac* was carried by many pioneers as they made their way west on the National Road.

Hagerstown, the county seat, was originally named for the founder, Jonathan Hager's, wife, Elizabeth, and was incorporated in 1791. On January 26, 1814, the Maryland Legislature passed an act "to alter and change the name of Elizabeth Town, in Washington County, to Hager's Town, and to incorporate the same." At some point in the 1800's, the name evolved into the present-day Hagerstown.

The first courthouse for Washington County, built sometime in the late 1700's, sat in the public square of Hagerstown. This put it right in the middle of the National Road, the main transportation artery of the nation at that time. We have this description of the building from *History of Western Maryland*, J. Thomas Scharf, 1882, Philadelphia: Louis H. Everts, "The courtroom was on the second floor, and was reached by a flight of steps on the outside...The windows on one side of the courthouse were protected with wire from random balls, there being a public alley for ball playing on that side of the building. The lower story was open and was used as a market house."

In *The First Two Centuries of the Washington County Courthouse* by The Commissioners of Washington County (1974, Hagerstown, Maryland) we find that "While workmen were digging in the Public Square on January 29, 1974, they found what appeared to be the foundation of the first Hagerstown Courthouse and marketplace."

This courthouse stood until the early 1800's when it was decided that it was time to build a new one. Samuel Ringgold and William Gabby were among the commissioners appointed by the Maryland General Assembly to select and purchase a lot for the

Maryland, Prior to 1880

new courthouse. At this time, Ringgold was also serving as a Congressman in Washington, DC. It was there, no doubt, that he met the famous architect of the White House, Benjamin Henry Latrobe, who was subsequently commissioned to draw up the plans for the new courthouse in Hagerstown. It was completed in 1822.

This building was used until a fire destroyed it on the night of December 5, 1871. Luckily, the court books, along with many other records, were stored in the fire vault and were saved. These records were then temporarily stored in townspeople's homes and attics until the completion of the third courthouse a year later.

The town of Williamsport, in southern Washington County, was founded in 1787 and named for General Otho Holland Williams, an officer on the staff of General George Washington. General Williams initially proposed to George Washington that Williamsport become the national capital,[1] but the plan had to be abandoned when it was discovered that the Potomac River was not navigable to sea vessels at this point. *The First Two Centuries of the Washington County Courthouse* tells us that, though Williamsport did not become the national capital, it prospered through another project backed by George Washington - the Potomac Company and later by its successor, the Chesapeake and Ohio Canal Company. The Canal was begun in 1828 and completely finished in 1850 from Georgetown to Cumberland. "For nearly one hundred years, until 1924, the canal brought progress and prosperity, recognition and importance to the little historic community of Williamsport - almost the nation's capital."

> ☞ The Lutheran Church will be open on next Lord's Day. The service in the morning will be in the German Language, and at candle light in the English Language.

---

[1] Letter from Otho Holland Williams to George Washington, dated November 1, 1790

Naturalizations of Washington County
How To Use This Book

Each entry begins with an immigrant's last name, followed by his first name, and contains all known naturalization information pertaining to that person.

Column headings indicate the following:

Last Name	Immigrant's last (or surname) name
First Name	Immigrant's first (or Christian) name
Place of Birth	Place of birth of immigrant
Age	Age of immigrant at time of Report
Birth Date	Date of Birth of immigrant
Report Date	Date that immigrant made his Report in Court
Natural. Date	Date that immigrant was granted Naturalization (citizenship) by the Washington County Court
Sig.	An "s" means that the immigrant was able to sign his name. An "x" means that he could only make an X for his mark.
Page No.	Page number in the Court Minutes and Proceedings where this entry is located.
Departure Port	Port where immigrant sailed out of Europe
Arrival Port	Port in American where immigrant landed
Other	Any notations that don't fit in other columns
Departure Date	Date that immigrant sailed out of Europe
Arrival Date	Date that immigrant landed in America
Witness	Person who "stood up" for immigrant at the naturalization ceremony, attesting to his good character
Witness	2nd Witness, if there was one

Maryland, Prior to 1880

The Hagerstown Mail   January 31, 1834

War on the Canal

The Williamsport Banner, of Saturday, gives the following particulars of the affray, among the workmen on the Canal, noticed in our last:

If we learn aright, there are two national parties among them, composed respectively of those from the North and those from the South of Ireland. The former are designated the *Fardouns* and *Longfords*; the latter, *Corkonians*. Their antipathies are, we understand, of ancient origin, probably growing out of the measure of the union with the British Crown. Be this as it may, these parties have assumed a hostile attitude on the Canal. -- The first demonstration by numbers and arms was made early on Monday morning last, about five or six miles below this place, in which the *Fardouns*, if we have been correctly informed, were the attacking party. The forces consisted, as accounts variously state, from one hundred to two hundred men, some of whom were armed with fire arms. The onset was fierce, and the first accounts received, much exaggerated of course, excited great alarm among the friends of the work and the citizens generally. The party attacked were engaged on the work at the time the assault was made, having no warning of the approach of the enemy till the latter was upon them. They were routed and dispersed, four or five were badly bruised and wounded, one man escaped by swimming the river, though unusually high and rapid, to the opposite shore. The victorious party was left in possession of the field. A company of mounted citizens, in aid of the civil authority, repaired to the scene of action, and apprehended about fifty persons supposed to be engaged in the affray. They were brought to this place, examined by *C. Hesletine*, Esq. and thirty-five of them regularly committed. These were conducted to prison, in Hagers Town, on the following day, under guard of the two Hagers-town volunteer companies, Captains, *Artz* and *Robertson*, upon whom a requisition had been made early on Monday, and who instantly and gallantly obeyed the call and marched to this place to render such service as should be required.

The cause of the above battle was, a beating received by one man, a *Fardoun*, on the Thursday previous, from some of the opposing party, on the section attacked. This individual, named John Irons, has since died of the wounds received, and an inquest been held over the body - the verdict, "he came to his death from blows received on several parts of his body and head, from persons unknown."

Naturalizations of Washington County

No injury was done to the work, with the exception of the partial destruction of one or two shantees. Nor was there any other cause, than the one here given, of the disturbance.

Since the foregoing event, great commotion has existed among the hands. Very little work has been done, and a state of alarm and warlike preparation has taken its place. On Thursday last, we are informed, a party of *Corkonians* committed excesses along the line above this place. Yesterday morning a small party were seen approaching this place from above, and were met on the Aqueduct and driven back by an opposing party of their countrymen in the town. In this affray one man was very seriously beaten and wounded. The citizens of the town, with commendable alacrity, soon put themselves in military order, under arms for the protection of the peace of the place, and remained under arms for the balance of the day, and the greater part of the night.

This scene was soon followed by another which resulted in a disastrous battle and several deaths. A party of *Fardouns* or *Longfords*, consisting of about three hundred men, headed by intrepid leaders, were announced as approaching from below. Their design they stated to be, to pass up the line of the Canal to the upper dam, for the purpose of exhibiting their strength, and not to commit a breach of the peace unless attacked. They were armed in part with guns; but principally with helves, clubs, &c. They passed up quietly over the Aqueduct, and on their way, as we learn, three or four hundred more of the same party fell into their ranks. At the upper dam, in a field on the other side of Middlekauff's they met the enemy in battle array, drawn up on the top of a hill, about three hundred in number, and armed, in part, with military weapons. The information we have is, that the attack or at least a challenge to the combat, was made by the latter party. Volleys of shot were exchanged; some men were seen to fall, and the party above began to fall back and disperse before the superior forces of their enemy. A pursuit ensued through the woods, where frequent firing was heard, and no doubt many lives were taken. Persons who traversed the field after the battle was over observed five men in the agonies of death, who had been shot through the head, several dead bodies were seen in the woods, and a number wounded in every direction. Those who observed the battle described it as one of great rage and most deadly violence. All the dead and wounded are reported to have been of the *Corkonians*.

Postscript. -- Since writing the above, a principal leader of one of the parties has been arrested for examination. The volunteer companies have arrived from Hagers-town, commanded by Col. Wm. H. Fitzhugh, who is also Sheriff of the county, and are now in readiness

Maryland, Prior to 1880

to act in aid of the civil authority. An express has been despatched to the seat of government for a sufficient regular force to be sent on and stationed here or at other suitable points along the line of the Canal, to preserve order among the laborers, and for purposes of general protection.

On Monday a meeting was held at Williamsport, for the purpose of adjusting the difficulties between the contending parties, which resulted in concluding a treaty of peace. We have not room for it this week.

On Tuesday intelligence was received that a force of several hundred men, Corkonians, had passed Harpers' Ferry on their way up the Canal, to assist their friends at Middlekauff's dam -- they were met at Hollman's dam, and made acquainted with the terms of the treaty, whereupon they gave up their arms, and returned to their work.

Peace and quiet appears to be restored.

The Hagerstown Mail   **January 31, 1834**

Proceedings of a Meeting held in Williams-Port.
January 27th, 1834

On motion of Col. J.R. Dail - General O.H. Williams was called to the Chair, and *Thomas F. Purcell* was chosen Secretary.

The Chairman then addressed the Irish Deputies from the Cork and Longford parties. He stated the object of the meeting, and urged on the parties concerned, the necessity of a speedy and complete reconciliation of the difficulties and disagreements that led to the late riotous proceedings on the Canal.

The Secretary then prepared a paper in the form of an agreement, the object of which is not only to remove the misunderstandings that have already occurred, but to prevent like results in future; to this was attached a recognizance to keep the peace. This agreement was then signed by the deputies from each party.

On motion of Wm. D. Bell, Esq. - it was Resolved - That a written copy of the articles of agreement be furnished forthwith to each party thereto.

On motion of Mr. Warfield - it was Resolved - That 200 copies of the foregoing agreement be printed for distribution on the line of Canal.

It was further Resolved - That the proceedings of this meeting be published in the public prints of the county.

Gen. O.H. Williams again addressed the Irish deputies. He explained to them the solemnity of the obligation they had just executed in the presence of the Magistrates; the necessity of their

Naturalizations of Washington County

preserving inviolate the pledge they had thus entered into - and at the same time he apprised them, that in case the agreement was violated, it was the determination of the citizens and the military to unite with the opposite side, and drive entirely from the county, the party who were guilty of the infraction.

On motion, the meeting then adjourned.

The above is a correct sketch of the proceedings. Thos. F. Purcell, Sec'ry.

The Agreement

Whereas great commotions and divers rigorous acts have resulted from certain misunderstandings, and alledged grievances, mutually urged by two parties of labourers and mechanics engaged on the line of the Chesapeake and Ohio Canal, and natives of Ireland; the one commonly known as the Longford men, the other as the Corkontans; and whereas it has been found that these riotous acts are calculated to disturb the public peace, without being in the least degree beneficial to the parties opposed to each other, but on the contrary is productive of great injury and distress to the workmen and their families.

Therefore, we the undersigned, representative of each party, have agreed, and do pledge ourselves to support and carry into effect the following terms of agreement: --

We agree for ourselves, that we will not, either individually or collectively, interrupt or suffer to be interrupted in our presence, any person engaged on the line of the Canal, for or on account of any local difference, or national prejudice, and that we will use our influence to destroy all these matters of difference growing out of this distinction of parties, known as Corkonians and Longfords; and we further agree and pledge ourselves in the most solemn manner, to inform on and bring to justice, any person, or persons, who may break the pledge contained in this agreement, either by interrupting any person passing along or near the line of Canal, or by secretly counselling, or assisting any person, or persons, who may endeavour to excite riotous conduct among the above parties; and we further bind ourselves to the State of Maryland, each in the sum of twenty dollars, to keep the peace towards each other, as well as towards the citizens of the State. In witness whereof, we have hereunto signed our names, at Williamsport, this twenty-seventh day of January, eighteen hundred and thirty-four. Timothy Kelley, William O'Brien, Michael Collins, John Barnes, Thomas Bennett, Michael Driscoll, Jeremiah Donevan, John Namack, Garret Donahue, Patrick McDonald, James Slaman, John O'Brien, Edward Farrell, Thomas Hill, Michael Tracy, Thomas McKey, James Riley, Daniel Murry, Murty Dempsey, James Carroll, Thos. Cunningham,

Maryland, Prior to 1880

Bathu. S. McMade, James Clarke, Michael Kain, Pat Purcell, William Moloney, William Brown, Peter Conner.

Signed before us two Justices of the Peace in and for Washington County and State of Maryland, this 27th day of January, 1834. Charles Hesletine, William Boullt.

The Hagerstown Mail
Vol. IX No. 4   Friday, December 11, 1840

The case of Patrick M'Laughlin vs. the Chesapeake and Ohio Canal Company, which has been going on for some days in the Circuit Court, was decided on Monday. The case was given to the Jury about 7 o'clock in the evening, and between 11 and 12 o'clock they agreed upon a verdict of damages for the plaintiff, to the amount of $3,500. The suit was brought by M'Laughlin, in consequence of damages sustained by him in the destruction of his property during the Canal riots, when his goods were used and destroyed by troops who were sent to quell the rioters and secure peace.   Balt. Rep.

- *All preceding newspaper articles were taken from microfilm at the Washington County Free Library; bound indexes also are there*

 **Appendix E**

Original Letter tucked into the Chronological Index, Naturalization Book 1798-1860, at the Washington County Courthouse

Commissioners Office   Sept. 2, 1840   To Genl. O.H. Williams
Sir   In compliance with the request of the Commissioners of Washington County, I send you the following resolutions which were passed by them on yesterday.

It being evident that frauds have been committed by one of the deputy Clerks in regard to naturalization certificates be it therefore resolved

That the Clerk of the Court Genl. O.H. Williams be requested to furnish nine certified copies of all the persons naturalized by the Court of this County since the first day of April 1839, and the sheriff be requested to deliver the same to the return Judges of the several election districts.   Very Respectfully   Your Obed Ser.
   Geo. W. Post   Clk Cos. Wash Co

- Additional information can be found in *The Hagerstown Mail*, July 10, 1840.

Maryland, Washington County, to wit:

At a County Court of the Fifth Judicial District of the State of Maryland, begun and holden at Hagerstown, in and for the County aforesaid, on the *fourth* Monday of *March*, being the *twenty sixth* day of the same month, in the year of our Lord, eighteen hundred and forty *nine*;

PRESENT:

The Hon. John ~~Buchanan, Esq. Chief Judge,~~
" Hon. ~~Thomas Buchanan,~~ } Associate Judges.
" Hon. ~~Richard H. Marshall,~~

The Hon. *Robert H. Martin, Esq. Chief Judge,*
" " *Richard H. Marshall, Associate Judge,*
" " *Daniel Weisel, Associate Judge,*
Daniel South, Esq. Shff. and Isaac Nesbitt, clerk;

In the record of proceedings of the same Court, amongst others is the following, to wit:

BE IT REMEMBERED, That now here on this *twenty sixth* day of *September*, Eighteen hundred and forty *nine*, *Henry Speaker* ———— in open Court, having made his application before the said Court, to become a citizen of the United States, and having at the same time made oath on the Holy Evangely of Almighty God, that it is his bona fide intention to become a citizen of the United States, and renounce forever, all allegiance and fidelity to any foreign Prince, Potentate, State or Sovereignty whatsoever, and particularly to the *King of Prussia*, ———— and also having made oath that he emigrated to the United States three years previous to his arriving at the age of twenty-one years; and also that it has been his intention for the last three years, to become a citizen of the United States, as required by law, establishing a uniform rule of naturalization, and prays to become a citizen of the United States; and it appearing to the satisfaction of the Court, here, on the testimony of *Dr. Samuel H. Kerch,* ———— a citizen of the United States, sworn in open Court, here, that *the said Henry Speaker hath* ———— resided five years and upwards last past, within the limits and under the jurisdiction of the United State; and also resided one year and upwards last past, within the State of Maryland, that during that time, he has behaved as a man of good moral character, attached to the principles of the Constitution of the United States, and well disposed to the good order and happiness of the same; and the said *Henry Speaker* ———— having declared on oath, that he will support the Constitution of the United States, and that he doth absolutely and entirely renounce all allegiance and fidelity to any foreign Prince, Potentate, State or Sovereignty whatsoever, and particularly to *the King of Prussia;* ———— The Court thereupon admit the said *Henry Speaker* ———— to naturalization, as a citizen of the United States.

WASHINGTON COUNTY, TO WIT:

I hereby certify that the foregoing is a correct copy, taken from the record of proceedings of the County Court aforesaid.

In Testimony Whereof, I hereunto subscribe my name and affix the seal of the said County Court, this *twenty sixth* day of *September* ———— eighteen hundred and forty *nine*. *Isaac Nesbitt, Clk.*

Western Maryland Room, Washington County Free Library

Naturalizations of Washington County, Maryland Prior to 1880

Last Name	First Name	Report Date	Departure Port	Departure Date	Witness(es)
Place of Birth	Date of Birth	Natural. Date	Arrival Port	Arrival Date	
Age		Sig. Page No.	Other		
Aap	Casper	27 Nov 1820		27 Jul 1817	
Town of Brockennaugh, Germany			Name may be Asp or Arp. Owes allegience to the Emperor of		
23		s 43	Austria.		
Abilshouser	Leanhart	20 Nov 1820		04 May 1816	
Vine/Nime, Germany					
28		s 21			
Acker	Adam	01 Oct 1850	Bremen	1840	
Bavaria			Baltimore	1840	
37		s 28			
Adam	Henry	03 Jan 1798	Living in Hagerstown.		
Prince of Hesse					
		13			
Adam	Peter	24 Aug 1844	Bremen	1841	
Coln on the Rhine, Hohenzollen			Baltimore	1841	
37	1807	s 43			
Adams	John	02 Jun 1876	Hamburg	1861	Samuel Ulrick
Wittenburg, Germany		06 Oct 1879	New York	1861	David Heller
36	1840	s 16			
Agen	John	16 Sep 1844			Robert Terry
		05 Oct 1846			
		24	Owes allegiance to Great Britain & Ireland		

Name				
Ahlborn Frederick	16 Sep 1844	Bremen	1837	George Philip Schmander
Ossenfeld, Hanover	20 Sep 1847	Baltimore	04 Dec 1837	
33 1811	s 61			
Albert Francis Joseph	16 Sep 1844	Bremen	1839	
Wurtburg, Bavaria	s 55	Baltimore	15 Nov 1839	
37 1807				
Allen John	21 Nov 1840			
	-- IN			
Altemuller Herman H.	28 Mar 1840	Bremen	1834	
West Casselin, Germany	02 Apr 1842	Baltimore	1834	
33 1807	s 21			
Anderson James	23 Nov 1831	New York	May 1824	
Cornan, Ireland	s 27		Jun 1824	
31 12 Mar 1800				
Andres Adam	08 Mar 1858	Bremen	1856	John Schleigh
Hesse Cassel	03 Oct 1861	Baltimore	18 Jun 1856	
54 1804	s 10			
Andrews Stephen	26 Sep 1844			Reuben Lighter
	123			
	Arrived as a minor. Owes allegiance to Great Britain & Ireland			
Anhalt Nicholas	22 Nov 1843			Caspar Swope
Prussia	05 Oct 1846			
	22			

Last Name / Place of Birth / Age	First Name / Date of Birth	Report Date / Natural. Date / Sig. Page No.	Departure Port / Arrival Port / Other	Departure Date / Arrival Date	Witness(es)
Anniba Amsterdam 36	William	27 Nov 1827 s 56	Amsterdam New York 12 yrs. old at arrival in U.S. Lived in New York for 11 yrs. Moved to Washington County, Maryland in 1814.	Feb 1803	Hartman Hase
Anthony Hesse Cassel	Conrad	16 Sep 1844 69	Index reads "Certificate" in Report Date column.		
Arviller Germany	William	09 Jan 1799 15	Farmer. Living in Licking Creek.		
Arnold Wirtemburgh 56	Joseph 1796	13 Oct 1852 01 Dec 1854 s 6	Havre de Grace New York	1849 Aug 1849	Gerson Levi
Arnold Wirtemburgh 21	Julius 1834	29 Nov 1855 29 Nov 1855 s 9	Havre de Grace New York Arrived as a minor.	1849 1849	Moyer Enstein
Artle County of Bishossheina, Baden 30	George	25 Mar 1822 *26 Mar 1827* s 1		26 Sep 1817	
Ash Ireland	James	*07 Nov 1811* 07 Nov 1811 39			

TO FOREIGNERS.

A last notice is hereby given to all foreigners residing in Washington county, who desire to become citizens of the United States, that they yet may be naturalized at the ensuing April court, on their bringing proof into court, to certify that they have resided in the limits and under the jurisdiction of the United States, since January 1795. Those who do not avail themselves of this notice, do wilfully exclude themselves from the rights of citizenship, for the long term of fourteen years.

—A CITIZEN.

Hagerstown Newspapers

AUGUST, 8th Month.

Weeks and Days.	Month Days, &c.	Hi. wa. h	Moon cis.&sets h. m	Moon's place. sign,de.	Remarks and miscellaneous Particulars.	SUN slow. m
Monday	1 Lammas day	8	11 56	♋ 15	☽ 1st ♀ sets 9, 0	6
Tuesday	2 Stephen	9	Morn.	♋ 29	♃ South 12, 36	6
Wednesd	3 Augustus	10	12 39	♌ 13	Sirius rises 4, 44	6
Thursday	4 Dominick	11	1 26	♌ 28	Moon in perigee 	6
Friday	5 Oswald	12	2 22	♍ 13	☍ ☊ ☉	6
Saturday	6 Annun.of Chr.	1	3 24	♍ 27	Orion rises 2, 15	6

32	10th Sunday after Trinity. Luke 19.	Days' length 13 hour

Sunday	7 Godfrey	2	SETS	♎ 12	7th ☌ sets 7, 46	6
Monday	8 Emily	2	7 41	♎ 26	☌ ☽ ♂	5
Tuesday	9 Ericus	3	8 19	♏ 10	☌ ☽ ♄	5
Wednesd	10 St. Lawrence	4	8 53	♏ 23	☌ ☽ ♀ ☍ ♃ ☉	5
Thursday	11 Titus	5	9 23	♐ 6	7* rise 10, 50	5

The American Farmers' Almanac, Hagerstown, Maryland

I Edward McCartin do hereby make the following Report of myself to the Clerk of Washington County Court agreeably to an Act of Congress, for the purpose of being naturalized. I arrived in the United States of America on the 22nd August 1818. I migrated from the County Armagh in the Kingdom of Ireland — am about the age of 22 years — have been in allegiance to the King of Great Britain & Ireland and intend settling in Washington County in the State of Maryland

25th Sept. 1820.
$1.00 (pd) (See oath 54) Edward M. Cartin

I Bernard McCormack do hereby make the following Report of myself to the Clerk of Washington County Court, agreeably to an Act of Congress for the purpose of being naturalized — I arrived in the United States of America on the about on the 25th December 1818 — I

 An Original Naturalization Certificate

Maryland, Prior to 1880
Key to Abbreviations and Definitions:

- A question mark ? indicates that I was unsure as to the spelling or the date, because the handwriting in the original court records was unclear.

- Anything in quotations marks " " is a direct and exact quotation from the court records.

- If the Report column has the word "certificate" in it, it indicates that the report was filed somewhere outside of Washington County and that the immigrant brought a certificate with him attesting to this to present to the Court.

- An italicized date in either the "Report Date" column or the "Natural. Date" column indicates that the date was not available in the existing court records. This date was listed only in the alphabetical *Index to Naturalization Book 1798-1860*. (Example: *02 Mar 1824*) An "IN" in the Page No. column indicates that the date was available only in the chronological index, *Naturalization Book 1798-1860*.

- In some naturalization records, you will see several references to the "rough bundle" in the "Other" column. This bundle of papers no longer exists as it was also lost in the Washington County Courthouse fire of 1871.

- The "Page No." column identifies the page number where the Report is located in the *Court Minutes and Proceedings* book. If the report was filed in another county or state, the page number corresponds to the Naturalization proceedings which occurred in Washington County.

- The term "Arrived as a minor" is often listed in the "Other" column. It describes someone who arrived in America while under the age of 21 years. These immigrants only had to appear once in court and were naturalized at that time.

Naturalizations of Washington County

Appendix A

Washington County Court Minutes and Proceedings Records of Naturalization Proceedings

Editor's note: This is an exact transcription of several entries in the Washington County Court Minutes and Proceedings. Unusual punctuation, phrases, and spelling have been reproduced exactly as they were written by the Clerk of the Court so many years ago.

April 1793
Dennis Cahill, a Native of Ireland came into Court and on application to be naturalized. The Oath directed to be administered by an Act entitled 'An Act for Naturalization ['] was taken and subscribed by him in open Court. And he at the same time subscribed a declaration of his belief in the Christian religion.

April 1794
Donald McPhaill a Native of Scotland came into Court and on application to be naturalized. The oath directed to be administered by an Act entitled "an Act for Naturalization" was taken and subscribed by him in open Court, And he at the same time subscribed a declaration of his belief in the Christian religion.
                        Cert. given under seal   5 p pd.

April 1797
The Reverend Mr. George Bower Native of Ireland appeared in open Court, and was naturalized under the Act of Congress entitled "an Act to establish an uniform rule of Naturalization and to repeal the Act heretofore passed on that Subject" by taking the several Oaths prescribed by the second section of the said Act; and in all thing having complied with the requisites in the said second section - The said George Bower being Resident within the limits and under the Jurisdiction of the United States at the passage of the said Act.

January 1798
Charles Seltzer of Hagers Town, Washington County Maryland a Native of Germany, and formerly a Subject of the Prince of Hess Appeared in open Court and was Naturalized under the Act of Congress entitled "An Act to Establish an Uniform Rule of Naturalization and to Repeal the Act heretofore passed on that Subject." by taking the several Oaths prescribed by the Second Section

Dennis Cahill a Native of Ireland, came into Court — and on application
to be Naturalized — — — — His Oath directed to be administered by an Act
entitled "An Act for Naturalizing persons taken and published by him &
In open Court — And he at the same time subscribed a declaration of his
belief in the Christian religion — — —

(See the minutes of the minutes for Job Simnett Esq.)

Dr. Philip Bodmann,

RESPECTFULLY offers his professional services to the inhabitants of Hagers-town and its vicinity.

His office is in the house formerly occupied by Mr. Downey, three doors below Mr. Martin Newcomer's tavern, opposite the Court house.

April 14. 25-6m.

Doctor Philipp Bodmann,

Bietet seine Dienste in der Heilkunde dem geneigten Publikum von Hägerstaun und dessen Nachbarschaft an.

Seine Office ist in dem Hause des Hrn. Samuel Downey, drey Thüren unterhalb des Hrn. Neukomer's Gasthof, und dem Courthause gegenüber, gelegen.

April 14.

THE CHOLERA.

AN ORDINANCE.

WHEREAS, at a meeting of the citizens of Hagers-town, held at the Court-house, on Saturday the 27th inst. 1833, it was " resolved, that the Moderator and Commissioners be requested to pass an Ordinance declaring it a nuisance to bring any persons within the limits of the Corporation, who have died upon the line of the Canal, or in any other infected district, without said limits"—Therefore,

Maryland, Prior to 1880

of the said Act, and in all things having complied with the Requisites in the said second Sections, The said Charles Seltzer being a Resident within the limits and under the jurisdiction of the United States at the passage of the said Act.

1799

John Peterpenner, A Shoemaker, of Boonsburg in Washington County, a German under the Emperor of Germany appeared in Open Court and declared his intention of becoming a Citizen of the United States and made oath that he has resided within the United States fifteen years and within the State of Maryland fourteen years that he will support the Constitution of the United States and that he doth absolutely and entirely renounce and objure all allegiance and fidelity to the Emperor of Germany.   15 P paid

1803

Peter Swartz, an alien makes application to become a Citizen of the United States. The Court being satisfied by the oath of Jacob Zellar, that the said Peter Swartz a native of France and formerly a subject of Louis the sixteenth King of France has resided within the United States for the Term of five years, and within the State of Maryland one year at least.

March 1808

George Michael Boyer, an alien a native of Germany makes application to the Court to become a citizen of the United States. The Court being satisfied by the Oaths of the said George M. Boyer and Lodwick Emerick, that the said George M. Boyer formerly a subject of the King of Prussia, has resided within the United States prior to the 14 April 1802 and ever since, and the two last years within the State of Maryland.

March 1853

To the Honorable the Judge of the Circuit Court for Washington County:
The undersigned begs leave to report that he was born in the County Cork, in the year 1831, and that he is now about 22 years of age, and owes allegiance to the Queen of Great Britain, that he emigrated from Liverpool in the year 1850 and arrived at New York, in October, of same year, that he now resides in Washington County, and intends residing therein. Given under his hand this 17th day of March, in the year eighteen hundred and fifty three.

       Signed   Thomas Desmond

Naturalizations of Washington County

And at the same time the said Thomas Desmond made oath on the Holy Evangely of Almighty God that it is bona fide his intention to become a citizen of the United States and to renounce forever all allegiance and fidelity to any foreign Prince, Potentate, State or Sovereignty whatsoever and particularly to the Queen of Great Britain.

1853

Lewis Deitrick, now here on the day and year aforesaid, in open Court, having made his report as above, and made his application before the said Court, to become a citizen of the United States, and having at the same time on the Holy Evangely of Almighty God, that it is bona fide his intention to become a citizen of the United States, and to renounce forever all allegiance and fidelity to any foreign Prince, Potentate, State or Sovereignty whatsoever, and particularly to the Grand Duke of Hesse Cassel, and also having made oath that he emigrated to the United States, three years previous to his arriving at the age of twenty one years, and also that it has been his intention for the last three years to become a citizen of the United States, as required by law, establishing a uniform rule of naturalization, and prays to become a citizen of the United States, and it appearing to the satisfaction of the Court here, on the testimony of Mrs. Elizabeth Deitrick, sworn in open Court here, that the said Lewis Deitrick hath resided five years and upwards last past, within the limits and under the Jurisdiction of the United States, and also resided one years and upwards, last past, within the State of Maryland, and during that time he has behaved as a man of good moral character, attached to the principles of the Constitution of the United States, and well disposed to the good order and happiness of the same, and the said Lewis Deitrick having declared on oath, that he will support the Constitution of the United States, and that he doth absolutely and entirely abjure and renounce forever all allegiance and fidelity to any foreign Prince, Potentate, State or Sovereignty whatsoever, and particularly to the Grand Duke of Hesse Cassel, the Court thereupon admit the said Lewis Deitrick to naturalization, as a citizen of the United States.

March 1853

Be it remembered, that now here on this 8th day of March in the year of our Lord Eighteen hundred and fifty three, appears here in open Court John Kolbacher, he having heretofore on the tenth day of December, 1850, declared his intention before Washington County Court, to become a citizen of the United States, and having at that time made oath on the Holy Evangely of Almighty God, that it was bona fide his intention to become a citizen of the United States and to renounce

Maryland, Prior to 1880

forever, all allegiance and fidelity to any foreign Prince, Potentate, State or Sovereignty whatsoever and particularly to the Grand Duke of Darmstadt as required by law, establishing a uniform rule of naturalization, and prays to become a citizen of the United States, and it appearing to the satisfaction of the Court here, on the testimony of Henry Freaner, a Citizen of the United States, sworn in open Court, that the said John Kolbacher hath resided five years and upwards last past, within the limits and under the Jurisdiction of the United States, and also resided one years and upwards, last past, within the State of Maryland, and during that time he has behaved as a man of good moral character, attached to the principles of the Constitution of the United States, and well disposed to the good order and happiness of the same, and the said John Kolbacher having declared on oath, that he will support the Constitution of the United States, and that he doth absolutely and entirely abjure and renounce forever all allegiance and fidelity to any foreign Prince, Potentate, State or Sovereignty whatsoever, and particularly to the Grand Duke of Darmstadt, the Court thereupon admit the said John Kolbacher to naturalization, as a citizen of the United States.

April 10, 1868
Frederick Feilman a Native of Muhlenburg appeared in open Court here, and applied to be admitted to become a Citizen of the United States under the provisions of the Act of Congress passed July 17th 1862. And it appearing to the satisfaction of the Court here that the said Frederick Feilman hath been in the Military Service of the United States and honorably discharged therefrom on the 4th day of December 1862 as appears from the Certificate in his possession and now produced to the Court Here has evidence of the fact. And it also appearing to the satisfaction of the Court here, by the testimony of John Cook that the said Frederick Feilman hath Continued to reside with the limits and under the Jurisdiction of the United States one year at least immediately preceeding this Application, and that during the said period he has Conducted himself as a man of good Moral Character attached to the principles of the Constitution of the United States and well disposed to the good order and happiness of the same, and the said Frederick Feilman, having declared on Oath taken in open Court here, that he will support the Constitution of the United States and that he doth absolutely and entirely renounce all allegiance and fidelity to every foreign Prince Potentate, State or sovereignty whatever and particularly all allegiance and fidelity to the King of Prussia of whom he was heretofore a subject. The Court here, thereupon admits the said Frederick Feilman to become a Citizen of the United States.

Naturalizations of Washington County

Appendix B

Naturalization Laws

The Laws of Maryland with The Charter, The Bill of Rights, The Constitution of the State, and Its Alterations, The Declaration of Independence, and The Constitution of the United States, and Its Amendments; with a General Index. In Three Volumes., Volume I., Revised by Virgil Maxcy, 1811, Baltimore, Published by Philip H. Nicklin & Co.

At a Session of the General Assembly of Maryland, begun and held at the City of Annapolis, on Thursday, the 22d of July, in the year of our Lord 1779, and ended the 15th day of August, the following laws were enacted. Thomas Johnson, Esq., Governor.

Chap. VI. An Act for naturalization.
Supplementary and other acts: 1789, ch. 24. November, 1792, ch. 14. 1793, ch. 26. 1797, ch. 60.

Whereas the increase of people is a means to advance the wealth and strength of this state: And whereas many foreigners, from the lenity of our government, the security afforded by our constitution and laws to civil and religious liberty, the mildness of our climate, the fertility of our soil, and the advantages of our commerce, may be induced to come and settle in this state, if they were made partakers of the advantages and privileges which the natural born subjects of this state do enjoy:

II. Be It Therefore Enacted, by the General Assembly of Maryland, That every person who shall hereafter (a) come into this state, from any nation, kingdom or state, and shall, before the governor and council, or before the general court, or any one of the judges thereof, or before any county court of this state, (b) repeat and subscribe a declaration of his belief in the christian religion, and take, repeat and subscribe, the following oath, or affirmation if a quaker, menonist or tunker, [Quaker, Mennonite or Dunkard] to wit: "I, A.B. do swear or affirm, that I will hereafter become a subject of the state of Maryland, and will be faithful and bear true allegiance to the said state, and that I do not hold myself bound to yield any allegiance or obedience to any king or prince, or any other state or government," (which said oath or affirmation, and subscription aforesaid respectively, the governor and the council, the general court, or any one judge thereof, or any county court, are hereby empowered to administer and take,) shall thereupon and thereafter be deemed, adjudged and taken, to be a natural born subject of this state, and shall be thenceforth entitled to all the immunities, rights and

Maryland, Prior to 1880

privileges, of a natural born subject of this state; provided that no person who shall become a natural born subject of this state by virtue of this act, shall be appointed to any civil office, or eligible as governor, member of the council, or general assembly, or as a delegate to congress, unless such person shall have resided within this state seven ;years previous to such election or appointment, and shall have the property and estate required by the constitution and form of government to execute any of the said offices respectively.

III. And Be It Enacted, That the clerk of the council shall, before the session of every general court, return a list of the names of the persons who shall take and subscribe the said oath or affirmation, and make the said declaration respectively, before the governor and the council, and the time when taken and made, to the clerk of the general court, to be entered by him among the minutes of the said court; and any judge of the general court, administering and taking the said oath or affirmation, shall return to the next general court a list of the names of the persons who shall take and subscribe the said oath or affirmation, and make the said declaration respectively before him, and the time when taken and made, to the clerk of the general court, to be entered by him among the minutes of the said court.

IV. And Be It Enacted, That a certificate by the clerk of the council, or by any judge of the general court, or by the clerk of the general or any county court, of any person's having taken and subscribed the said oath or affirmation, and having made and subscribed the said declaration, or a certificate by the clerk of the general court, that it appears by the return of any judge of the said court entered among the minutes, of any person's having taken and subscribed the said oath or affirmation, and ;having made and subscribed the said declaration, shall be deemed and taken to be a sufficient testimony and proof thereof, and of his being a natural born subject, and as such shall be allowed in every court of this state.

V. And, to encourage such foreigners to come and settle in this state, Be It Enacted, That no tax shall be imposed on any such foreigner coming into this state, and taking and subscribing the declaration, and oath or affirmation, aforesaid, or his property, for the term of two years after his arrival in this state.

VI. And, to encourage such foreigners, tradesmen, artificers and manufacturers, to come and settle I this state, Be It Enacted, That no tax shall be imposed on any such foreigner, being a tradesman, artificer or manufacturer, coming into this state, and taking and subscribing the declaration, and oath or affirmation aforesaid, or his property, for the term of four years after his arrival in this state. [Maryland State Law Library]

Naturalizations of Washington County
1790 Law from the Maryland State Law Library:
Chap. 30 [III.] An act to establish an uniform rule of naturalization.
[Sect. 1.] *Be it enacted by the senate and house of representatives of the United States of America in congress assembled,* That any alien, being a free white person, who shall have resided within the limits and under the jurisdiction of the United States for the term of two years, may be admitted to become a citizen thereof, on application to any common law court of record, in any one of the states wherein he shall have resided for the term of one year at least, and making proof, to the satisfaction of such court, that he is a person of good character, and taking the oath or affirmation prescribed by law, to support the constitution of the United States, which oath or affirmation such court shall administer; and the clerk of such court shall record such application, and the proceedings thereon; and thereupon such person shall be considered as a citizen of the United States. And the children of such persons so naturalized, dwelling within the United States, being under the age of twenty-one years, at the time of such naturalization, shall also be considered as citizens of the United States. And the children of citizens of the United States, that may be born beyond sea, or out of the limits of the United States, shall be considered as natural born citizens: Provided, That the right of citizenship shall not descend to persons whose fathers have never been resident in the United States: Provided also, That no person heretofore proscribed by any state, shall be admitted a citizen as aforesaid, except by an act of the legislature of the state in which such person was proscribed."   Approved March 26, 1790
[Maryland State Law Library]

**The Laws of Maryland with The Charter, The Bill of Rights, The Constitution of the State, and Its Alterations, The Declaration of Independence, and The Constitution of the United States, and Its Amendments; with a General Index. In Three Volumes., Volume II.,
Revised by Virgil Maxcy, 1811, Baltimore, Published by Philip H. Nicklin & Co.**

At a Session of the General Assembly of Maryland, begun and held at the City of Annapolis, on Monday, the 5th of November, and ended the 23d day of December, in the year of our Lord 1792, the following laws were enacted.
Thomas Sim Lee, Esq., Governor.   Chap. XIV.

Maryland, Prior to 1880

An Act for the relief of certain foreigners who have settled within this state, further supplementary to the act for naturalization. Another act, 1793, ch. 26.

Whereas the act for naturalization, passed at July session, in the year seventeen hundred and seventy-nine, declares, that every person who shall thereafter come into this state from any nation, kingdom or state, and shall repeat and subscribe a declaration of his belief in the Christian religion, and take, repeat and subscribe, the oath or affirmation in the same act prescribed, before the governor and the council, or before the general court, or any of the judges thereof, or before any county court, shall thereupon and thereafter be deemed, adjudged and taken, to be a natural born subject of this state, and shall be thenceforth entitled to all the immunities, rights and privileges, of a natural born subject of this state, subject nevertheless to the restrictions provided by the said act: And whereas, since the passage of the said act, divers foreigners have come into this state, and have settled and become inhabitants thereof, and have been induced, from the various advantages afforded by our government, climate, soil and commerce, to employ their money in the purchase of property, both real and personal, and to improve the same, thereby acquiring a just and equitable title to such property, but through ignorance of the provisions contained in the beforementioned act, or apprehending that taking and subscribing the oath of allegiance in the usual manner would entitle them to the advantages of property, the said foreigners have not taken and subscribed the oath prescribed by the act for naturalization, under the particular circumstances required by the same, whereby their titles to such real property as they have acquired since their settlement in this state may be drawn in question, to their great prejudice and injury: And whereas the said foreigners have always manifested a firm attachment to our government and laws, and it is conceived that by securing their interest in our soil, their affections to this country will be more fully confirmed, and that justice and policy require that the hardships and inconveniences, under which they respectively labour should be remedied; therefore,

II. Be It Enacted, by the General Assembly of Maryland, That all and every the said foreigners, who, since their settlement in this state, have purchased and acquired, by any lawful and fair means, any portion of property, real, personal or mixed, and have since possessed and enjoyed the same, and have still a just and equitable title thereto, whether such title be derived from grant, gift, purchase or devise, shall, by virtue of this act, hold possess and enjoy, such property, real, personal and mixed, as fully and amply, and to all intents and purposes, as rightfully as the said foreigners would have been entitled to hold,

Naturalizations of Washington County

possess and enjoy the same, if they had respectively naturalized themselves according to the express provisions contained in the said act for naturalization.

III. And Be It Enacted, That in case any real property, purchased or acquired by foreigners since the passage of the aforesaid act, hath been escheated, it is hereby declared, that all the right and title of this state to the said property so escheated, and to any property so escheatable, shall be and the same are hereby relinquished, and vested for ever hereafter in the said foreigners, their heirs and assigns, saving nevertheless to all persons whatsoever, who may have heretofore acquired titles to any such escheatable property under the laws of this state, their several and respective rights, and all and every person and persons, who may have purchased, or otherwise acquired any real property from or under the said foreigners, or any of them, shall be, and they are hereby declared to be, entitled to all and every advantage, with respect to such property, as if the same had been purchased or acquired from or under any foreigners who have naturalized themselves according to the provisions of the said original act.

IV. Provided Nevertheless, That the said foreigners respectively, before they shall receive the benefit of this act, shall naturalize themselves in the mode prescribed by the original act, on or before the first day of August ensuing, any law to the contrary thereof notwithstanding.

V. And Provided Also, That no application within the period limited by this act to prejudice the rights of the said respective foreigners, or others, shall be admitted ore received.

VI. And, in order to carry the good intentions, as well of this, as of the said original act, into complete execution, Be It Enacted, That the governor and council shall and they are hereby required to cause the said respective acts to be printed and published in the several newspapers within this state, for the space of six weeks, after the end of this session of assembly, in the English, French and German languages, and shall also cause the said original act to be published in like manner, for the space of three weeks, in the month of August, in every year hereafter.

[Maryland State Law Library]

The Laws of Maryland From the End of the Year 1799, with A Full Index, and The Constitution of This State, As Adopted by the Convention, with The Several Alterations by Acts of Assembly: and an Appendix Containing the Land Laws; with the Resolutions Considered Proper to be Published, Volume V. Annapolis

Maryland, Prior to 1880

Revised and Prepared, Under the Authority of the Legislature, by William Kilty, Thomas Harris and John N. Watkins.

Chapter CV., Passed January 17, 1814,
An Act for the benefit of certain Persons who emigrated into or settled in this State before the adoption of the Constitution of the United States. Lib. TH. No. 4, fol. 120

1. Be It Enacted, by the General Assembly of Maryland, That all free white persons, who emigrated into, or settled within the limits of this state, before the adoption of the constitution of the United States of America, and who have continued and remained inhabitants of this state, shall be deemed, construed, and taken to have been, and they hereby are declared to have been, and to be respectively entitled, to all and singular the immunities, privileges, rights and advantages, of natural born citizens, so far as to enable such persons to acquire right, title and interest in, and to hold, possess and enjoy, lands, tenements and real estate, within this state, and to transmit and transfer the same in the same manner as natural born citizens of this state; and all property, real, personal and mixed, acquired and transferred by, from, through, or under the said person, or any of them, or their or any of their descendants, shall be held, possessed, enjoyed or transferred, in like manner as if the said persons had respectively been and were at the several times of acquiring and transferring such property natural born citizens of this state; and all and every person or persons whatsoever, being citizens of this or some one of the United States, claiming any real estate by, from or under, the said persons first herein before described, or their or any of their descendants, by gift, grant, purchase, descent or otherwise, shall hold, possess and enjoy the same, in like manner as if the said persons had respectively been and were, at the several times of acquiring and transferring such real estate, natural born citizens of this state; Provided, that nothing herein contained shall be construed to interfere with or affect the rights of any person or persons acquired before the passage of this act.

Chapter LXXIX., Passed January 13, 1815
An Act for the benefit of Persons who have emigrated into this State since the adoption of the Constitution of the United States. Lib. TH. No. 4, fol. 331.
Be It Enacted, by the General Assembly of Maryland, That in all cases where any alien hath emigrated into this state since the adoption of the constitution of the United States, and hath acquired or become entitled to lands and tenements therein, if such person after such acquisition as aforesaid, hath been naturalized according to the laws of the United

Naturalizations of Washington County

States, then and in such case, he or she shall quietly have, possess and enjoy, such lands and tenements, in the same manner as he or she might or could have done if he or she had been a naturalized citizen at the time of such acquisition; Provided always, that nothing herein contained shall be construed to interfere with or affect the rights or interest of any other person or persons acquired before the passage of this act.
[Maryland State Law Library]

Written in the Chronological Index, Naturalization Book 1798-1860:

Act of Congress, approved May 26, 1824 - Chapter 186, Sec. 3 *enacts as follows:* "That the declaration required by the first condition specified in the first section of the act, to which this is in addition, shall, if the same has been bona fide made before the Clerks of either of the Courts in the said condition named, be as valid as if it had been made before the said Courts, respectively." *Note - by Washington County Court:*
The 'Court is inclined to think this section will embrace the future as well as past, but that it would be safest to declare in Court.'

Appendix C

Extant Washington County Court Minutes and Proceedings records prior to 1800:

March 1778	December 1792	April 1795	January 1798
August 1778	April 1793	December 1795	April 1798
November 1778	December 1793	April 1796	January 1799
March 1779	April 1794	December 1796	April 1799
August 1779	December 1794	April 1797	December 1799
November 1779			

All Washington County Court Minutes and Proceedings records are available for 1800 - 1879 *except*:

November 1825	March 1835	November 1841
March 1828	March 1838	March 1842
November 1832	November 1840	November 1843
March 1833		

NEW-YORK, June 10.

On Thursday last arrived here his Majesty's ship Solebay, Capt. Symonds, in 15 days from Savannah, by whom we have the following important intelligence.

Extract of a letter from Capt. Henry, senior Officer of his Majesty's ships in Georgia, to Sir George Collier, dated Savannah, May 23, 1779.

"The King's troops, under Major General Prevost, crossed Savannah river on the 28th of April, and marched from Purysburgh towards Charles-Town, the Rebels abandoning every strong post as our army approached. We are now without loss, in possession of James Island, John's Island, and all the south side of Charles-Town harbour, the rebels having abandoned and burnt Fort Johnson. General Moultrie is in Charlestown with 1000 men, and General Lincoln at Dorchester, afraid to come on Charlestown Neck, left we should get behind them.

"His Majesty's armed ship the Germaine remains at Port-Royal, for the protection of the inhabitants, who together with all the other islands, have sent in their submissions. When the Vigilant and armed vessels sailed from hence, they went through Callibogie Sound and Skull Creek into Broad River, and on their approach the Rebels burnt Fort Lyttleton, in Port Royal, and abandoned another fort on St. Helena, leaving it entire. We have taken the guns out of both.

"Charles-Town has offered to capitulate, if they might remain neuter during the war, this was refused. Our army is in possession of several vessels on Ashley-river, &c.

Extract of a letter from an officer of the Royal Navy, dated Savannah, May 23, 1779.

"I am going round to five fathom hole, in company with the Rose and victuallers. I hope to give a good account soon of the town and fort—as the enemy have left Fort Johnson, and we are in possession of Mount Pleasant, which commands Fort Moultrie."

PHILADELPHIA, June 22.

An open boat called, the ____, mounting a gun, with 17 men, belonging to Egg Harbour, lately sent there a vessel with a valuable cargo, which makes her nineteenth prize since she was fitted out.

IN CONGRESS, June 12, 1779.

Congress took into consideration the report of the Committee to whom was referred the memorial Doctor John Morgan, late Director General and Physician in Chief in the General Hospitals of the United States, and thereupon came to the following resolution:

Whereas by the report of the Medical Committee confirmed by Congress on the 9th of August 1777, it appears that Doctor John Morgan, late Director General and Chief Physician of the General Hospitals of the United States, had been removed from office on the 9th of January, 1777, by reason of the general complaint of persons of all ranks in the army and the critical state of affairs at that time; and that the said Doctor John Morgan requesting an inquiry into his conduct, it was thought fit that a Committee of Congress should be appointed for that purpose:

TO be SOLD, on Friday the 2d of July, at the Coffee-House, in Baltimore-Town, a LOT, 24 feet ____ high; it being a corner Lot, has thereon, two stories high; it being a corner Lot, has thereon, two Store or a Tavern, and stands in a pleasant part of the Town, near Griffith's Bridge; subject to a ground rent of fifteen pounds currency. The Sale to the highest bidder, for ready money, will be at 7 o'clock. Attendance will be given by

JAMES YOUNG.

Baltimore, June 26, 1779.

T Hereby acquaint the public, that I carry on the nailing business in this town, and shall be able, in a few weeks, to furnish any Gentleman with what quantity of nails he may want, and of all kinds, whether for his own private use, or retailing.—I have now on hand upwards of thirty thousand, well assorted, for retailing.

ROBERT WOOD.

N. B. I am in want of eight NAILERS, who have served an apprenticeship to the business, or can make good work, and according to the rule of nailing. R.W.

Frederick Town, Maryland, June 22, 1779.

Maryland Newspaper

POUGHKEE[PSIE], June 14.

*Three deserters from the ene[my ca]me in on the [__]
instant, on examination, a[s rea]d as follows, viz.*

That they left the enemy [__] between 12 and [__] o'clock that morning, that [Sir H. C]linton was then [at] Verplank's Point, togeth[er with] Generals Vaugh[an] and Matthew, Lords Raw[don and] Cathcart.—3000 [at] the Point.—That they are [buildi]ng a battery and n[o] doubt at Stoney-Point, on th[e oth]er side of the river.—That in the ferry way a[re tw]o gates, and about [__] smaller vessels, one 64 gun [ship, o]pposite Tarry-Tow[n] 17th regiment li[ght] dragoo[ns, Lo]rd Cathcart's legio[n] Emerick's corps, [Qu]een's r[angers], two regiments [of] Hessians, 7th, 17th, and 2[3d B]ritish regiments, a[nd] with Sir W. Erskine, who [is w]ith the flying army, [at] Dobbs's Ferry.—A Lieut. [Colon]el commands on th[e] other side, o[ppo]site King's [Bridge,] who, with the other principal officers, lodge [abo]ard their vessels eve[ry] night.—It is reported am[ong the] soldiers, that they [are] to continue at the Point ab[out th]ree weeks—44th a[nd] 57th British regiments, an[d on]e Hessian ditto are [at] King's Bridge.

The troops which came [from] Virginia, not bei[ng] furnished with proper cloa[thing] for the campaig[n] are permitted to return to [nor]k for fifteen days [and] then to come up the river [__]

WILLIAMSBURG, *June 19.*

On Saturday last several [of th]e enemy's privateer[s] that have been some days i[n our ba]y, chaled into W[i]comico river the Lady W[__] ten brig, and a flo[op] commanded by Capt. R. [__] the brig unluckil[y] run aground and was [__] her own crew: t[he] sloop ran up the warehouse [doc]k, but was pursued [by] boats manned for the purp[ose] and carried her o[ff.] These two vessels were [both ou]t-bound, loaded wi[th] tobacco. The enemy th[en la]nded a body of me[n] and set fire to and totally de[stro]yed the warehouse [on] that river, wherein was a la[rge] quantity of tobacc[o] they burnt the Protector, g[alley] belonging to this sta[te] which was repairing at that [place]; they then procee[d]ed to the burning several g[entl]emen's houses in th[e] neighbourhood. Capt. G[__] [Bla]ckburn and Mr. [__] Haynie, whose houses they [__] [bu]rnt, were taken [__] endeavouring to save som[e of hi]s property; the latt[er] was found dead floating in [the] river two days ag[o.] After carrying off a numb[er of sla]ves, and what sto[ck] they could, they pushed [off, o]n seeing the mili[tia] assembling.

Elk-Ridge, Maryland, June 25, 1779.

A MINISTER of the Established Church of England, of good Character, is much wanted, and will be genteelly provided for, in Queen-Caroline parish, Anne-Arundel County, by appl[y]ing to the Vestry of said parish. Signed, by ord[e]r,

W. COALE.

Maryland, Prior to 1880

Appendix D

The Torch Light and Public Advertiser   August 10, 1791

Philadelphia, August 1
In the Ship Ann, Captain A. Miller, junior, arrived yesterday from Londonderry, came 363 passengers, all in perfect health, meaning to settle in America, having paid their passage money before they embarked.

The Washington Spy   Thursday, February 24, 1791

    According to the several enumerations of the inhabitants of various districts of the United States, the population of this country exceeds all the estimates heretofore published on the subject. Some persons may say the amazing increase in particular places, is owing in a great degree to emigrations. Grant this to be the case, where is the spot in those states which have furnished the largest number of emigrants, that has not made advances in its population. The fact is, that this country is advancing to the sovereignty of the globe with a rapidity that baffles all calculation.
    There is a profession, which it has become a good deal fashionable to rail against, to whom civil society is under no small obligations, both on account of their public spirit, and as assertors of the rights of freemen - I mean lawyers. It is said the present glorious revolution of France owes its rise in a great measure to the gentlemen of the bar - and in our own country they have always borne a conspicuous part in the council, and in the field. - Penns. Mercury

The Maryland Herald & Elizabeth-Town Weekly Advertiser
March 28, 1799

To Foreigners.
A last notice is hereby given to all foreigners residing in Washington county, who desire to become citizens of the United States, that they yet may be naturalized at the ensuing April court, on their bringing proof into court, to certify that they have resided in the limits and under the jurisdiction of the United States, since January 1795. Those who do not avail themselves of this notice, do wilfully exclude themselves from the rights of citizenship, for the long term of fourteen years.
A Citizen.

Naturalizations of Washington County

The Torch Light and Public Advertiser
Vol. XVII No. 11 Thursday, January 6, 1831

A German Newspaper

It affords us pleasure to have it in our power to inform the public, that efforts are now making to establish *a German Newspaper in Hagers-town.* --- The "Western Correspondence," a very respectable German paper, printed for many years by Messrs. Gruber & May of this place, was permitted to languish, and ultimately to sink, about a year ago, for want of patronage. This, it must be confessed, reflects no credit upon the German population of Washington county. Surely, in a county like ours, containing thousands of the descendants of German ancestors, and hundreds who are able to read and understand the noble, and copious, and expressive language of their fathers, we ought to be *willing* to support at least *one Germany newspaper* at the very moderate subscription price *of one dollar and fifty cents per annum*! As respects our *ability* to sustain such a paper, no one who has the slightest acquaintance with Washington county can entertain a doubt. A goodly portion of the property and wealth of this rich and prosperous region of country, has descended to the possession of the children of honest, industrious and thrifty Germans, and a considerable number of these are still able to read and understand German. Why then not be willing to patronize a paper published in the ancient language of their worthy progenitors? -- in that language which is at this moment the living language of half of Europe? -- the favorite language of the far-famed court of St. James? -- and which is also the medium of communication for at least three-fifths of all the solid and profound erudition of this enlightened age? There are many individuals in this county, whose partial and limited knowledge of the English language disqualifies them to read an English newspaper *understandingly,* but who yet are not sufficiently numerous to sustain the publication of a paper in their vernacular tongue. To them the reading of a paper judiciously conducted, would doubtless be a source of no small gratification and benefit: and are there no generous citizens among us, who, while they might also derive some satisfaction from the perusal of a German paper, will be willing to join themselves to their less favored neighbors, and lend their aid in supporting a paper, which, without their co-operation, may not meet with adequate encouragement?

But the contemplated enterprize appears to us to present peculiar claims to our patronage. It is to be published by our former well known and truly exemplary fellow-townsman, Mr. May, co-editor of the late "Western Correspondence. He has resolved to devote all his time and his best efforts to it, and has the promise of respectable

Die Westliche Correspondenz und Hägerstauner Wochenschrift.

Hägerstaun, Maryland, alle Freytag herausgegeben von J. Gruber und D. May, in der Süd-Potomacstraße.

Freytag, December 30, 1825.

Botschaft

Washington, December 6, 1825.

Des Präsidenten der Ver. Staaten beym Anfange der ersten Sitzung des 19ten Congresses dem Senate und Hause der Repräsentanten mitgetheilt.

(Beschluß.)

Die Acte des Congresses vom 26sten May, 1824, welche die Beschickung, Weisung, &c. des Hafens von Charleston in Süd-Carolina, von St. Marys in Georgien, und von Mobile anzeigt, hat sich bewährt.

unter die wichtigsten Verbesserungsmittel. Moralische, politische und geistige Verbesserung aber sind Pflichten, welche von dem Urheber unseres Daseyns sowohl der menschlichen Gesellschaft im Allgemeinen, als jedem Einzelnen vorgeschrieben sind. Zur Erfüllung dieser Pflichten sind die Regierungen mit Macht betraut, und zur Erreichung dieses Zwecks ist die vorzüglichste Verwendung der Regierungsgewalt, die Anwendung der Lage der Macht, eine eben so heilige und unerläßliche Pflicht, als die Anmaßung einer nicht zugestandenen Gewalt verbrecherisch und haßenswerth ist. Zu den erstgenannten gehört die—

so frieden, als im Kriege, die Kosten und abwartet—und für die persönliche Publication (einer Beobachtung, die sich gar keinen Beruhigungen zu machen. Es geschieht freywillig aus seinem Gefühle des Ernstes, wenn man als Amerikaner der Bemerkung anschlagen, wuß sie die Dienste, welche sie sich zu seinen vorgenommen, erwägt, daß sich auf seinem Verhältnisse muß, wie sollen vor die Rolle durch die der Staatengesellschaft Europas nicht als 3 tels rischer Unternehmungen berechnen? und der Staatsgarten bestehen, während auf welche Belohnung kann steuern, oder ihrem der jetzigen amerikanischen Halbkugel auch —————für ihr freyes werden? Gibt ———zur jetzt vorhanden ist. Wenn anders als sie im bekanntgegeben sind, wir ganz Augenblick, aber die Einschranes unzweifelhaft— Beobachtung in halten? Giebt ges nachdrücklich, welche die europäischen eine größere als die Nachahmung jen Neuerungen in der politischen Welt ein zu einer schöpferischen Gebaude und zu einem Gesuch?—indem er einige unser Umschwung mittelst dieser Gebäude und der Handwerker in dem Stand setzen, die darin angestellter Beobachter gemacht der Handwerker zu verfolgen, und ihr Lewerden, können wir dann an ihnen, jeder menschliche Natur zu befolgen, und ihr Retrollen, gewahren Nutzen ziehen—?

First Washington County Courthouse   Print by Douglas Stone, Funkstown, Mary

Maryland, Prior to 1880

assistance in the editorial department. He intends, moreover, to open and continue a correspondence with Europe, and thus impart the earliest European news, which, at the present momentous crisis - big with transpiring events of immense magnitude, cannot fail to prove deeply interesting to his readers. It is also his determination to make his paper a vehicle of conveying moral truth; and so far as is compatible with the general design, to render it subservient to the dissemination of correct and virtuous principles -- the suppression of vice and the advancement of good morals. Who can calculate the advantages which may arise to the cause of ethicks, and the consequent benefits which must accrue to the public from a weekly periodical of this character?

We would only yet add that subscribers to "Der Americanische Burgerfreund" (American Citizen-friend) will be received at the office of the Herald, and that a prospectus has been left at the Store of Messrs. Hager & Kausler, and another at the Bookstore of Mr. P. Blood.   HERMAN

The Maryland Herald & Hagers-Town Weekly Advertiser
March 14, 1806

Blue & Black Dying.

The subscriber informs the public, that he has begun the Dying business in the house formerly occupied by Daniel Nead, two doors from Mr. Mittelkauff's Tavern in Hagers-town.

He carries it on in all its various branches in Dying Cotton, Linen and Woolen Yarn and Stuffs blue and all other colours. Having learned the above business in Germany, and carried it on in that country extensively, he feels a confident assurance of rendering satisfaction to all who will favor him with their custom, in making bright, real and lasting colours at the most reduced prices. All that he will be intrusted with shall be colour'd at the shortest notice.

G. M. Conradt.   Hagers-town, March 12, 1806

N.B. Farmers from the back parts who keep Wagons going to Baltimore, can get their Dying done by the time they return.

The above mentioned keeps Turkey Red Cotton for sale.

The Torch Light and Public Advertiser   May 14, 1829

To the Irishmen of Hagers-town and Washington County.

It may be soothing to you Fellow Citizens, to hear that the Land of your Fathers, has, by a solemn set of the British Parliament,

Naturalizations of Washington County

been admitted to the unalienable rights of Freemen: -- Nor are we, who felt an interest and expressed our sympathy in the sufferings of your transatlantic friends, the unfit organs whereby this cheering intelligence should be communicated. You left your loved and lovely Isle under the most gloomy auspices. The arm of intolerance drove you from your green fields; and looking either upon the past or to the future, you had nothing to hope for, but every thing to fear. Weary and worn out by physical debility, and mental suffering, you landed upon the beach, and though the hand of fellowship was proffered you, and the asylum of the oppressed was opened for your reception -- yet the reflection of your country's wrongs, and the difficulties that were in prospect to beset you, weighed heavily upon your minds. Inured to hardships: familiar with adversity, yet unshackled in spirit or in mind: tutored in a religion, whose dictates are pure, holy and heavenly -- your resignation to your fate has been equalled only by your devotion to the land of your adoption. By your upright conduct in times of peace, and gallant bearing in the hour of danger, you have endeared yourselves to every American bosom, and found in a land of strangers, God your friend and many your ally. No sooner were you taken into the American brotherhood, than we felt a redoubled interest, and an increased sympathy in the wrongs of your native country. We mingled our fervent orisons with yours to the God of nations, that Erin might be freed of her yoke. How oft have the sea breezes wafted our sighs and sympathies to your mourning isle! How oft has the little bark (proud of its charge) scudded along the main, bearing not only our prayers for your deliverance, but a mite from our coffers, to feed your hungry, clothe your naked, and enlighten your ignorant. America has surely been your friend - you were hers. When on her martial fields she beheld the bleached bones of your brave warriors; reckless of every ennobling sentiment would she have been, had she not enrolled her name among the earliest of your benefactors. Long has been the day of your disasters , severe and unmerited has been your fate. With every requisite, to make you a contented, a happy, and a glorious people - your fields teeming with abundance; your isle laved by the ocean; your mountains and your meads forming a scenery at once picturesque and lovely: your people warm-hearted, generous and brave; proverbial for their piety and unrivalled in genius. Your history notwithstanding, has been marked by a series of calamities; by a system of oppression, unfelt before in any other clime, and by the mercy of Heaven we hope never again to be felt by you. The aristocracy of an intolerant kingdom (to use the language of one of venerated memory,) ___ ? booted and spurred over your coun___? your holy altars have been pilfered, and your sacred rights despised. But the day of your disenthrallment has at

Maryland, Prior to 1880

length dawned in glory; that dark and murky cloud which so long lowered over your devoted land, is fleeing fast away before the light of liberty: a wonderful and glorious revolution has been wrought, free from the stain of blood or the imputation of crime. This moment is one of pure joy and real exultation, to Irishmen and to freemen of every clime. In pouring forth the grateful thanks of our hearts, to the master spirits, who "rode in the whirlwind and directed the storm," the O'Connells, the O'Conners, the Doyles, and the Shiels -- Let us not be unmindful of that all controuling and uncontrouled Spirit, who gave authority to their persons, inspiration to their eloquence, and triumph to their struggle.

We subscribe ourselves, in joy, Your friends and fellow citizens, R.M. Harrison, Henry Lewis, E. Fitzpatrick.

The Hagerstown Mail   Vol. I No. 25   May 17, 1833

The cause of Ireland. -- A public meeting of the friends of Ireland, opposed to the "bloody coercion bill," we perceive is to be held at Washington City this evening. The call is headed by George W. P. Curtis, Esq. and is signed by some of the most respectable people of the place, Cannot -- rather, *will not*, something be done for the generous, patriotic and warm harted sons of the "green emerald isle," in Lancaster? -- *Lancaster Intelligencer.*

The Torch Light and Public Advertiser   July 5, 1833

Cheasapeake and Ohio Canal.
The National Intelligencer says, Forty-six miles, distributed into ninety-two sections, have been placed under contract. Upon this line, about eighteen hundred laborers, masons, and stone cutter, are emplyed. The wages of the first vary from 10 to 13 dolls. per month, the last earn from $2 to $2.50 per day. Not a death, except one, and that by accident and carelessness, has occurred upon the canal since the work began, which was in August last. Four thousand additional hands might now find employment on it, provisions having been made for the expenditure of one hundred thousand dollars per month in its construction. At the Great Falls of the Potomac, and especially on the 12th section of canal, let to Mr. George Ketchum, of New York, a most interesting spectacle is daily presented. The hill, along the face of which the canal extends, is blasted by kegs of powder used at a blast, separating immense masses. The stone is lifted from he quarry by a

Naturalizations of Washington County

crane worked by horses -- it is run along to where it is needed, upon wooden rails, and laid in a perpendicular wall of fifty feet elevation by the same power, guided, indeed, by human ingenuity, which is no where in this case as conspicuously displayed as here.

The Torch Light and Public Advertiser   July 5, 1833

Persons dying of Cholera, along the line of the Canal, have generally been brought to the Catholic burying ground in this place for interment. This practice has heretofore been tolerated, because there was no other burying ground belonging to that sect, in the neighborhood. This is not now the case. A piece of ground has been purchased and set apart as a burying ground, near the line of the Canal, in the neighborhood of Williams-port, in which it is the request of the Rev. Mr. Ryan, that future interments of those dying along the Canal, may be made. And, it may be proper to say, that if this reasonable request be disregarded, prompt measures will be adopted, by the authorities of our town, to put a stop to a practice, for the continuance of which no reasonable excuse longer exists.

Agents of the Canal Company, Contractors, and others interested, will be so good as to give to this subject the attention to which its importance entitles it.   *Torch Light.*

The Hagerstown Mail   Vol. I No. 33   July 12, 1833

The cholera re-appeared among the laborers on the Canal near this place on Monday last, owing probably to the intense heat of that day. The attacks were of the most malignant character, and resulted almost invariably in death after a few hours. We are unable to state precisely their number, but they might be put down at fifteen or twenty in all. The disease abated so far, that on Thursday no new case occurred. Yesterday, however, there was a rumor of three new cases in one shantee. It has caused considerable dispersion among the hands, and must materially delay the progress of the work, if it continue. We learn that the cases have generally been attended with the usual premonitory symptoms, which have been neglected until incipient collapse, too late for relief form medical aid. They are also but slightly attended with cramps or spasms. The citizens of the town continue to enjoy uninterrupted good health.

The disease in the west has greatly abated. Many places that have been sorely visited, are now entirely exempt from the pestilence. - - *Williamsport Banner.*

Maryland, Prior to 1880

The Hagerstown Mail   Vol. I No. 36   August 2, 1833

The Committee appointed to examine into the health of the citizens of Hagerstown, beg leave to submit the following report,

That after full enquiry and careful investigation, they find that from the Spring of the present year, down to this date, the citizens of the town have, under Providence, enjoyed an unusual amount of good health, and that no case of epidemic cholera has been engendered in the town during this entire season. -- Your Committee will not conceal the fact that three deaths from cholera have occurred within the corporate bounds, but they were all brought from the line of the Canal, where the disease had been contracted. We would further remark, that so far as our enquiries have extended, the citizens of the county have, with us, been blessed with unusually good health, except on a few sections of the Canal, where the cholera raged with considerable violence, which we believe is mainly to be attributed to the shameful intemperance and extreme filthiness of the laborers. The Committee feel pleasure in saying that the present state of cleanliness of the town does great credit to the exertions of the corporate authorities and the cheerful co-operation of the citizens. To the public we would give the solemn assurance that there exists not a shadow of cause for alarm, as no disease of an Epidemic character is known to exist in the town.

G.W. Boerstler, Wm. Hammond, R.W. Davis, Frederick Dorsey, Charles MacGill, John C. Dorsey, T.B. Duckett, James Buchanan, Joseph Martin.

The Hagerstown Mail   Vol. I No. 36   August 2, 1833

The Cholera   An Ordinance

Whereas, at a meeting of the citizens of Hagers-town, held at the Court-house, on Saturday the 27th inst. 1833, it was "resolved, that the Moderator and Commissioners be requested to pass an Ordinance declaring it a nuisance to bring any persons within the limits of the Corporation, who have died upon the line of the Canal, or in any other infected district, without said limits" --Therefore,

Be it enacted and ordained by the Moderator and other Commissioners of Hagers-town, That the bringing into the limits of said town, or its additions, the dead body or bodies of any person or persons for interment, who may have died along the line of the Canal, or in the neighborhood of said line, or in any other infected district, out of the limits of Hagers-town, be, and the same is hereby declared to be a nuisance.

Naturalizations of Washington County

And be it enacted and ordained, That it shall be the duty of the Market Master and the Constables of Hagers-town, or any one of them, to prevent the introduction of all such nuisances, within the limits of the Corporation, and if brought within said limits, to cause the same to be removed, without delay -- and in case the Market Master or Constables, shall be resisted in the execution of such duty, he or they are hereby authorised, to call out the *posse* to enforce this ordinance. - Passed, July 31, 1833.
W.D. Bell, Mod'r.   Test - S. Herbert Cl'k.

The Hagerstown Mail   Vol. I No. 37   August 9, 1833

A laboring man, from the line of the canal, arrived in Town on Sunday last, was attacked by cholera that night, and died, at the Hospital, on Monday. Two old colored women, died of cholera, same day. -- And on Tuesday, an old black man died -- making, in all, four deaths, within the last week. The three colored people were old and dissipated, and resided back of the Hospital in one of the remote, detached, out-skirts of the town. -- There has not yet been a case among our regular citizens, or in the business part of the town -- which continues unusually healthy, and free from alarm.   *Torch.*

The Hagerstown Mail   **January 24, 1834**

War on the Canal

On Monday morning last our town was thrown into commotion by the announcement that a "war" had broken out among the workmen on the line of the Canal, near Williamsport. The excitement was much heightened by Madam Rumor, who, soon after the receipt of the news, gave a graphic description of the order of the battle, together with a statement of the number of killed, wounded, and missing. The "Union Riflemen" and "Hagerstown Infantry" were called out, and with becoming promptness marched to Williamsport. Upon their arrival, they learned that there had been a *battle-royal* between the workmen employed on two different sections of the canal, but that the riot was quelled and a number of the aggressing party captured. On Tuesday the volunteers returned, having in charge 34 prisoners, who were safely lodged in jail, to await, probably, an investigation of the affair.

We understand no lives were lost, but that a number of individuals have been severely beaten.

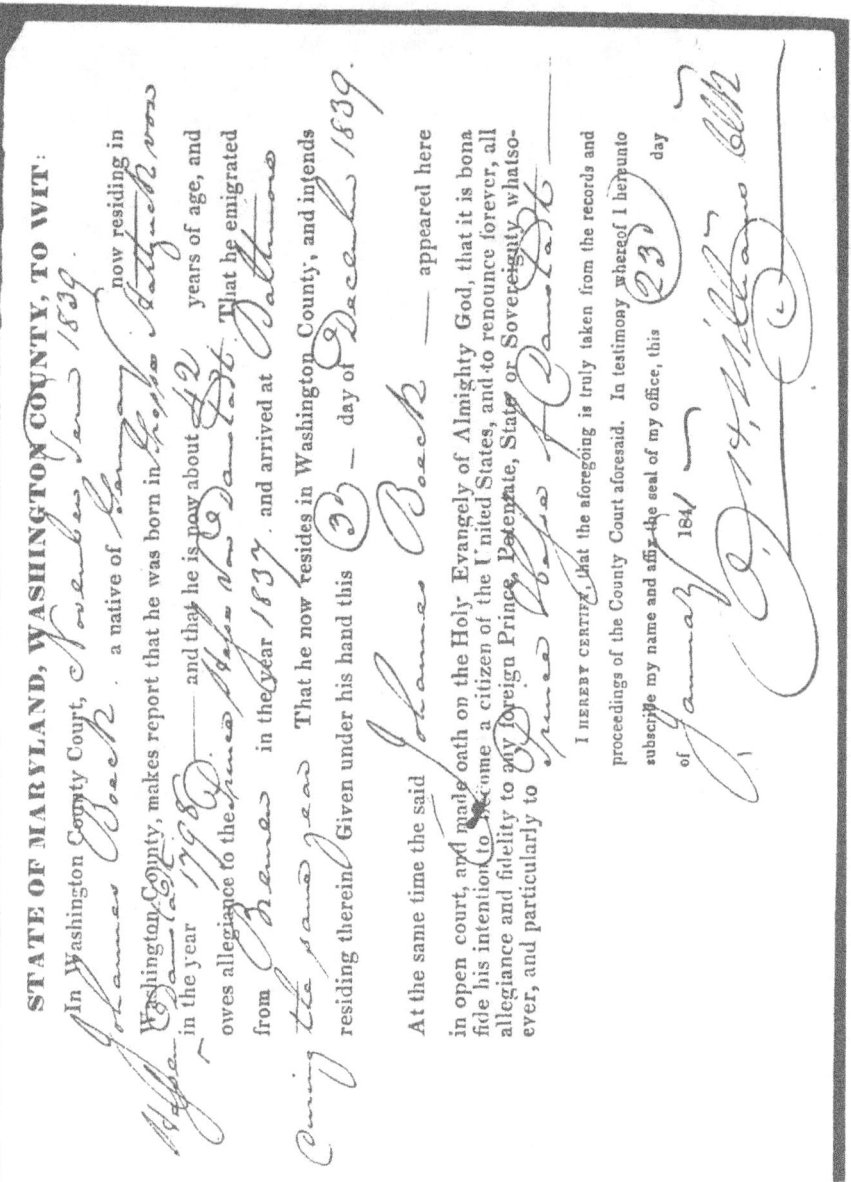

This is a copy of an original Certificate. If an immigrant decided to move between the time he made his Report to the Court and the time he was naturalized, he was given a Certificate. He carried this with him to his new home and submitted it to the Court as proof that his Report had been properly made.

Stonework on the C & O Canal, Built by Irish Stonemasons

Ashton	William	02 Apr 1831	16 Sep 1829	
Lancestershire, England		05 Oct 1835	Alexandria,DC	Oct 1829
22	1809	s 35	Alexandria, District of Columbia	
Atwell	James	22 Nov 1838	Liverpool	1826	John Atwell
County Cavan, Ireland		22 Nov 1838	Philadelphia	1826	
25	1813	x 11			
Augenstein	Jacob	23 Nov 1829			
Averbach, Baden		04 Apr 1833			
34		s			
Awell	David	17 Aug 1840	Bristol	1832	Daniel Evans
Bridly Hill, Wales		17 Aug 1840	New York	1832	
26	1814	x 67			
Bachtell	Martin	03 Sep 1838			
		03 Sep 1838			
65		IN			
Bain	George	21 Nov 1840			
		--			
		IN			
Bain	John	21 Nov 1840			
		--			
		IN			
Bain	William	21 Nov 1840			
		--			
		IN			

Last Name / Place of Birth / Age	First Name / Date of Birth	Report Date / Natural. Date / Sig. Page No.	Departure Port / Arrival Port / Other	Departure Date / Arrival Date	Witness(es)
Baker	Christian	01 Feb 1841 / 12 Feb 1844 / IN			
Baker	Christopher	16 Nov 1841 / -- / IN			
Baker / Darmstadt, Hesse Darmstadt / 31	Daniel / 1806	30 Nov 1836 / 01 Apr 1839 / s 33	Bremen / Baltimore	1831 / 1831	Frederick Fishach
Baker / Oldendoiff, Hanover / 23	Henry / 1821	16 Sep 1844 / 28 Sep 1847 / s 59	Bremen / Baltimore	1842 / 04 Jun 1842	Valentine Reichard
Baker / Prince of Nassen	Nicholas	05 Apr 1798 / 05 Apr 1798 / 10	Farmer. Living in Williamsport.		
Baker, Jr. / Hesse Darmstadt	George	01 Oct 1850 / 30	Arrived as a minor.		Henry C. Smith / George Baker Sen.
Baker, Sen. / Hesse Darmstadt	George	22 Jul 1848 / 01 Oct 1850 / 32			Henry C. Smith

Name	First	Date 1	Port	Date 2	Notes
Balz	Ernst	05 Jan 1853	Antwerp	1848	
Murrhardt, Wirtemburgh			New York	Jul 1848	
42		s 24			
Baner	Michael	24 Oct 1871	Havre de Grace	1852?	J. B. Costenberger
Wirtemburgh		24 Oct 1871	New York	1852?	Henry Kyper
36	1835	s 34	Arrived as a minor.	The 2 in 1852 is unclear - it could be something else.	
Banett?	Thomas	04 Oct 1870	Queenstown	1867	
Ireland			New York	1867	
56	1814	s 25			
Banner	Christopher	04 Oct 1848			Marke Banner
Wirtemburgh		23	Arrived as a minor.		
Banner	Marks	10 Apr 1838			
		10 Apr 1840			
		IN			
Banzaf	George	04 Oct 1838			Name may be Banzhaf. Report column reads "Certificate"
		30 Sep 1842			
		IN			
Barkstrasser	Adam	01 Nov 1806			
		01 Nov 1806			
		IN			
Barns/Burns	Marcus	23 Oct 1815		July 1801	
County Down, Ireland					
		x 16			

Last Name / Place of Birth / Age	First Name / Date of Birth	Report Date / Natural. Date / Sig. Page No.	Departure Port / Arrival Port / Other	Departure Date / Arrival Date	Witness(es)
Barr / Ireland /	Christopher /	23 Oct 1810 / / 15		<14 Apr 180_ /	James Garrett Samuel Geedy
Barr / /	William /	27 Sep 1802 / / 50	Owes allegiance to Great Britain & Ireland		
Barringer / Town of Stugart, Wirtemburgh / 32	Boldus /	04 Apr 1825 / / s 39		/ 25 Aug 1820	
Barry / Ireland / 25	David /	05 Jan 1854 / 12 Aug 1856 / 15	Report was made in St. Louis, Missouri.		Hugh McKosker
Barry / Ireland / 26	John / 1826	19 Oct 1852 / / s 7	Liverpool / New York /	1850 / 01 Jun 1850	
Barry / Co. Limerick / 28	Richard / 1826	10 Jun 1854 / / s 10	Liverpool / New York /	1851 / Jun 1851	
Barietz / Prussia / 25	John /	26 Oct 1815 / / s 24	Hamburgh / /	/ Nov 1805	

Barth	Jacob	18 Nov 1833		Everhart Rigley
		19 Nov 1835		
		12		
Bartlett	John	26 Oct 1813		
		20	Name may be Bartles. Owes allegiance to Great Britain	
Bartlett	Richard	31 Mar 1817	Plymoth	
County Cornwall, England		05 Apr 1822		Sep 1802
38		s 43		
Bassett	George	27 Nov 1851	Liverpool	1848
England		01 Dec 1853	New York	Sep 1847
34	1817	s 3		Charles G. Downs
Basten	James	02 Dec 1837	Limerick	1829
County Clare, Ireland			Baltimore	1829
39	1798	x 36		John Reidnour
Battle	Michael	25 Sep 1876	Dublin	1866
Ireland		25 Sep 1878	New York	1866
34	1842	x 25		David A. Peters, Thomas Eagan & Charles Gross
Battle, Jr.	Michael	20 Dec 1879	Liverpool	1876
Co. Mayo, Ireland			New York	1876
38	1841	s 17		
Baxton	Daniel	cert.		
		16 Sep 1844		

Last Name Place of Birth Age	First Name Date of Birth	Report Date Natural. Date Sig. Page No.	Departure Port Arrival Port Other	Departure Date Arrival Date	Witness(es)
Bayhah Wirtemburgh	John Martin	10 Dec 1856 14 Mar 1859 8			Adolph Kneuss
Bayly/Bayley Ireland 42	John	24 Oct 1810 20 Nov 1817 s 20		1800	
Baxton	Daniel	*Certificate* *16 Sep 1844*			
Bea	Conrad	03 Oct 1838 -- IN			
Beard	George	27 Mar 1833 03 Oct 1836 45			Michael McSherry
Beard Town of Lamburgh, Co. Kreitz 1784 50	Jacob	18 Nov 1833 s 6	Laaburgh Baltimore Owes allegiance to King Frederick. Has lived in Maryland since his arrival in U.S.	Jul 1829 Nov 1829	
Beard Wettswiller, Germany 30	Louis 1810	05 Apr 1840 05 Sep 1842 s 36	Havre de Grace New York	1834 1834	

Surname / Origin	Given name	Date / Age	Port / Destination	Notes	Witness
Beard Germany	Michael	02 Jan 1798 02 Jan 1798 9			
Beard	Robert	01 Mar 1804 57	Living in Washington County. Owes allegiance to Great Britain & Ireland		John Smith
Beber Wirtemburgh 31 1827	Edward	13 Sep 1859 s 5	Havre de Grace 1853 New York 23 Oct 1853		
Beckelharb Arback, Hesse Darmstadt 32 1812	Philip	30 Sep 1844 05 Oct 1846 s 121	Bremen 1832 New York 17 Jun 1832 Name could be spelled Beckelharp.		Hugh Murphy
Becker	Henry	Certificate 22 Nov 1841 IN			
Beetmun Ireland 23 1833	Marshall	25 Jan 1856 x 22	Liverpool 1849 New York 03 Mar 1849 Name may be Michael Beetman		
Behler Strasburg, France 36 1814	Andrew	25 Mar 1850 30 Mar 1852 s 1	Havre de Grace 1847 New York 01 Oct 1847		Nathan McDowell Christian Katzel
Beigle Bishoss, Baden Doriach 23	George	26 Mar 1824 x 81	Oct 1816		

71

| Last Name | First Name | Report Date | Departure Port | Departure Date | Witness(es) |
| Place of Birth | Date of Birth | Natural. Date | Arrival Port | Arrival Date | |
Age		Sig. Page No.	Other		
Beinstine	Charles	01 Apr 1840	Bremen	1830	
Warsaw, Hesse Darmstadt		26 Sep 1842	Baltimore	1830	
29	1811	s 30			
Belch	William	15 Apr 1799			
		15 Apr 1799			
		54	Farmer. Living in Salisbury Hundred. Owes allegiance - Great Britain		
Belekheimer	Henry	*27 Nov 1841*			
		05 Feb 1844			
Bellman	Henry	05 Nov 1842			Michael Foye
Prussia		26 Nov 1844			
		12			
Belser	Augustus Fred	05 Apr 1820		01 Nov 1819	
Stutgard, Wirtemburgh, Germany					
30		s 43			
Bemford	Thomas	04 Nov 1828			
		04 Nov 1828			
		IN			
Bender	Christian	27 Mar 1816			
Germany		31			

Bender	John	19 Nov 1834	Havre de Grace	1833
Rhinebyer, Germany			New York	Aug 1833
31	1803	s 13	Owes allegiance to Prince Ludwig.	
Benner	John Peter	28 Feb 1803		
		28 Feb 1803		
Bennet?	Lewis	05 Apr 1840		
		05 Sep 1842		
		IN		
Bensinger	Frederick	25 Mar 1823		Sep 1819
Village Vilay, Wirtemburgh				
35		s 51		
Bentz	Andrew	19 Nov 1844	Hamburg	1839
Darmstadt, Hesse Darmstadt			New York	08 Jun 1839
43	1801	- 2		
Berger	John G.	11 Aug 1866	Bremen	1857 Lewis Heist
		11 Aug 1866	Baltimore	07 Sep 1857 John Costenberger
Bavaria	1833	s 3	Honorably discharged from military service 29 May 1865.	
Berk	Daniel	04 Apr 1832	Amsterdam	Jul 1830
Darmstadt, Hesse Darmstadt			Baltimore	Oct 1830
39	Feb 1793	s 43		
Bert	Pierre	25 Mar 1835		
		--		
		IN		

73

Last Name First Name	Report Date Natural. Date	Departure Port Arrival Port	Departure Date Arrival Date	Witness(es)
Place of Birth Date of Birth		Other		
Age	Sig. Page No.			
Besermer Christian	27 Sep 1847	Havre de Grace	1847	
Unterturkheim, Wirtemburgh		New York	Jun 1847	
31 1816	s 29			
Bestard William	28 Nov 1842	Bremen	1839	John Markoe
Cossell, Hesse Castle, Germany	30 Nov 1844	Baltimore	1839	
40 1802	s 17			
Betekleimer Henry	27 Nov 1841			
	05 Feb 1844			
	IN			
Beutelspacher Everhart	08 Dec 1842	Havre de Grace	1839	
Leonberg, Wirtemburgh	*08 Sep 1845*	Philadelphia	1830	
39 1803	s 33			
Beydel John	01 Dec 1832			Jacob Gruber
	23 Nov 1836			
	13			
Beyer Egidus	15 Jun 1841	Bremen	1839	
Eckersdorf, Bayrenth, Bayern		Baltimore	25 Sep 1839	
26 1815	s 58			
Bier Peter	17 Nov 1841			
	--			
	IN			

Surname / Origin	Given name / Year	Date	Port / Destination	Year / Date	Sponsor / Notes
Binder	Charles Henry	08 Oct 1855	Havre de Grace	1854	
Vachongen, Wirtemburgh			New York	09 May 1854	
28	1827	s 20			
Birmingham	Daniel	21 Nov 1839	Liverpool	1836	
County Longford, Ireland			New York	1836	
28	1811	s 10			
Bish	Henry	02 Oct 1860			Joseph S. Smith
Hesse Darmstadt		07 Nov 1864			
		4			
Black	James	10 Aug 1844	Belfast	1839	William Hawthorn
Dowss, Parish of Dramorra		01 Sep 1846	New York	24 May 1839	
55	1789	s 42	Born in Ireland.		
Black	Samuel	08 Oct 1859	Liverpool	1846	
Ireland			New York	29 May 1846	
28	1831	s 5			
Blaine	John T.	01 Oct 1835			
		01 Oct 1835			
		IN			
Blanout	Frederick	29 Nov 1858	Bremen	1854	
Prussia			Baltimore	18 Nov 1854	
28	1830	s 8			
Blaye/Bloyer	John	26 Sep 1844			John Ridenaur
Germany		114	Arrived as a minor.		

| Last Name | First Name | Report Date | Departure Port | Departure Date | Witness(es) |
| Place of Birth | Date of Birth | Natural. Date | Arrival Port | Arrival Date | |
Age		Sig. Page No.	Other		
Blenttinger	Conrad				
Prussia		03 Jan 1798			
Bloom	Moses	11 Aug 1854	Havre de Grace	1839	Nathan Kahn
Westhoffen, France		11 Aug 1854	New York	1839	
22	1832	s 13	Living in Hagerstown.		
Blourouck	Andrew	*04 Oct 1845*	Arrived as a minor.		
Boadman	Godfried	*Certificate*			John Russaamen
Baden		26 Sep 1844			
		119			
Bocher	Laurence	05 Oct 1840	Dublin	1822	
Kings Co., Ireland		05 Oct 1842	New York	1822	
38	1802	x 100			
Bock/Boek	George	29 Mar 1839			
		30 Sep 1842			
		IN			
Bodmann	Ferdenand	30 Mar 1825			
City of Hanan, Hessen Cassel		24 Sep 1828		03 Aug 1822	
24		s 14			

Name	Given	Date1	Date2	Place1	Place2	Notes	Witness/Other
Bodmann Henau, Hessen Cassell 21	Philip	30 Sep 1829	30 Sep 1829	Rotterdam	Baltimore	1822 1822	William Bodmann
Bodmann	William	May 1808 s	24 Sep 1828 24 Sep 1828 IN			Arrived in Baltimore at age of 14 yrs.	
Boeck Grosse Hartzuk, Hesse Darmst. 42	Johannes	1798	03 Dec 1839 s 31	Bremen Baltimore		1837 1837 Report Certificate issued 23 Jan 1841 - Perhaps moving out of county?	
Boehler Bavaria 56	George Conrad	1799	06 Mar 1855 s 1	Havre de Grace Baltimore		1833 1833	
Boesler Prussia	Gottleib	24 Sep 1806 65					John Miller
Bolch	William	15 Apr 1799 15 Apr 1799				Owes allegiance to Great Britain	
Bolinger	Christian	*20 Nov 1822* 29 Nov 1827					Christian C. Fichtig
Bolinger Walheim in Wirtemburgh 24	John Christian	21 Nov 1822 s 29				02 Oct 1819	

| Last Name | First Name | Report Date | Departure Port | Departure Date | Witness(es) |
| Place of Birth | Date of Birth | Natural. Date | Arrival Port | Arrival Date | |
Age		Sig., Page No.	Other		
Bolinger	John G.	24 Sep 1838			
		24 Sep 1838			
		IN			
Bolinger	John Jacob	24 Mar 1829	Bremen	May 1827	
Walheim, Wirtemburg		26 Nov 1832	Baltimore	Aug 1827	
44	1785	s	Has lived in Maryland since arrival in U.S.		
BonnerBanner	John Peter	28 Feb 1803			
Prussia		38			
Bopp	Charles	30 Mar 1857	Antwerp	1854	
Wirtemburgh			New York	26 Apr 1854	
23	1834	s 23			
Boswell	F. C.	19 Nov 1867	Bremen	1855	Dr. J.F. Smith
Hanover		02 Oct 1874	New York	1855	
37	1830	s 8	J.G.P. Krouse		
Bovehich	Patrick	02 Apr 1838	Could also be spelled Bordrich		
		--			
		IN			
Bower	Conrad	15 Oct 1855	Bremen	1854	
Bavaria			Baltimore	28 Oct 1854	
43	1812	s 21			

Name	Origin	Date	Place	Notes
Bower Ireland	George	05 Apr 1797		
Bowers France 54	Jacob 1781	26 Mar 1839 26 Mar 1841 x 2	Havre de Grace Baltimore	Clergyman. "The Rev. Mr. George Bower" 1833 Abraham Folker 1833
Bowers Hesse Darmstadt, Germany 32	Peter 1804	29 Mar 1837 17 Aug 1840 s 11	Bremen Baltimore	1833 Martin Hotz 1833
Bowman Windsheim, Bavaria 32	John Leonard 1812	16 Sep 1844 s 58	Bremen Baltimore	1841 31 Aug 1841
Bowman Linden, Bavaria 39	John Michael 1806	16 Sep 1844 s 55	Bremen Baltimore	1838 30 Dec 1838
Bowser Canten of Basil, Switzerland 35	Henry	14 Apr 1816 29 Mar 1821 s 66		1806 Christian Boestler Witness for report was Henry Dillman.
Bowser Switzerland	Henry	03 Jan 1798 03 Jan 1798 12		Living in Salisbury Hundred.
Boyd County Limerich, Ireland 42	Michael 1798	28 Mar 1840 31 Mar 1842 x 20	Limerich Baltimore	1825 1825

Last Name / Place of Birth / Age	First Name / Date of Birth	Report Date / Natural. Date / Sig. Page No.	Departure Port / Arrival Port / Other	Departure Date / Arrival Date	Witness(es)
Boyer	Egilus	15 Jun 1841			
Boyer Prussia	George Michae	29 Mar 1808 ? 21		<14?Apr1802	Lodwich Emerich
Boyle Ireland 28	Joseph	02 Nov 1815 25 Oct 1828 s 37		1807	
Bradley County Donegall, Ireland 24	William	30 Nov 1822 23 Nov 1836 x 64		May 1822	George Beltzhoover
Brady County Longford, Ireland 25	James 1808	11 Jan 1834 s 65	Liverpool New York	1829 Apr 1829	
Brady County Mannahan, Ireland 22	James 1817	01 Apr 1839 x 18	Liverpool New York	1836 1836	
Brady Ireland	John	31 Mar 1810 34		<14 Apr 1802	Michael M. Kieman

Name		Date		Place	Sponsor
Brady	John	16 Sep 1844			John Egan
		98		Owes allegiance to Great Britain & Ireland	
Braiesch	John	27 Nov 1837			Henry Lyday
		02 Apr 1840			
		31			
Brant	John	14 Jan 1799			
Germany				Gunsmith. Living in Funkstown.	
Brarutigam?	Johannes	28 Nov 1827		Amsterdam	Apr 1827
Hessen Cassel				New York	07 Jul 1827
27		s	62	Name may be Braentigand	
Brazill	James	06 Jan 1834		Dublin	1819
Kings County, Ireland				New York	1823
36	1797	x	49		
Breisch	Jacob	30 Mar 1824			12 Feb 1819
Stutgard, Wirtemburgh		*Nov. Ct. 1829*		Naturalization was during November Court 1829	
33		s	84		
Breisch	John	27 Nov 1837		*Holland	1827
Wirtemburgh, Germany		*02 Apr 1840*		Baltimore	1827
37	1800	s	19	* - "a port of Holland". Owes allegiance to Prince William.	
Breitweiser	George	20 Feb 1855		London	1851	Adam Vogle
Hesse Darmstadt		09 Mar 1857		New York	07 Jan 1852
42	1813	x	17		

Last Name / Place of Birth / Age	First Name / Date of Birth	Report Date / Natural. Date / Sig. Page No.	Departure Port / Arrival Port / Other	Departure Date / Arrival Date	Witness(es)
Brendhiem	Auschell	30 Mar 1872	Averbach	1868	
Prussia, Germany			New York	1868	
22	1850	s 24			
Breneman	Christian	24 Oct 1871	Basle	1852	P.A. Brugh
Switzerland		24 Oct 1871	New York	1852	Dr. A.K. Eberly
27	1844	s 36	Arrived as a minor.		
Breslen	Patrick	01 Apr 1839	Liverpool	1837	
County Donnegal, Ireland			New York	1837	
22	1817	x 19			
Bretzler	Charles	12 Dec 1855	Bremen	1853	
Wirtemburgh			Baltimore	1853	
21	1834	s 19			
Bretzler	Christian G.	*27 Oct 1857*			
Bretzler, Sen.	Charles	12 Dec 1855	Bremen	1853	
Wirtemburgh			Baltimore	1853	
48	1807	s 19			
Breudella	William	*05 Aug 1844*			William Freaver
Hanover		01 Sep 1846			
		40	Name may be Brendeka		

Brey Bavaria 33	John 1822	24 Jul 1855 s 4	Bremen Baltimore	1852 09 Sep 1852	
Brey Bavaria	John Wolfgang	14 Sep 1857 09 Oct 1865 11			Henry Howard David Crist
Bridges Fifeshire? Scotland 30	Robert F.	30 Mar 1826 1 Oct 1828 s		Mar 1817	
Brien Ireland 32	Henry 1836	01 Jun 1868 24 Oct 1870 x 26	Tralee New York	1857 1857	Thomas H. Moore Patrick Kelly
Briesch Wertemburg 33	Frederick 1795	19 Nov 1828 22 Aug 1837 s 64	Amsterdam Philadelphia Has lived in Washington Co. for the last 5 yrs.	1818	George Earnst
Briesch	John	*27 Nov 1837* *02 Apr 1840*			
Briesch Wirtunburg	John Jacob	30 Mar 1824 18 Nov 1829			George Shirp
Brill	George	24 Sep 1838 05 Oct 1840 106			Herman Westerhouse

83

Last Name Place of Birth Age	First Name Date of Birth	Report Date Natural. Date Sig. Page No.	Departure Port Arrival Port Other	Departure Date Arrival Date	Witness(es)
Brining "near Stutgard", Wirtemburgh 45	Christian	27 Mar 1821 28 Nov 1827 s 28		Dec 1818	John King
Brinkman Ipping, Baden, Germany 26	Adam 1812	29 Nov 1838 30 Mar 1841 s 26	Bremen Baltimore	1832 183	George Gassman
Brinkman	Henry	01 Apr 1831 20 Aug 1835 IN	Name may be Brenkman		
Brinkman	John George	01 Apr 1831 20 Aug 1835 IN	Name may be Brenkman		
Brinning Baden 40	Andrew 1817	30 Nov 1857 s 9	Frankfort New York	1852 24 Oct 1852	Paul Decker
Britch Stein, Germany 45	Jacob 1792	30 Nov 1837 29 Jun 1840 s 28	Bremen Baltimore	1832 1832	
Brodrick	Patrick	02 Apr 1838			

Surname, Origin, Age	Given Name, Birth	Date / #	Port	Year	Notes
Broidelman Prussia 42	John 1812	13 Dec 1854	Havre de Grace New Orleans	1852 06 Apr 1852	
Bromet Holland	Michael	s 11 26 Oct 1815 22			
Brondeka Rina, Hanover 43	William 1801	05 Aug 1844 x 41	Bremoley Baltimore	1835 1835	Name may be Brendeka
Brookhart Swyburgh, Germany 23	John 1811	28 Nov 1833 s 33	Havre, France New York	Aug 1831 Oct 1831	Has lived in Washington County since his arrival in U.S. Owes allegiance to King Lewis.
Brown Bavaria 26	Augustus 1844	18 Oct 1870 s 28	Pottsheim New York	1866 1866	
Brown Province Darmstadt, Germany 34	Michael 1806	01 Oct 1840 s 91	Bremen Baltimore	1833 1833	
Brown Bavaria 38	Philip 1811	12 Sep 1849 *24 Sep 1851* s 22	Bremen Baltimore	1839 14 Nov 1839	
Brown Bavaria	Philip	12 Sep 1849 24 Sep 1851 25			Michael Freize

Last Name / Place of Birth / Age	First Name / Date of Birth	Report Date / Natural. Date / Sig. / Page No.	Departure Port / Arrival Port / Other	Departure Date / Arrival Date	Witness(es)
Brown	William	05 Nov 1828 24 Jul 1837 57			Charles Sweeney Adam Shoof
			Report made in Albany County, NY.		
Bruck Sontra, Hesse Cassel 28	Charles 1816	16 Sep 1844 10 Aug 1847 s 52	Bremen Baltimore	1839 1839	John Robertson
			Signature reads Carl. Clerk has written Charles.		
Bruen County Sligo, Ireland 36	Redmon	06 Apr 1821 x 76		Jun 1806	
Bryerton Co. Cildsar, Ireland 30	Christopher 1810	05 Oct 1840 x 99	Liverpool New York	1837 1837	
Bryhah Wirtemburgh 45	John Martin 1811	10 Dec 1856 s 21	Amsterdam Baltimore	1831-1832 1831-1832	
			He left Amsterdam in "1831 or 1832" and arrived in Baltimore in "1831 or 1832."		
Bubeck Stukate?, Wurtemburgh 48	Joseph	27 Oct 1813 s 24		01 Oct 1803	
Buchanan	John	*03 Apr 1821*			

Name	Origin	Year	Date 1	Date 2	Place 1	Place 2	Year 1	Year 2	Sponsor
Bucher			29 Dec 1849						Gotleib Heigis
Bavaria			13 Mar 1855						
			6		Report made in Baltimore City.				
Buckley	Dennis		19 Nov 1835		County Cork		1830		Anthony Loftus
County Cork, Ireland		1812	05 Dec 1837		Baltimore		1830		
23			s 11						
Buckley	John		19 Nov 1835		County Cork		1830		
County Cork, Ireland		1811			Baltimore		1830		
24			s 10						
Bunce	Richard		18 Nov 1839		Liverpool		1829		John Park
Berkshire, England		1812	18 Nov 1839		Baltimore		1829		
27			x 2						
Bunkman	Henry		01 Apr 1831		Rotterdam		10 Jun 1829		
Epinghan, Baden		1803	*20 Aug 1835*		Baltimore		18 Aug 1829		
28			s 33		Name may be Brenkman				
Bunkman	John George		01 Apr 1831		Rotterdam		10 Jul 1826		
Epinghan, Baden		1805			Baltimore		10 Aug 1826		
26			s 32		Name may be Brenkman				
Bunkman	John George		01 Apr 1831		Rotterdam		10 Jul 1826		
Epinghan, Baden		1801			Baltimore		10 Apr 1828		
29			s 32		Name may be Brenkman				
Bunner	Marks		10 Apr 1838						John Leitz
			10 Apr 1840						

Last Name Place of Birth Age	First Name Date of Birth	Report Date Natural Date Sig. Page No.	Departure Port Arrival Port Other	Departure Date Arrival Date	Witness(es)
Burger Bavaria 46	Conrad 1809	12 Nov 1855 s 22	Bremen Baltimore	1854 27 Sep 1854	
Burger Bavaria 30	Conrad 1836	18 May 1866 18 Aug 1866 s 12	Bremen Baltimore Honorably discharged from military service 29 May 1865.	1860 1860	John Peter Rauth John G. Wiles
Burger Bavaria 23	John Michael 1843	18 Aug 1866 18 Aug 1866 s 10	Bremen Baltimore Arrived as a minor. Full name is John Michael Rhoderick Burger.	1858 1858	John Peter Rauth John G. Wiles
Burkhardt Hesse Darmstadt 23	Christian 1832	01 Aug 1855 s 12	Havre de Grace New York	1854 01 Dec 1854	
Burkhardt Hesse Darmstadt 26	J. L. 1829	01 Aug 1855 s 13	Havre de Grace New York	1855 21 May 1855	
Burley	John	10 Oct 1828 10 Oct 1828 IN			
Burmgart	Casper	07 Dec 1837 28 Mar 1840 18			Jacob Sweitzer

Name	Origin	Age/Date	Port	Arrived	Notes
Burns James		25 Nov 1837	Belfast	1828	
County Antrim, Ireland			Baltimore	1828	
32	1805	s 17			
Burns Patrick		17 Aug 1840	Liverpool	1835	
Kings Co., Ireland			New York	1835	
25	1815	x 63			
Bury James C.		25 Nov 1833	City of Cork	1827	
City of Cork, Ireland		20 Aug 1835	New York	May 1827	
26	1807	s 26			
Buser Michael		16 Sep 1834			John I. Briesch
		29 Mar 1837			
		13			
Busser Michael		11 Oct 1834	Havre de Grace	1827	
Belmersen, Germany			New York	23 Oct 1827	
36	1796	s 87	Owes allegiance to the King of Berne.		
Butz Jacob		22 Nov 1838	Bremen	1833	John Seitz
Town Brooksall, Baden, Germany		26 Mar 1841	Baltimore	1833	
32	1806	x 9			
Byers Jacob		28 Nov 1836	Bremen	1833	
Wirtemburg, Germany			Baltimore	1833	
27	1809	s 24			
Byrne Pierce		28 Mar 1835			
		28 Mar 1835			
		IN			

Last Name	First Name	Report Date	Departure Port	Departure Date	Witness(es)
Place of Birth	Date of Birth	Natural. Date	Arrival Port	Arrival Date	
Age		Sig. Page No.	Other		
Cahill	Dennis	10 Apr 1793			
Ireland					
Calahan	John	19 Nov 1834	Limerick	1831	
Limerick, Ireland			New York	1831	
29	1805	x 18	Name may be Callahan		
Callnan	Richard	03 Oct 1838			
		-- IN	Name may be Callman		
Cameron	John	25 Aug 1876	U.S.	1856	Samuel Johnson
Ontario, Canada		25 Aug 1876			George T. Leiter
	1842	s 21	Enlisted in Volunteer Forces, Company B, 3rd Maryland Infantry in 1861. Honorably discharged 31 Aug 1862. "Gun shot wound rendering him unable to perform soldier duties." Moved to Maryland 1861.		
					Philip Fitzpatrick
Campbell	Michael	*Certificate*			
		16 Sep 1844	Owes allegiance to Great Britain & Ireland		
		78			
Campbell	Thomas	05 Dec 1837	Liverpool	1832	
County Longford, Ireland			New York	1832	
25	1812	s 43			

Can/Carr	Patrick	24 Oct 1871	Donegal	Michael Dillon
Ireland		24 Oct 1871	New York	Cornelius Shehan
31	1840	x 33	1857	1857

Cane	John			

Apparently, someone sold him forged naturalization papers and this case came to court on 04 Jul 1840. There is no record of him being officially naturalized. See Appendix E.

Cane	Laurence			

Apparently, someone sold him forged naturalization papers and this case came to court on 04 Jul 1840. There is no record of him being officially naturalized. See Appendix E.

Canlahan	James C.	08 Apr 1833		

Cardan	James	24 Nov 1834		

Cardan	Thomas	24 Nov 1834	Dublin	1827
County Meath, Ireland			New York	1827
40	1794	x 38		

Last Name / Place of Birth / Age	First Name / Date of Birth	Report Date / Natural. Date / Sig. Page No.	Departure Port / Arrival Port / Other	Departure Date / Arrival Date	Witness(es)
Carey	Cornelius	25 Nov 1834			
Carey Ireland 35	Dennis 1823	09 Aug 1858 x 8	Cork Fall River, MA	1845 1845	
Carey County Longford, Ireland 23	James 1817	24 Mar 1840 x 7	Liverpool New York	1837 1837	
Carey County Cork, Ireland 27	Joseph 1809	16 Apr 1836 24 Sep 1838 x 39	City of Cork White Hall, NY	1828 1828	
Carn Germany	Nicholas	06 Jan 1798 06 Jan 1798 24	Farmer. Living in Hagerstown.		
Carney County Donegal, Ireland 33	Patrick	26 Oct 1813 18 Nov 1818 - 16	Londonderry Naturalization date comes from notation on page 48 of Oct 1813 Minutes.	15 Aug 1804	
Carolan County Meath, Ireland 36	James 1798	24 Nov 1834 s 37	Dublin Alexandria, DC Name may be Cardan	1827 1832	

Name		Date 1	Place	Date 2	Notes
Carson	John	29 Nov 1820		Aug 1816	
County Songford, Ireland					
25		s	49		
Carson	Thomas	29 Mar 1824		1811	
County Longfew, Ireland					
21		s	82		
Carsteve	Frederick	30 Oct 1812	Amsterdam		
Bremen					
27		s	23	Name may be Carstine. Owes allegiance to Emperor of France	
Cary	Cornelius	25 Nov 1832	Cove of Cork	1825	
County Cork, Ireland			Sago, NY	Aug 1826	
32	1802	x	47		
Cassidy	James	31 Mar 1836	Belfast	1830	
County Londonderry, Ireland			Lewistown, NY	1830	
28	1808	s	9	Born in the Parish of Ardtrea. Name may be Cassady	
Cassini	M.C.	03 Dec 1830	Leghorn	Feb 1816	
Leghorn		31 Mar 1835	Norfolk	Dec 1816	
31	1799	s	62	No country listed - only the name Leghorn.	
Cencil	Peter	12 Jan 6798			
Germany		12 Jan 1798			
			39	Farmer. Living on Ringgold's Manor.	
Cestenberger	Baltzer	26 Nov 1832			George Earnst
		22 Aug 1837			
			65		

| Last Name | First Name | Report Date | Departure Port | Departure Date | Witness(es) |
| Place of Birth | Date of Birth | Natural. Date | Arrival Port | Arrival Date | |
Age		Sig. Page No.	Other		
Chambers	John	08 Aug 1855	Cork	1845	
Co. Waterford, Ireland	1813	x 17	Boston	1845	
42					
Chambers	Samuel	27 Jul 1827	Belfast	Apr 1819	
County Down, Ireland	26 Feb 1798	s	East Port, ME	May 1819	
31					
Chehan	Michael	24 Nov 1837	Limerick	1829	
County Limerick, Ireland	1802	s 16	Troy, NY	1829	
35					
Christ	Adam	02 Oct 1850	Bremen	1845	
Hesse Darmstadt	1801	s 33	Baltimore	Jun 1845	
49					
Christ	Henry	29 Mar 1821			Daniel Schnebly
Switzerland		43			
Christ	Jacob	30 Nov 1822		Sep 1803	
Switzerland		s 65			
23					
Christ	John	02 Oct 1850	Arrived as a minor.		Adam Christ
Hesse Darmstadt		34			

Name		Date 1	Date 2 / Age	Place 1	Place 2	Date/Year	Sponsor/Notes
Christen	Zachariah	05 Oct 1844?					Christian Bickley
Heitzock of Minering		05 Oct 1846					
			21				
Christeor?	Zachariah	05 Oct 1842					Index reads Report made 05 Oct 1842. Natural. record reads 1844.
		05 Oct 1846					
			IN				
Christman	Michael	11 Apr 1799					
Germany		11 Apr 1799					
			47	Miller. Living in Salisbury Hundred.			
Clark	James	25 Mar 1834		Belfast		Jun 1833	
County Down, Ireland		23 Sep 1838		New York		Jun 1833	
53	1787	s	13				
Clarke	Peter	23 Nov 1836		Dublin		1830	
County Meath, Ireland				St. Albans, VT		1830	
30	1806	s	12				
Clarkson	Edward	25 Mar 1852		Liverpool		1849	Andrew Kershner
Co. Cork		08 Aug 1856		Baltimore		Sep 1849	
31	1821	s	2				
Clarkson	Patrick	11 May 1854		Liverpool		1849	William O'Neill
Old Castle, Great Britain		09 Aug 1858		Philadelphia		1849	
35	1819	x	10				
Clay	Francis	27 Dec 1842		Bremen		1830	Ulrich Leinkand?
Gaisa, Saxe Weimer, Germany		20 Sep 1847		Baltimore		Jan 1840	
49	1793	s	37				

95

Last Name Place of Birth Age	First Name Date of Birth	Report Date Natural. Date Sig. Page No.	Departure Port Arrival Port Other	Departure Date Arrival Date	Witness(es)
Cleary Kings Co., Ireland 30	James 1810	05 Oct 1840 s 99	Liverpool New York	1837 1837	
Clement Bavaria	John	11 Aug 1866 3	Honorably discharged from military service 29 May 1863.		Lewis Heist John Costenberger
Clinch Germany	Frederick	05 Jan 1798 05 Jan 1798 21			
Cline Germany	Daniel	13 Jan 1798 13 Jan 1798 44	Labourer. Living in Hagerstown.		
Cline Germany	Henry	13 Jan 1798 13 Jan 1798 43	Farmer. Living in Funkstown.		
Coleman Ireland 23	John 1847	22 Oct 1870 22 Oct 1870 x 29	Butcher. Living in Hagerstown. Queenstown New York	1862 1862	James J. Hurley John Murphy
Coleman County Teprierly, Ireland 32	William 1805	24 Nov 1837 s 16	Waterford Sligo, NY	1827 1827	

Coles	George	06 Jan 1875	London	1851
Somerset Shire, England			New York	1851
47	1828	s 20		
Colgan	James	05 Apr 1838		
		-- IN		
Collins	Bernard	*05 Apr 1833*		
Collins	John	25 Mar 1834	Limerick	Apr 1832
County Limerick, Ireland			Albany, NY	May 1832
24	1810	x 8		
Collins	Michael	09 Apr 1834	Cork	1825
County Cork, Ireland			New York	19 Aug 1825
33	1801	s 63		
Collins	Oscar E.	29 Oct 1867	Canada	1840 Michael Stine
Canada		29 Oct 1867	Vermont	1840
27	1840	s 14	Honorably discharged from military service 19 Nov 1864.	
Collins	Patrick	08 Apr 1867	Limerick	1853
Kilker, Co. Clare, Ireland		04 Oct 1870	New York	1853
35	-	s 16		
Colvin	Andrew	28 Mar 1836	Waren's Point	1823
County Cavin, Ireland		31 Mar 1838	White Hall, NY	1823
37	1800	x 1	Born in the Parish of Drumgone, Ireland.	

Last Name Place of Birth Age	First Name Date of Birth	Report Date Natural. Date Sig. Page No.	Departure Port Arrival Port Other	Departure Date Arrival Date	Witness(es)
Commous Hilden, Hanover 42	Caspar Henry 1807	30 Nov 1842 28 Sep 1847 x 21	Bremen Baltimore	1837 1837	
Coudy County Down, Ireland 23	James ca. 1804	27 Nov 1827 27 Nov 1827 s 69	Was 13 yrs. old when arrived with his father and family. Went first to Dauphin Co., PA. Moved to Washington Co. 7 yrs. ago.	Aug 1817	John Repley
Coneaughton	Michael	23 Mar 1840 5	Report made in Adams Co., PA.		Daniel Coffee
Conn Ireland	William	08 Apr 1800	Living in Lower Antietam Hundred.		
Connelly Kings County, Ireland 27	John 1807	23 Nov 1836 x 12	Dublin New York	1827 1827	
Connelly County Manahan, Ireland 37	Patrick 1801	22 Nov 1838 x 9	Belfast Philadelphia	1822 1822	
Connelly County Mayo, Ireland 35	Roger 1800	06 Jan 1836 s 39	Slago White Hall, VT	Jun 1830 1830	

Name	Given	Date	Place	Year	Notes
Connelly	Terrence	01 Apr 1839	Liverpool	1836	
County Mannahan, Ireland			New York	1836	
26		x 18			
Conrad	Andrew	01 Oct 1828			
		01 Oct 1828			
		IN			
Conrad	Henry	05 Nov 1828			
		05 Nov 1828			
		IN			
Conrad	John	01 Apr 1837	Bremen	1820	Owen Barnes
Wirtemburgh		26 Mar 1839	George Town,	1820	
42	1795	s 25	Arrived at George Town, District of Columbia		
Conradt	George Jacob				Augustus Copich
Germany		29 Mar 1810		<14 Apr 1802	
		25			
Cook	John	24 Mar 1841	Bremen	1837	
Bysore, Germany			Baltimore	1837	
37	1804	s 24	Owes allegiance to King Byron of Germany.		
Cookman	William	11 Apr 1843	Liverpool	1836	
Emiscartley Co. of Wesford			New York	1836	
28	1815	s 23	From Wesford, Ireland.		
Cooper	Philip	12 Apr 1799			
Germany		12 Apr 1799			
		50	Farmer. Living on Lower Antietam Hundred.		

Last Name Place of Birth Age	First Name Date of Birth	Report Date Natural. Date Sig. Page No.	Departure Port Arrival Port Other	Departure Date Arrival Date	Witness(es)
Copich Germany	Augustus	29 Mar 1810 23		<14 Apr 1802	Christian Lautz
Copp	Jacob	-- Aug 1824 04 Nov 1828 IN			
Cornyar County Caven, Ireland 27	Murty	06 Apr 1821 s 75	Name may be Cornyn	Aug 1817	
Cosens England 32	Henry John 1838	07 Nov 1870 02 Oct 1876 s 37	Liverpool New York	1861 1861	Dr. George Fechtig William H. Armstrong
Cost Bavaria	Andrew	19 Nov 1846 19 Nov 1846 3	Arrived as a minor.		Jacob Funk
Cost Baden 44	Charles 1811	07 Mar 1855 s 3	Havre de Grace New York	1850 May 1850	
Costenberger	Baltzer	26 Nov 1832 22 Aug 1837 IN			

Couton	Arthur	01 Oct 1835		
		01 Oct 1835		
		IN	Name may be Cowton	
Couton	John	10 Oct 1835		
		10 Oct 1835		
		IN	Name may be Cowton	
Cowen	Timothy	01 Oct 1840	Cork, Ireland	Joshua Turner
Cork, Ireland		01 Oct 1840		
27	1813	x 88		
Cowon	Arthur	23 Nov 1831	Liverpool	07 Aug 1830
Yorkshire, England		01 Oct 1835	New York	21 Sep 1830
25	26 Oct 1806	s 30		
Cowton	John	01 Apr 1823		
Yorkshire, England		*10 Oct 1835*		07 Oct 1820
23		s 38		
Cox	James	26 Nov 1836	Londonderry	1827
Larga, Ireland		*06 Apr 1840*	New York	1827
27	1809	s 20		
Craddock	John	02 Apr 1831		16 Oct 1822
Yorkshire, England		26 Mar 1835	New York	03 Jan 1822
32	18 Nov 1798	s 36		
Cramer	Ambrose M.C.	--		George R. Beall
		05 Oct 1840		

| Last Name | First Name | Report Date | Departure Port | Departure Date | Witness(es) |
| Place of Birth | Date of Birth | Natural. Date | Arrival Port | Arrival Date | |
Age		Sig. Page No.	Other		
Cramer	Thomas	12 Apr 1822			
County Waterford, Ireland				1816	
25		x 51			
Crass	John	16 Sep 1844	Bremen	1839	
Graffengehaig, Bavaria			Baltimore	02 Oct 1839	
28	1816	s 56	Name may be Cross		
Creager	Henry	03 Jan 1798			
Prince of Hanover		03 Jan 1798			
		16	Living in Hagerstown.		
Creek	Peter	26 Mar 1838			
		26 Mar 1838			
		IN			
Crilley	John	19 Mar 1870	Derry, Ireland	1865	
Co. Donegal, Ireland			New York	1865	
26	1844	s 16			
Crilly	William	02 Nov 1874	Derry, Ireland	1865	Nelson Sprecher
County Donegal, Ireland		03 Nov 1876	New York	1865	John Spickler
28	1846	s 25			
Crisman	George	09 Jan 1798			
German		09 Jan 1798			
		30	Butcher. Living in Hagerstown.		

Name	Origin	Date	Age	Port of departure	Port of arrival	Year	Notes
Crist Henry	Canten of Basil, Switzerland	27 Mar 1816					
		29 Mar 1821				1803	
	42	s	65				
Croft Conrad	City of Domstadt, Domstadt	04 Dec 1833		Bremen		10 May 1830	
				Baltimore		11 Aug 1830	
	40	1793	s	38			
Crogan Patrick	Kinnenore, Ireland	20 Feb 1852		Waterford		1846	
				Quebec, Canad		1846	
	33	1819	x	23		Name may be Coogan	
Cronise Patrick	Ireland	01 Oct 1851		Liverpool		1838	
				New York		1838	
	37	1844	x	27			
Crosson John	County Tyrone, ireland	23 Oct 1815				02 May 1812	
	30		s	17		Name may be Crossen	
Crow Dennis	County Carlow, Ireland	31 Mar 1820				04 Jul 1814	
	23		s	25			
Crow Henry	Hesse Darmstadt	28 Nov 1839		Bremen		1832	
				Baltimore		1832	
	48	1791	s	23			
Crow James	Ireland	05 Nov 1867		Liverpool		1864	
				New York		1864	
	55	1812	s	19			

Last Name / Place of Birth / Age	First Name / Date of Birth	Report Date / Natural. Date / Sig. Page No.	Departure Port / Arrival Port / Other	Departure Date / Arrival Date	Witness(es)
Crow / County Carlow, Ireland / 20	Michael	31 Mar 1820 / / 25		01 Aug 1819	
Crow	Patrick	16 Nov 1840 / ---	Michael says he is brother of Dennis Crow.		
		IN			
Crowley	John	16 Sep 1844 / / 96	Owes allegiance to Great Britain & Ireland		Timothy Cohen
Crowther / England / 42	D. W. / 1834	30 Mar 1876 / 30 Mar 1876 / s 18	Liverpool / New York / Arrived as a minor.	1834 / 1834	Allen Yingling, M.A. Berry, C.W. Henneberger
Cullen / Ireland / 26	James / 1824	04 Dec 1850 / 20 Mar 1855 / s 5	New Ross / Baltimore	1849 / Feb 1849	Levi Moore
Cummons / Hanover	Caspar H.	30 Nov 1842 / 28 Sep 1847 / 36			John J. Breisch
Cunning	John	05 Nov 1828 / 05 Nov 1828 / IN			

Cunningham James		29 Mar 1836	Dublin	1830	
County Roscommon, Ireland			Oswago, NY	1833	
28	1808	s	4		
Cunningham Samuel		20 Nov 1820			
County Armagh, Ireland				12 Jul 1817	
22		s	21		
Cunningham William		27 Mar 1820			Thomas Flemming
County Armagh, Ireland		28 Mar 1825		01 Jul 1816	
24		s	3		
Curley Patrick		06 Dec 1837	Dublin	1832	Thomas Howard
County Galway, Ireland		05 Oct 1840	New York	1834	
26	1811	x	44		
Curren Peter		30 Nov 1840			Bernard McKinnly
		06 Dec 1842			
			30	Owes allegiance to Great Britain and Ireland.	
Daab Conrad		18 Nov 1830	Bremen	31 May 1830	
Great Beven, Hessen Darmstadt			Baltimore	20 Aug 1830	
25	1805	s			
Daily John					
Germany		12 Jan 1799			
Danheiber Isaac		22 Oct 1856	Havre de Grace	1852	Abram Seir
France		30 Jul 1859	New York	1852	
35	1821	?	19	Next to his signature, the clerk has written "Signed in Hebrew."	
				Name could be spelled Danheiser.	

Last Name / Place of Birth / Age	First Name / Date of Birth	Report Date / Natural. Date / Sig. Page No.	Departure Port / Arrival Port / Other	Departure Date / Arrival Date	Witness(es)
Danner	Andrew	05 Dec 1837	Bremen	1836	
Weiden, Wirtemburgh	1806		Baltimore	1836	
31		s 40			
Danzer	William	23 Nov 1837	Bremen	1832	Conrad Simler
Calba, Prussia	1811	25 Sep 1840	New York	1832	
26		s 10	Name could be spelled Dantzer.		
Daughanay?	James	04 Oct 1838			
		--			
		IN			
Davis	Daniel	13 Apr 1835	Name may be Doughterty		
		--			
		IN	Name may be Doris		
Davis	Richard	28 Nov 1831	Liverpool	1831	William D. Bell
County Radnorshire, England	1803	24 Nov 1836	Baltimore	1831	
28		s 41			
Davis	Thomas	19 Nov 1824			
County Hereford, England				Jan 1822	
27		s 26			
Davis	William	6 Apr 1826			
County Derry, Ireland		05 Nov 1828		Sep 1818	
40		x			

Davis	William	29 Nov 1839			
		29 Nov 1839			
Deary	Edward	01 Apr 1839		Liverpool	1836
County Mannahan, Ireland				Baltimore	1836
34	1805	x	18		
Decker	Paul	24 Jul 1837		Bremen	1832	Peter Hammen
Braden, Germany		12 Aug 1839		Baltimore	1832
26	1811	s	56	Owes allegiance to Prince Leopold.
Deflinger	E. Andrew	09 Oct 1849		Bremen	1837
Barbrickwald, Bavaria		26 Jul 1852		Baltimore	1837
49	1800	s	32		
Degnan	Michael	26 Mar 1840		Liverpool	1834	Patrick Kelly
Co. Latron, Ireland		16 Sep 1844		New York	1834
34	1806	x	14		
Deitlehouser	Lewis	14 Aug 1866		Bremen	1854	Andrew Nail
Bavaria		20 Oct 1869		Baltimore	1854	William Schlotterbeck
37	1829	s	9		
Deitrick	Elizabeth	19 Mar 1852		Bremen	1833	George W. Smith
Hesse Cassel		20 Mar 1854		Baltimore	1833
50	1802	s	24	One of only 2 women naturalized prior to 1880 in Washington Co.
Deitrick	Frederick	05 Apr 1809		Bordeaux*	
Upenhaur, Germany					30 May 1806
27		s	38		

* - "Bordeaux, France". Signature reads Frederic Dietrich

Last Name	First Name	Report Date	Departure Port	Departure Date	Witness(es)
Place of Birth	Date of Birth	Natural. Date	Arrival Port	Arrival Date	
Age		Sig. Page No.	Other		
Deitrick	Frederick	29 Sep 1845			
		29 Sep 1845			
Deitrick	George	11 Mar 1856			Andrew Sibald
Bavaria		01 Aug 1859			
		4			
Deitrick	Lewis	22 Mar 1853	Bremen	1833	Elizabeth Deitrick
Hulseheusen, Hesse Cassel		22 Mar 1853	Baltimore	Jun 1833	
21	1832	x 11	Arrived as a minor.		
Deitz	John	29 Oct 1812			
Basil, Switzerland				01 Sep 1806	
41		s 22			
Delp	Henry	18 Nov 1830	Amsterdam	05 Sep 1827	
Ninter Casten, Hessen Darmstad			Baltimore	11 Nov 1827	
35	1795	s 34			
Delzell	John	24 Sep 1806			William Moore
Ireland		67			
Denbel	Henry	21 Nov 1821		Aug 1819	
Wirtemburgh, Germany					
27		s 31			

Name	Origin	Age/Year	Date	Port/Dest	Year	Witness/Notes
Denbel William	Wirtemburgh, Germany		21 Nov 1821		Aug 1819	
35			s 31			
Deneaf Patrick	County Kilkenny, Ireland		04 Dec 1833	Waterford *	1825	
36	1797		x 41	New York	1825	
				* City of Waterford		
Denholm Charles			11 Sep 1850			Daniel South
			24			
				Arrived as a minor. Owes allegiance to Great Britain & Ireland		
Dennhoefer Simon S.	Bavaria		13 Sep 1867	Hamburg	1861	Lewis Heist
			13 Sep 1867	New York	1861	Lewis Monath
32	1835		? 5	Honorably discharged from military service 27 Feb 1867		
Depra/Depoi August	Salbert, Hesse, Germany		27 Sep 1837	Bremen	1837	
48	1789			Baltimore	1837	
			s 68	Signature reads Depoi.		
Dermody William			26 Sep 1833			Joel B. Cahoun
			22 Nov 1836			
			5			
Desmond Thomas	Co. Cork		17 Mar 1853	Liverpool	1850?	
22	1831		s 8	New York	Oct 1850?	
Despres Cerf	France		05 Nov 1855	Havre de Grace	1853	
39	1817		s 21	New York	23 Oct 1853	
				Name may be Deprès		

Last Name	First Name	Report Date	Departure Port	Departure Date	Witness(es)
Place of Birth	Date of Birth	Natural. Date	Arrival Port	Arrival Date	
Age		Sig. Page No.	Other		
Despres	Leon	05 Nov 1855	Havre de Grace	1853	
France			New York	23 Oct 1853	
35	1821	s 22	Name may be Deprès		
Deitelback	Sclickman	30 Mar 1842			
		30 Mar 1842			
		IN			
Devine	Patrick	02 Nov 1814			
County Tyrone, Ireland				02 Sep 1812	
32		s 34			
Devine	Thomas	05 Oct 1840	Liverpool	1839	
Kings Co., Ireland			New York	1839	
18	1822	s 101			
Devins	Frankin	24 Mar 1840	Sligo	1826	
Sligo Co., Ireland			New York	1826	
35	1805	x 7			
Dick	John	28 Nov 1808			Christian Fechtig
Germany		28 Nov 1808		<5 Jul 1804	
		40			
Dickey	William	02 Apr 1814	County Derry,		Joseph Hemphill
Ireland		30 Mar 1821		14 May 1807	
24		s 43			

Name	Origin	Birth/Age	Departure	Arrival	Date	Notes	Sponsor
Diederick Fritzler, Hesse Cassel	Francis	1791	02 Apr 1852 08 Aug 1856 s 10	Bremen Baltimore	1832 1832	Name may be Deiderick	George W. Smith
Dieterich Bavaria	George	1795	11 Mar 1856 s 6	Bremen Baltimore	1833 15 Aug 1833		
Diffenbaugh Eppinghan, Baden	Martin	Sep 1800	19 Nov 1828 26 Nov 1832 s	Amsterdam Baltimore	1819 Aug 1819	Has lived in Maryland since arrival in U.S.	
Dillon Ireland	Michael	1834	11 Dec 1856 s 23	Liverpool New York	1853 10 Sep 1853		
Dillon	Michael		28 Oct 1872 46			Weaver. Living in Hagerstown.	
Dilman Holland	Henry		11 Jan 1798 11 Jan 1798 36				
Doarnberger Hesse Darmstadt	Adam	1842	11 Aug 1866 11 Aug 1866 s 5	Bremen Baltimore	1854 1854	Arrived as a minor.	Lewis Heist John Costenberger
Doarnberger Hesse Darmstadt	Henary	1845	11 Aug 1866 11 Aug 1866 s 6	Bremen Baltimore	1854 1854	Arrived as a minor.	Lewis Heist John Costenberger

Last Name Place of Birth Age	First Name Date of Birth	Report Date Natural. Date Sig. Page No.	Departure Port Arrival Port Other	Departure Date Arrival Date	Witness(es)
Doarnberger Hesse Darmstadt 21	Peter 1847	15 Mar 1869 s 25	Bremen Baltimore	1854 1854	
Dolin	Charles	14 Nov 1825 10 Oct 1828 IN			
Dolzell	Samuel	*17 Aug 1844*			
Domel Wirtemburgh	Matthias	22 Feb 1848 28 May 1850 22			Baltis Castenbader John J. Breisch
Donnelly Ireland 28	Daniel	19 Nov 1817 25 Nov 1822 s 22	Londonderry	10 Nov 1816	
Donnelly New Castle, Ireland 28	Edward 1816	14 Sep 1844 05 Oct 1846 x 50	Liverpool New York	1839 1839	William Hawken
Donnelly Ireland 46	James 1810	29 Oct 1856 x 21	Galway New York	May 1851 12 Aug 1851	

Surname	Given	Origin	Date 1 / Date 2	s/x	age	Port / Notes	Sponsor
Donnelly	Patrick	Parrish of Daunmore	25 Nov 1820 / 27 Mar 1827	s	41	Jul 1817 Born in Parrish of Daunmore, County Tirone, Ireland.	Henry C. Schnebly
38							
Donnelly	Patrick	Ireland	01 Nov 1815	s	35	17 Oct 1809	
Doris	John	County Tyrone, Ireland	06 Apr 1821	x	73	Aug 1818	
27							
Dorley	Joseph		19 Jan 1835 / 20 Nov 1838		3	Report made in Dauphin Co., PA. Name may be Dooley	Luke O'Brien
Dougherty	Conn	County Donegal, Ireland	04 Apr 1822	x	37	1811	
38							
Dougherty	James	County Lathem, Ireland	19 Nov 1833	x	13	Slago / New York	1823 / 1823
30		1803					
Doyle	James		28 Sep 1840 / 05 Oct 1846		24	Allegiance to Gr. Britain & Ireland. Report made in Morgan Co. WV	David Rush
Dozell	Samuel	Glocestershire, England	17 Aug 1844	s	43	Liverpool / Boston	1835 / 1835
48		1796					

Last Name / Place of Birth / Age	First Name / Date of Birth	Report Date / Natural. Date / Sig. Page No.	Departure Port / Arrival Port / Other	Departure Date / Arrival Date	Witness(es)
Dress	William	29 Oct 1812			
28		s 22	Born in County Derry, Ireland.	1803	
Drexler	Frederick	17 Nov 1824			
Wirtemburgh, Germany		01 Oct 1828		1819	
35		s 24			
Driefus	Raphael	22 Oct 1856	Havre de Grace	1853	Nathan Kahn
France		01 Nov 1860	New York	1853	
42	1813	s 19			
Drinnen	Thomas	19 Nov 1839	Dublin	1827	
County Queens, Ireland		16 Nov 1841	Alexandria,DC	1827	
30	1809	x 4	Name may be Drennon. Arrived Alexandria, District of Columbia		
Driscoll	Michael	19 Nov 1835	County Cork	1832	
County Cork, Ireland			Albany, NY	1832	
25	1809	s 13			
Druss	Lewis				
		24 Oct 1840			

Duffey Wickliff Co. 27	Edward 1825	16 Aug 1852 x 3	Liverpool 1847 New York Jan 1847 I question whether he could leave Liverpool in 1847 and arrive by Jan. 1847.	
Duffy	John	06 Nov 1817 29 Mar 1823 25		John Allen
Duignan Ireland 25	James 1842	29 Oct 1867 31 Oct 1867 s 15	Report was made in York County, PA. Queenstown, Ir 1849 New York 1849 Departed Queenstown, Ireland	Bernard Reilly
Dundy	James	30 Nov 1831 15 Mar 1837 65		William D. Bell
Dunn	Edward	03 Oct 1838 05 Oct 1840		Thomas Dunn
Dunn	Henry	16 Sep 1844 85		John H. Kidwell
Dunn	James	05 Oct 1842 05 Oct 1842 IN	Arrived as a minor. Owes allegiance to Great Britain & Ireland Beside his name is the notation "minor"	
Dunn France	Lewis	16 Sep 1844 99	Arrived as a minor.	Michael Friese

Last Name / Place of Birth / Age	First Name / Date of Birth	Report Date / Natural. Date / Sig. Page No.	Departure Port / Arrival Port / Other	Departure Date / Arrival Date	Witness(es)
Dunn / Ireland / 33	Peter / 1839	22 Nov 1872 / 03 Mar 1875 / s 6?	Liverpool / New York	1866 / 1866	Edward Donnelly / William O'Neil
Dunn / Co. Kildare, Ireland / 36	Richard / 1808	08 Apr 1844 / / s 26	Dublin / Ogdensburgh * / * Ogdensburgh, New York	1831 / 1831	
Dunn / /	Thomas /	23 May 1831 / 27 Mar 1834 / 23	Report made in Huntingdon County, PA.		James D. Farrell
Durdy / County Derry, Ireland / 41	James / 1790	30 Nov 1831 / 15 Mar 1837 / s 47a	Londonderry / NewBrunswick / Left New Brunswick, Canada and arrived Norfolk, VA in 1831.	1830 / 1830	
Durney / Halifax, Novia Scotia, Canada / 27	Richard / 1814	27 Sep 1841 / 26 Sep 1844 / s 61	Halifax / Boston	1834 / 25 Dec 1834	John Gall
Duttrow / Bavaria / 43	John / 1812	29 Dec 1855 / / s 21	Bremen / Baltimore	1839 / 08 Oct 1839	
Dwyer / County Tipperary, Ireland / 32	John / 1802	04 Apr 1834 / / x 49	Waterford / Philadelphia	1827 / Nov 1827	

Name		Birth	Arrival	Origin/Port	Year	Sponsors
Dwyer	Simon	17 Nov 1835		Limerick	1822	
County Clare, Ireland				Rochester, NY	1822	
32	1803	s	5			
Dyer	Henry	02 Oct 1838				Terrance Roke
		05 Oct 1840		Report made in Morgan Co., VA (now WV).		
Eagan	Thomas	20 Sep 1870		Galway	1861	James I. Hurley
Ireland		11 Sep 1872		New York	1861	George Sias
30	1840	s	23			
Earhart	John	03 Feb 1852				John Baltz
Hesse Darmstadt			20	Arrived as a minor.		
Earle	Thomas	15 Oct 1870		New Ross, Irel.	1849	Charles E. Weiss
Ireland		15 Oct 1870		Baltimore	1849	F.T. Houser
34	1836	s	27			
Earnest	Jacob	26 Nov 1832				
		---		IN		
Earnst	John	28 Nov 1848		Bremen	1843	
Nakkertentzzlengen, Wirtemburg				Philadelphia	04 Jul 1843	
29	1819	s	2			
Earnst/Earnest	John George	26 Nov 1832				John Leitz
		29 Aug 1836				
			42			

Last Name Place of Birth Age	First Name Date of Birth	Report Date Natural. Date Sig. Page No.	Departure Port Arrival Port Other	Departure Date Arrival Date	Witness(es)
Eartinhousin Germany	Conrad	05 Apr 1798 05 Apr 1798 7			
Ebb	John	27 Nov 1846 27 Nov 1846	Weaver. Living near Beaver Creek.		
Ebberts Germany	John Samuel	26 Aug 1802			
Ebbrecht Leana, Hanover 32	William 1812	16 Sep 1844 20 Sep 1847 s 54	Bremen Baltimore	1839 1839	Christian Moost
Eber Byren, King of Byre, Germany 31	John 1808	26 Mar 1839 30 Sep 1842 s 5	Bremen Baltimore	1837 1837	
Eber Bavaria 36	John Henry 1819	10 Apr 1855 s 20	Bremen Baltimore	1852 02 Feb 1853	
Eck Bavaria 32	John Michael 1812	16 Sep 1844 28 Sep 1847 s 63	Bremen Baltimore	1840 30 Sep 1840	Ulrich Leinkand

Surname	Given Name	Dates	Place	Notes
Eckstein	John	03 Dec 1825		David Rohrer
		16 Nov 1830		
Ecland	George	Certificate		
		22 Nov 1841		
		IN		
Effland	George	*certificate*		
		22 Nov 1841		
Egan	John	16 Sep 1844	Dublin	1830
Balydaly, Ireland			Baltimore	15 Aug 1830
139		1805 s 62		
Eggers	Louis Gustus	27 Nov 1827	Baltimore	Jun 1822
Sessen, Dukedom of Brunswick			Made 2nd Report on 04 Nov 1828	
22		s		
Einick?	Joseph	27 Feb 1839		Report Column reads "Certificate." Name may be Eirich.
		26 Sep 1842		
		IN		
Einstein	Henry	16 Dec 1843		
		02 Apr 1846		
		IN		
Eisenbriess?	Charles	3 Apr 1826		Jun 1822
Town of Ortwiler?, Prussia				
38		s		

Last Name Place of Birth Age	First Name Date of Birth	Report Date Natural. Date Sig. Page No.	Departure Port Arrival Port Other	Departure Date Arrival Date	Witness(es)
Elliott Ireland 28	William 1825	20 Oct 1853 12 Aug 1856 s 14	Liverpool Boston	41 Jun 1841	Hugh McKusker
Endriss Wirtemburgh 21	Gotleib 1833	19 Jul 1854 s 10	Havre de Grace New York	1853 15 Nov 1853	
Engert Saxony, Germany 28	John A. 1816	08 Apr 1844 s 26	Bremen New York	1839 1839	
Erstine Wirtemburgh	Henry	02 Apr 1846 6			John Uleis/Weis
Erbb/Ebb Wirtemburgh	John	27 Nov 1846 9	Arrived as a minor.		George Gassman
Ernde Soultz, Wirtemburgh 21	Lewis 1819	10 Aug 1840 10 Aug 1840 s 59	Bremen Baltimore	1834 1834	Gotleib Stutts
Ernst	Frederick	*10 Nov 1857*			

Name	Given	Date	Port	Year	Notes
Ernst	Henry	13 Mar 1855	Havre de Grace	1852	
Neckerdenslingen, Wirtemburgh			New York	07 Apr 1852	
23	1832	s 6			
Ernst	John	28 Nov 1848	Bremen	1843	John B. Castenbader
Nakkartent, Wirtemburg		31 Mar 1851	Philadelphia	04 Jul 1843	
29	1819	s 7			
Evans	David	17 Aug 1840	Liverpool	1834	Josiah James
Wales		17 Aug 1840	New York	1834	
23	1817	s 68			
Evans	John	21 Nov 1842			John S. Pollard
121		1			
Evans	Richards	17 Aug 1840	Liverpool	1833	
Wales		03 Oct 1842	Philadelphia	1833	
29	1811	x 70			
Everlein	Adam	25 Oct 1836	Bremen	1833	
County Darmstadt, Germany			Baltimore	1833	
25	1811	s 50	Name may be Everling		
Ewald	Kaspar	25 Mar 1841	Bremen	1839	
Munnerstower, Bavaria			Baltimore	01 Sep 1839	
35	1806	s 26	Signature reads Ewats.		
Exner	Joseph	08 Apr 1840	Bremen	1833	
Waldeim, Baden, Germany			Baltimore	1833	
32	1808	x 39			

Last Name Place of Birth Age	First Name Date of Birth	Report Date Natural. Date Sig. Page No.	Departure Port Arrival Port Other	Departure Date Arrival Date	Witness(es)
Facken Heckenghen, Germany 25	Thomas 1817	21 Nov 1842 s 2	Bremen Baltimore Name may be Fangher	1839 1839	
Facksberger Bavaria	Adam	26 Jul 1853 27 Jul 1855 6			David H. Wiles Samuel Johnson
Fagan Ireland	John	01 Feb 1871 02 Oct 1876 - 26	Report made in Pittsburgh, Western Districk of Pennsylvania.		William McK Keppler P. Sweeney
Faik/Fait Bavaria	John	20 Sep 1847 24	Arrived as a minor.		David Rush
Faith Bavaria	Adam	*16 Sep 1844* 16 Sep 1844 71	Arrived as a minor.		Hartman Hase
Fannreuther	Frederick	*20 Feb 1849*			
Fanthorp Lekurshire County, Great Brit. 31	Henry	26 Nov 1821 s 48		11 Dec 1818	

Farrell	Edward	26 Aug 1827			
		31 Mar 1834			
		38		Report made at Northumberland County, PA.	
Farrell	James D.	26 Aug 1827			Thomas Dunn
		27 Mar 1834			
		24		Report made in Huntingdon County, PA.	
Farrell	John	26 Aug 1829			Peter Ganahan
		31 Mar 1834			
		33		Report made at Northumberland County, PA.	
Fate	John	*12 Mar 1855*			Elisha Miles
Bavaria		12 Mar 1855			
		5			
Faulder	John	*22 Nov 1822*			
		22 Nov 1822		Arrived as a minor.	
Febrey	George	02 Dec 1847	Havre de Grace	1845	Michael Freize
Schurtzheim, Baden		01 Oct 1850	New York	01 Oct 1845	
28	1819	s 20			
Febrey	Lewis	19 Dec 1854	Havre de Grace	1852	
Baden			New York	18 Jul 1852	
29	1825	s 16			
Fecher	Joseph	03 Apr 1841	Bremen	1839	Christian Rosenstock
Hecham, Wirtemburgh		16 Sep 1844	Baltimore	1839	Elijah Swope
28	1813	s 45			

Last Name / Place of Birth / Age	First Name / Date of Birth	Report Date / Natural. Date / Sig. Page No.	Departure Port / Arrival Port / Other	Departure Date / Arrival Date	Witness(es)
Fechtig Wirtemburgh 36	Frederick	01 Nov 1808 01 Apr 1815 s 31		1805	
Feezler Scherzheim, Baden 32	John 1824	09 Oct 1856 s 19	Havre de Grace New York	1852 20 Jul 1852	
Feighl Wirtemburgh 45	Joseph 1795	01 Oct 1840 s 90	Bremen New York	1839 1839	
Feilman Muhlenburg, Prussia	Frederick	10 Apr 1868 24			John Cook
Felinger	Frederick	03 Sep 1838 05 Oct 1840 102	Honorably discharged from military service 04 Dec 1862.		Herman Westinhouse
Fernsner Sultzhanch, Prussia 21	Lewis 1828	26 Sep 1849 26 Sep 1849 s 24	Havre de Grace New York Arrived as a minor.	1837 1837	Patrick Whitney
Fess Sweibergh, Germany 33	Jacob 1803	15 Apr 1836 s 36	Havre de Grace New York	1832 1832	

Fessler Prussia	Charles Godhel	31 Oct 1808 04 Nov 1811 27	Has lived in Maryland since Oct. 1802
Fessler	John		
Fetterly	Philip	*27 Mar 1821*	
Fightig Germany	Christian	13 Jan 1798 13 Jan 1798 44	
Finegan	Bernard	26 Mar 1833 -- IN	Shoemaker. Living in Hagerstown.
Finekin County Clare, Ireland 26 1808	John	27 Mar 1834 x 20	Limerick 1831 White Hall, NY May 1831
Finekin County Clare, Ireland 23 1811	Michael	27 Mar 1834 x 21	Limerick 1831 White Hall, NY May 1831
Finkbinder Wertenburg, Germany 42 1794	Frederick	20 Nov 1835 02 Dec 1837 s 16	Havre de Grace 1829 Baltimore 1829 Jacob Barth

Last Name	First Name	Report Date	Departure Port	Departure Date	Witness(es)
Place of Birth	Date of Birth	Natural. Date	Arrival Port	Arrival Date	
Age		Sig. Page No.	Other		
Finnigan	Bernard	*26 Mar 1833*			
Firth	Robert M.	29 Nov 1839	Liverpool	1831	
Yorkshire, England		27 Nov 1841	Baltimore	1831	
31	1808	s 29			
Fisher	David	22 Nov 1823		1820	
Arnstadt, Wirtemburgh			Under Arrival Date, he said "3 years ago."		
23		s 38			
Fisher	Henry	31 Mar 1810	Waltenbaugh		
Hohenhe?, Germany		31 Mar 1810		1809	
39		s 35	Born in Waltenbaugh.		
Fisher	Joseph	05 Jul 1837	Havre de Grace	1830	
Sickinger, Germany			New York	1830	
42	1795	s 54			
Fitzgerald	Patrick	26 Nov 1832			
		--			
		IN			
Flartney	Peter	05 Oct 1840	Slygo	1834	
Co. Slygo, Ireland			New York	1834	
24	1816	x 115			

Fleder/Flater Andrew	16 Sep 1844	Bremen	1839	Christian Brining
Herlheim, Bavaria	05 Oct 1846	Baltimore	1839	
33 1811	s 51			
Fleming James	21 Nov 1821		Feb 1819	William Freaner
County Armaugh, Ireland	02 Dec 1834	Under Arrival Date, he listed "2 years and 9 months ago."		
21	s 39			
Flemming John	20 Nov 1827	New York	1816	Samuel Hays
County Armaugh, Ireland	01 Apr 1836			
36	s			
Flemming Thomas	31 Mar 1814		18 May 1812	
Ireland	25 *Oct 1828*			
125	s 34			
Flemming Thomas	31 Mar 1819			
	25 Oct 1828			
	IN			
Flinn James	12 Nov 1852	Liverpool	1849	Hugh Murphy
Ireland	28 Jul 1856	New York	Jan 1850	
22	x 8			
Flurschutz John Michael	01 Oct 1840	Bremen	1838	
Saxony, Germany		Baltimore	1838	
27 1813	s 90			
Flynn Michael	01 Jul 1869	City of Cork	1852	
Ireland	28 Oct 1872	New York	1852	
40 1829	x 46			

| Last Name | First Name | Report Date | Departure Port | Departure Date | Witness(es) |
| Place of Birth | Date of Birth | Natural. Date | Arrival Port | Arrival Date | |
Age		Sig. Page No.	Other		
Foard	William	13 Apr 1799			
Great Britain		13 Apr 1799			
		51	Labourer. Living on Upper Antietam Hundred.		
Fogel	Adam	27 Sep 1836	Bremen	1834	Frederick Fishach
Dukedom Darmstadt, Germany		01 Apr 1839	Baltimore	1823	
30	1806	s 45	Born Hesse Darmstadt.		
Fogle	Frederick	14 Dec 1838	Bremen	1835	
Stuckenburg, Hesse Darmstadt		26 Sep 1842	Baltimore	1835	
45	1793	s 38			
Fogle	John	14 Dec 1838	Bremen	1833	
Stuckenburg, Hesse Darmstadt		26 Sep 1842	Baltimore	1833	
43	1795	s 38			
Foglesong	George	23 Aug 1804			George Foglesong
France		27			
Folk	Alexander	cert			
		06 Aug 1857	Full name is F.W. Alexander Folk		
Foos	Jacob	02 Nov 1811	Amsterdam	01 Sep 1806	
Wurtemburgh					
35		s 41			

Name		Dates	Port	Witnesses
Ford	Franklin	16 Jun 1864		F.F. Mongan
County Mead, Ireland		24 Oct 1870		George W. Smith
37		34	Report made in District of Columbia.	
Ford	James	24 Nov 1834	Dublin	1827
County Longford, Ireland			New York	1827
27		s 41		
Foreman	Henry	03 Oct 1844	Bremen	1837
Osueburg, Hanover			Baltimore	Dec 1837
28	1816	x 124		
Forthman	Frederick	12 Sep 1853	Bremen	1845
Saxe Meininger Hidlgh, Germany		12 Sep 1853	Philadelphia	1845 Henry Spielman
21	1832	s 9	Arrived as a minor.	
Forthman	Jacob	01 Apr 1848	Bremen	1845
Meininger, Saxe Meininger			Philadelphia	19 Nov 1845
25	1823	s 3		
Forthman	John	10 Apr 1838		
		30 Sep 1842		
		IN		
Fose	John	05 Apr 1822		1814
County Tirone, Ireland				
35		x 39		
Foster	George	05 Apr 1836	Bremen	1831
Fulder, Hesse Cassel, Germany		24 Sep 1838	Baltimore	1831
28	1808	s 20		

Last Name Place of Birth Age	First Name Date of Birth	Report Date Natural. Date Sig. Page No.	Departure Port Arrival Port Other	Departure Date Arrival Date	Witness(es)
Foster Hesse Cassel	Henry	*01 Dec 1840* 07 Dec 1842 31			John N. Russe
Fox Bavaria	Alozins Andre	01 Oct 1850 01 Oct 1850 32			James Ward
Fox Prussia	Ernst A.C.	01 Oct 1850 28	Arrived as a minor.		James Gladhill
Fox	John	*05 Apr 1822*	Report was made in Frederick Co., Maryland. No date given.		
Fraker Austria	George	28 Mar 1818 41			John Shafer
Frantz Bavaria	John	23 Feb 1841 04 Apr 1844 17	Report made in Morgan Co., VA (now WV).		Horace Repley

Freaker	George	28 Mar 1818 28 Mar 1818		
Frederick	John	Certificate 25 Sep 1838 IN		
Frederick	John Jefferson	03 Oct 1838 03 Oct 1838 IN		
Frederick	Kettering	03 Oct 1838 05 Oct 1840 IN		
Freeman Germany	Stephen	18 Jun 1804 66	Christian Hawke	
Freiderici	Ernst	28 Aug 1832 09 Apr 1836 26	William A. Good	Report filed in Adams County, PA.
Freise Bavaria	Peter	16 Sep 1844 30 Aug 1848 17	Jacob Butts	Name may be Freize. Arrived as a minor.
Frey	Jacob	25 Jun 1840 26 Sep 1842 IN		Report columns reads "Certificate."

Last Name	First Name	Report Date	Departure Port	Departure Date	Witness(es)
Place of Birth	Date of Birth	Natural. Date	Arrival Port	Arrival Date	
Age		Sig. Page No.	Other		
Freyfogle	John	05 Dec 1820			Martin Newcomer
Village of Mesenbaugh, Bavaria		03 Apr 1827		26 Aug 1820	
28		s 67	Born in the Village of Mesenbaugh, Canton Sanotarl, Bavaria.		
Frick	Charles	--			
		24 Sep 1838			
		IN			
Fridinger	Charles	12 Oct 1839			Jacob Gassman
		47	"Came in a minor." Rest of page is blank.		
Fridinger	George	29 Nov 1839	Havre de Grace	1832	
Zwibricken, Bavaria		12 Feb 1844	New York	1832	
52	1787	s 28			
Fridinger	Henry	12 Feb 1844			
		12 Feb 1844			
		IN			
Fridinger	John	05 Oct 1846			Samuel Johnston
Bavaria		32	Arrived as a minor.		
Fridinger, Jr.	George	24 Nov 1845	Havre de Grace	1832	Charles Ulrick
Wolfersheimer, Bavaria		06 Nov 1848	New York	17 Jun 1832	
34	1811	s 6			

Name	Date	Place	Note
Friess Michael	05 Nov 1828 05 Nov 1828 IN		
Fritz Nicholas Germany	29 Oct 1813 29 Oct 1813 34		Name may be Frieze
Fury Dennis County Mayo, Ireland 50 1784	25 Mar 1834 x 12	Kilila White Hall, NY	1831 Jul 1831
Futterer Louis Baden, Germany 1326 1814	09 Jun 1840 09 Ju 1840 s 47	Havre de Grace New York Name may be Foutter	1833 1833
Fye Conrad Hesse Darmstadt 55 1801	27 Aug 1856 s 18	Bremen New York	1849 1849
Gaertner Michael	cert 22 Mar 1841		
Gafney Michael	26 Sep 1842 --- IN		
Gagle John Henry Hesse Darmstadt 40 1800	02 Apr 1840 26 Sep 1842 s 32	Bremen Baltimore	1831 1831

| Last Name | First Name | Report Date | Departure Port | Departure Date | Witness(es) |
| Place of Birth | Date of Birth | Natural. Date | Arrival Port | Arrival Date | |
Age		Sig. Page No.	Other		
Gaismar	Salomon	15 Sep 1855	Havre de Grace	1852	
France			New York	01 Jul 1852	
26	1829	s 19			
Galvin	Dennis	28 Nov 1833		1826	
City of Waterford, Ireland		20 Aug 1835	New York	Dec 1826	
35	1798	s 34	Has lived in Washington County since his arrival in U.S.		
Galvin	James	23 Nov 1836	Dublin	1830	
County Westmeath, Ireland			Sevago, NY	1830	
26	1811	x 10			
Ganahan	Peter	22 May 1827			Patrick Hopkins
		09 Apr 1834	Report made at New York, NY.		
		67			
Ganter	Thomas	25 Mar 1834	Havre de Grace	1830	
Schuten, Baden, Germany			Baltimore	Sep 1830	
50	1784	s 4	Owes allegiance to Prince Leopold.		
Gardner	George	16 Sep 1844	Bremen	1839	Andrew Flater
Elitzhum, Bavaria		05 Oct 1846	Baltimore	1839	
37	1807	s 51	Signature reads Gartner.		
Gareis	George	24 May 1858	Bremen	1857	William Biershing
Bavaria		08 Nov 1864	Baltimore	Sep 1857	
28	1829	s 23			

Surname	Given	Date 1	Date 2	Place	Notes	Other
Garman	Adam	02 Nov 1843				George Polch
Hesse Darmstadt		05 Oct 1846				
		21				
Garmeyer	Francis	04 Jan 1798				
Germany		04 Jan 1798				
		11		Shoemaker. Living near Antietam.		
Garraghan	Thomas	26 Nov 1832		Dublin 1829		
County Longford, Ireland				Leubeck, Main 1829		
30		1804				James Hughes
		s	49			
Garraham	Thomas	26 Nov 1834				
		01 Dec 1837				
		32		Name may be Ganahan		
Garrett	James	21 Aug 1804				Henry Dillman
Ireland		22				
Garrett	Thomas	27 May 1807				George Binkley
Ireland						
Garvey	Patrick	16 Sep 1844		Drogheda 1841		
Drungerries, Ireland				New York 21 Jun 1841		
24		1830				
		s	54			
Garvin	Andrew	24 Mar 1840				

Last Name / Place of Birth / Age	First Name / Date of Birth	Report Date / Natural. Date / Sig. Page No.	Departure Port / Arrival Port / Other	Departure Date / Arrival Date	Witness(es)
Gasman	George	24 Mar 1829	Rotterdam	Jun 1826	
Town of Essingen, Baden		26 Nov 1832	Baltimore	July 1826	
25	1804	s	Has resided in Maryland since arrival in U.S.		
Gasman	Philip	05 Apr 1833			
		--			
		IN	Name may be Gosman		
Gates	William	31 Oct 1872			Charles A. Ways
Germany		31 Oct 1872			
		35	Wendall Gates. Arrived as a minor.		
Gavey/Garvey	Michael	22 Oct 1838			James Hughes
		30 Mar 1841			
		33			
Gavin	Andrew/Edw.	24 Mar 1840	Liverpool	1837	
County Monnay, Ireland			New York	1837	
30	1810	x 7	Andrew and Edward are both listed as his first name in different places in the document.		
Geetle	Jacob	05 Oct 1846			John Leis
Bavaria		32	Arrived as a minor.		
Geiger	Norbert	06 Aug 1844			Michael P. Smith
Baden		05 Oct 1846			
		27	Report made in York Co., Pennsylvania		

Surname / Origin	Given name	Dates	Place	Witness
Geimbel	John	03 Oct 1838		Peter Heuyett
		05 Oct 1840		
Geist	Lewis K.	*01 Dec 1838*		
Gerbig	Heinrich	25 Sep 1875	Bremen	Justice Heimel
Erbech, Hesse Darmstadt		19 Mar 1878	Baltimore	Leonard Wagoner
59		s 20		
Gerloch	Justus	07 Oct 1856	Bremen	Andrew Shank
Bernsdorf, Hesse Cassel		29 Nov 1858	United States	Mar 1852
1805		s 19	Lived "a while in Canada."	
Germley	John P.	24 Sep 1838		
		24 Sep 1838		
		IN		
Gettle	Daniel	02 Sep 1844		George Fechtig
Bavaria		02 Sep 1844		
		46	Arrived as a minor.	
Gilaspy	Patrick	19 Nov 1827		1815
County Donegal, Ireland				
31		x		
Gillan	Dominick	05 Oct 1867	Liverpool	Hamilton Downs
Ireland		05 Oct 1869	New York	Jesse F. Thompson
35	1832	x 8		1851 / 1851

Last Name First Name	Report Date Natural. Date Sig. Page No.	Departure Port Arrival Port Other	Departure Date Arrival Date	Witness(es)
Place of Birth Date of Birth				
Age				
Gillchrist Michael	21 Jul 1845	Liverpool	1835	Henry Remley
Latham Co., Ireland	02 Dec 1851	New York	Mar 1836	
44 1811	x 23	Note the descrepancy in the age and date of birth.		
Gillespie Anthony	24 Sep 1839			Thomas Gilleeca
Great Britain & Ireland	26 Mar 1844			
	3	Report made in Morgan Co., VA (now WV).		
Gillna Henry	25 Oct 1814	Co. Langford		
Ireland			23 Jul 1799	
55	s 18			
Gilmartin Thomas	05 Oct 1840	Slygo	1837	
Co. Slygo, Ireland		New York	1837	
24 1816	s 103			
Gimbel John	03 Oct 1838			
	05 Oct 1840			
	IN			
Glanmeyer Joseph	20 Sep 1847	Bremen	1839	Andrew Miller
Hoherzollen, Sigmaringen	25 Mar 1850	Baltimore	Jul 1839	
41 1806	s 15	Born in Germany. Name may be Glenmyer		
Glockner Devault	11 Apr 1801			
Prince of Switburgh, Germany				
40		Wagonmaker. Living in Conococheague Hundred.		

Name			Date	Place	Witness/Notes
Glockner	Devault		18 Aug 1802		Ambrose Geoghagan
Germany				Resided in U.S. before 29 Jan 1795	
Goetle	Henry		03 Sep 1838		
			03 Sep 1838		
			IN		
Goheen	Thomas		02 Jul 1858	Waterford	
Ireland				Baltimore	
25	1832	x	24		
Goldsmith	Jacob		09 Apr 1840	Holland	1852
Teurlach, Baden, Germany			16 Sep 1844	Baltimore	05 Nov 1854
72	1768	x	41		John Steffle
					1832
					1832
Goll	John		04 Jan 1798		
Prince of Sandgrave, Germany				Living in Hagerstown.	
Goll	John Jacob		26 Mar 1822		12 Feb 1819
County of Winesburgh		s	9	Born in County of Winesburgh, Wirtemburgh, Germany.	
Gollecher	Michael		05 Oct 1840	Dublin	1827
Co. West Mead, Ireland			05 Oct 1842	Philadelphia	1827
42	1798	x	98		
Goodending	Daniel		16 Sep 1844		John Goodending
Hesse Darmstadt			75	Arrived as a minor.	

Last Name Place of Birth Age	First Name Date of Birth	Report Date Natural. Date Sig. Page No.	Departure Port Arrival Port Other	Departure Date Arrival Date	Witness(es)
Goodenting, Jr	John	30 Sep 1839 30 Sep 1839 46			Anthony McBride
		"Came in under 18 yrs. of age." The rest of the page is blank.			
Goodening, Sr Rohrbaugh, Hesse Darmstadt 48	John 1791	30 Sep 1839 16 Sep 1844 s 42	Amsterdam Baltimore	1827 1827	Charles M. Perry
Goodman	Philip	04 Jan 1840 03 Oct 1842 IN			
		Report column reads "Certificate"			
Gorman	John	*01 Apr 1837* *01 Apr 1837*			
Gormley	John P.	*24 Sep 1838* *24 Sep 1838*			
Gossman County Baitenn, Germany 22	Jacob 1815	24 Jul 1837 03 Sep 1838 s 55	Bremen Baltimore	1833 1833	
		Owes allegiance to Prince Leopold. Arrived as a minor.			
Grabner Bavaria 35	George 1821	15 Oct 1855 s 21	Bremen Baltimore	1854 28 Oct 1854	

Name	Origin	Age/Year	Dates	Port/Destination	Arrival	Sponsor
Grady Thomas	Ireland	30 / 1837	20 Sep 1867 / 20 Sep 1870 / s 7	Queenstown / New York	1859 / Aug 1859	James J. Hurley / George G. Middlekauff
Graffe Jacob	Mensher, Prussia	36 / 1808	30 Sep 1844 / 28 Sep 1847 / s 122	Rotterdam / Baltimore	1839 / 09 Jul 1839	Samuel Tall
Graham James	Ireland	26	31 Mar 1814 / - 34		10 Aug 1801	
Graidy Thomas			03 Oct 1838 / --	IN		
Grass Charles	Free City of Bremen		26 Sep 1844 / 116			Benedict Grimminger
Greiner Frederick			-- / 01 Oct 1840		Report was made in Dauphin Co., Pennsylvania.	
Greminger John			11 Jul 1836 / 27 Sep 1841 / 63	Report made in Philadelphia, PA.	1841	Frederick Greiner
Griese Conrad	Azzenburg, Bavaria	34 / 1810	16 Sep 1844 / 03 Jul 1848 / s 58	Bremen / Baltimore	1841 / 29 Jun 1841	Everhart Beitelspacher / Frederick Helzle

Last Name	First Name	Report Date	Departure Port	Departure Date	Witness(es)
Place of Birth	Date of Birth	Natural. Date	Arrival Port	Arrival Date	
Age		Sig. Page No.	Other		
Griffen	Thomas	09 Apr 1834	Cork	1827	
County Cork, Ireland			New York	Feb 1827	
35	1799	s 65			
Gronower	Joseph	22 Nov 1830	Bremen	24 May 1830	
Lindenbaugh, Baden			Baltimore	01 Jul 1830	
26	1804	s			
Gross	Charles	*28 Sep 1844*			
Gross	Jacob	29 Nov 1841			John Leis
Wirtemburgh		05 Oct 1846			
		22			
Gross	John	16 Sep 1844			David Smith
Bavaria		05 Oct 1846			
		18			
Grouse	Peter	10 Jan 1799			
Germany		10 Jan 1799			
		18	Farmer. Living in Upper Antietam Hundred.		
Gruber	Jacob	25 Mar 1824			
Canton of Basil, Switzerland		24 Sep 1828		Nov 1816	
31		s 79			

Gunnpart?	John	23 Nov 1840		William Price, Jr.
		12 Feb 1844		
Guth	Rev. Michael	16 Nov 1835		
		27 Sep 1841		
		64	Report made in Philadelphia, PA.	
Hager	Christian	23 Mar 1840	Bremen	1830
Eldingen, Wirtemburgh.		28 Mar 1842	Baltimore	1830
38	1802	s 3		
Hagerman	Frederick	09 Mar 1855	Bremen	1851
Luebsnan, Hanover			Baltimore	Jul 1851
23	1832	s 4		
Hagerman	Henry	13 Aug 1856	Bremen	1851	Frederick Hagerman
Hanover		13 Aug 1856	Baltimore	Jun 1851	
22	1834	s 18	Arrived as a minor.		
Haggerty	John Henry	17 Nov 1835		Theabold Eichelberger
		IN		
Hahn	Earhart	16 Sep 1844		Charles Macgill
Bavaria		70		
Hahn	Thomas	04 Apr 1820		Oct 1818
Wirtemburgh, Germany				
54		s 42		

Last Name Place of Birth Age	First Name Date of Birth	Report Date Natural. Date Sig. Page No.	Departure Port Arrival Port Other	Departure Date Arrival Date	Witness(es)
Haiges Hottshous, Wirtemburgh 26	Gottleib 1810	05 Dec 1836 05 Oct 1842 s 52	Bremen Baltimore	1833 1833	
Haiges Hottshous, Wirtemburg 35	Henry 1801	05 Dec 1836 *30 Sep 1839* s 52	Bremen Baltimore	1832 1832	
Hall Ireland	John	31 Mar 1814 36			
Halm Grassflorian, Austria 32	Dr. Reinhold 1821	17 Feb 1853 09 Dec 1857 s 25	Hamburg New York	1852 Feb 1852	Julius M. Dashiell
Halpin Limerick, Ireland 24	John 1844	07 Sep 1868 07 Sep 1868 s 184	Waterford Philadelphia	1852 1852	
Hanenkampf Hanover	Arnold	23 May 1808 07 Nov 1811			Owes allegience to George Welss, Elector
Hanff?	Frederick	28 Mar 1842	IN		

Surname	Given	Origin / Destination	Dates	Year	Sponsors
Hanly	Luke	Roscomman County, Ireland	27 Mar 1865	1851	William S. Williamson, Esq
			27 Mar 1865	-	
	27	1838	s 17		
Hanna	James		02 Dec 1836		
			02 Dec 1836		
Happel	Martin	Hamburg	31 Oct 1870	1866	Albert Heil
		New York	31 Oct 1872	1866	William Schlotter
	32	Saxony, Germany	s 36		
		Schlotterbeck.			
Harman	Peter		23 Nov 1825		David Rohrer
		Switzerland	16 Nov 1830		
Harmon	Conrad	Bremen	10 Apr 1846	1839	
		Baltimore		Sep 1839	
	29	Hesan, Hesse Cassel	s 14		
		1817			
Hart	Cyrus		Certificate		
			30 Nov 1843		
			IN		
Hartman	Michael	Bremen	12 Oct 1870	1861	Lewis Heist
		Baltimore	28 Oct 1872	1861	George Hartman
	62	Streitan, Bavaria	s 25		
		1808			
Hartnack	Conrad		07 Apr 1842		
			16 Sep 1844		
			IN		

| Last Name | First Name | Report Date | Departure Port | Departure Date | Witness(es) |
| Place of Birth | Date of Birth | Natural. Date | Arrival Port | Arrival Date | |
Age		Sig. Page No.	Other		
Hartnack	Conrad	16 Sep 1844			Henry Rice
Hesse Cassel		103			
Hartzack	Saphara	01 Oct 1849			
		01 Oct 1849			
Harvey	Henry	24 Aug 1852			Henry Rowland
Byron, Germany		11 Sep 1866			David Martin
		17	Report was made in Frederick Co., Maryland.		
Hassard	Thomas	19 Nov 1834	Liverpool	1824	
County Fermanah, Ireland			New York	Oct 1824	
30	1804	s 12			
Hassett	John	19 Oct 1852	Liverpool	1850	Joseph Myers
Co. Clare		24 Jul 1855	Baltimore	Apr 1850	
21	1831	s 6			
Hasslett	Thomas	29 Sep 1845			
		29 Sep 1845			
Hauff	Frederick	28 Mar 1842			

Name	Origin	Date	Age	Notes	Witness
Haupt John C.*	Prussia	18 Aug 1802			Jacob Sharor
					*John Christopher
Hawthorn David	County Down, Ireland	21 Nov 1827		1818	William Hawthorn
	22	21 Nov 1827 s		Arrived at 13 yrs. of age. Came with mother and family to Washington County	
Hawthorn John	County Down, Ireland	22 Nov 1820		05 Jul 1819	
	21	10 Oct 1828 s	30		
Hawthorn William		06 Nov 1828			
		06 Nov 1828 IN			
Hayword William H.		20 Sep 1847	25	Arrived as a minor. Owes allegiance to Great Britain & Ireland	Samuel Thompson
Heartzack Laphara	Canton Aargan, Switzerland	01 Oct 1849		Philadelphia 1817	James Heysey
	1813 36	01 Oct 1849 s	28	Arrived as a minor.	1817
Heberly Godfrey	County of Wybleing, Wirtemburg	26 Mar 1822			29 Sep 1817
	26	s	7		
Heckman Christian	Hesse Cassel	16 Sep 1844	104	Arrived as a minor.	John Martin

Last Name Place of Birth Age	First Name Date of Birth	Report Date Natural. Date Sig. Page No.	Departure Port Arrival Port Other	Departure Date Arrival Date	Witness(es)
Heely Ireland 30	Thomas 1840	22 Sep 1870 x 24	Ireland New York	1861 1861	Alexander Neill
Heferla Kresailie, Prussia 34	Nicholas 1810	30 Sep 1844 s 121	Havre de Grace New York	1835 Sep 1835	
Heffier Saxony 25	John August	20 Nov 1848 27	Bremen Philadelphia	1847 Jun 1847	
Heggerly	John Henry	01 Dec 1832 17 Nov 1835 IN			
Heibner Bavaria 39	Thomas 1826	15 Aug 1866 s 9	Bremen Baltimore	1858 1858	
Heibner Bavaria 39	Thomas 1826	12 Sep 1868 12 Sep 1868 ? 285	Bremen Baltimore	1858 1858	
Heider Bavaria 34	John Adam 1824	24 Aug 1858 s 9	Havre de Grace New York	1854 01 Jul 1854	

Name	Origin	Date	Port	Sponsor
Heigel Michael		30 Nov 1822		
Freystadt, Baden, Germany			Sep 1817	
51		s 64		
Heiges Henry		05 Dec 1836		Michael Friese
		30 Dec 1839		
		39		
Heihnlein John		07 Apr 1843		David Benshoof
Bavaria		17		
Heil Adelbert		28 Jul 1855		Lewis Heist
Hesse Cassel		28 Jul 1855		
		8		
Heimel Justus		24 Jun 1862	Bremen	
Hesse Cassel			New York	
30	1832	s 23		
Helana George		25 Mar 1835		
		--		
		IN		
Heleine John		06 Jun 1831		09 Aug 1827
Nembach, Hesse Darmstadt		*25 Sep 1840*	Baltimore	10 Oct 1827
39	28 Mar 1792	s 61		
Helena Benjamin		05 Apr 1833		
		24 Oct 1840		
		IN		

Last Name Place of Birth Age	First Name Date of Birth	Report Date Natural. Date Sig. Page No.	Departure Port Arrival Port Other	Departure Date Arrival Date	Witness(es)
Helena	George	*25 Mar 1835*			
		IN			
Helena	John	06 Jun 1831 25 Sep 1836			Charles Ulrich
Helena Rohrback, Hesse Darmstadt 144	John Daniel 1801	05 Nov 1844 27 Nov 1846 s 128	Bremen Baltimore	1838 29 Oct 1838	Adam Weaver
Helgoth Bavaria 43	George 1813	12 Mar 1857 s 11	Bremen New York	1833 1833	
Hellaine Darmstadt 24	George 1826	26 Nov 1850 s 2	London New York	1847 1847	
Helsley Switzerland 47	Frederick 1808	05 Apr 1855 *06 Aug 1857* s 20	Havre de Grace New York	1828 1828	
Hemp Prussia	Philip	12 Apr 1799 12 Apr 1799 49	Miller. Living in Sharpsburg.		

Hemphill	Joseph	20 Oct 1810			
Ireland		28 Mar 1818		Aug 1808	
19		s 34			
Henderson	Samuel	19 Nov 1828	Londonderry	1819	
County Fermanaugh, Ireland			Baltimore	1819	
	Dec 1793	s	Has lived in Maryland since arrival in U.S.		
Hennessy	Peter	07 Sep 1849	Liverpool	1848	
Co. Kildare, Ireland			New York	01 Jul 1848	
26	1823	x 21			
Hennesy	John	25 Mar 1834	Limerick	1832	
County Limerick, Ireland			Albany, NY	May 1832	
22	1812	x 9			
Herlehy	David	31 Jan 1856	Liverpool	1852	John Barry
Ireland		06 Mar 1858	New York	23 Mar 1852	
23	1833	s 22			
Herlehy	Richard	31 Jan 1856	Liverpool	1854	
Ireland			New York	05 May 1854	
22	1834	x 21			
Herr	Adam	16 Sep 1844			Lorenz Herr
Bavaria		91			Alphabetical Index reads "Report made by Certificate."

Last Name / Place of Birth / Age	First Name / Date of Birth	Report Date / Natural. Date / Sig. Page No.	Departure Port / Arrival Port / Other	Departure Date / Arrival Date	Witness(es)
Herr Ashuffenburg, Bavaria 36	Conrad 1808	16 Sep 1844 s 55	Bremen Baltimore	1836 18 Mar 1837	
Herr Bavaria	Lorenz	16 Sep 1844 92			Adam Herr
Hershberger	John S.	25 Sep 1838 25 Sep 1838 IN	Alpha. Index says Report made by Cert. but no record in Court Min.		
Hess Wirtemburgh 33	Felix 1805	04 Dec 1838 02 Apr 1841 s 37	Bremen Baltimore	1833 1833	John J. Keedy
Hess	Moritz	26 Nov 1842 15	Owes allegience to the King of Byron.		Lewis Hammerslough
Hetzel Wirtemburgh 38	Gotlieb 1812	26 Sep 1850 s 26	Bremen Baltimore	1833 Aug 1833	
Hickroat Prince of Hesse	Henry	04 Jan 1798 04 Jan 1798 17	Living in Williamsport. Name may be Heckrote		

Name	Origin	Age/Year	Date	From	To	Arrival	Sponsor
Higgins	Patrick		11 Apr 1837	Dublin		1830	Charles Sweeney
Kings County, Ireland			24 Jul 1837	New York		1830	John Patterson
30	1806	x	49				
Higgs	William		27 Mar 1838				
			IN				
Hiller	Frederick		22 Jan 1856	Havre de Grace		1853	
Wirtemburgh				New York		03 Jun 1853	
23	1833	s	21				
Himmel	Christian		03 Feb 1857	Bremen		1851	
Wirtemburgh				Baltimore		02 May 1851	
46	1811	s	28				
Hinds	John		28 Mar 1837				James Hughes
Gr. Brit. & Irel.			28 Mar 1837				
			3	Alpha. Index gives 06 Apr 1835 as date of report. Records missing.			
Hinkle	John		26 Sep 1846	Bremen		1836	Peter M. Spring
Hesse Darmstadt			22 Dec 1851	Baltimoe		01 Oct 1836	
30	1816	s	42	Robert Bennett			
Hirchmuller	John Christoph		15 Jun 1850	Rotterdam		1840	
Laufen, Wirtemburgh				Baltimore		1840	
36	1814	s	16				
Hirschfield	John		24 Jan 1851	Bremen		1849	
Trysa, Hesse Cassel				Baltimore		Jun 1849	
29	1822	s	15	See record of Christian Otto.			

Last Name Place of Birth Age	First Name Date of Birth	Report Date Natural. Date Sig. Page No.	Departure Port Arrival Port Other	Departure Date Arrival Date	Witness(es)
Hoes	Hartman	26 Mar 1838 27 Aug 1840			Charles Gelwix
Hoff Hessburgh, Prussia 25	Anthony 1815	26 Mar 1840 30 Mar 1842 s 11	Bremen Philadelphia	1833 1833	
Hoff Austria	Jacob Frederic	03 Oct 1839 02 Oct 1849 31	Page No. is for Natural. Date		Henry Enstine
Hoffman Epping, Baden 34	Frederick 1795	17 Nov 1830 01 Oct 1835 s			
Hoffman County Darmstadt, Germany 25	Henry 1815	29 Sep 1840 29 Sep 1840 s 81	Bremen Baltimore	1832 1832	Christian Wirt/Mirt
Hoffman Burckconstadt, Bavaria 33	Henry 1822	03 Sep 1855 *01 Aug 1859* s 19	Bremen New York	1843 1843	
Hoffman Darmstadt 46	Michael 22 Dec 1787	26 Nov 1833 s 31	Bremen Baltimore The report in the court records said that he left Bremen in 1833 and arrived in Baltimore in 1832.	10 May 1833 22 May 1832	

Surname / Origin	Given Name	Dates	Place	Notes / Sponsor
Hohanstein Darmstadt, Hesse Darmstadt 31	Leonard 1813	02 Nov 1844 s 127	Bremen New York	1840 Jun 1840
Holder Duke of Poltz	Martin	07 Apr 1798 07 Apr 1798 19		Weaver. Living near Newcomers Mill.
Holmes County Derry	John	29 Nov 1818 s 38		19 Oct 1817
Holsaple Hesse Cassel 223	Henry 1842	29 Aug 1865 29 Aug 1865 s 5	Germany Baltimore	Richard Sheckles, Esq. 1856 - 1857 - He left Germany in "1856 or 1857."
Hoobrick Germany 155	Charles	08 Jan 1798 08 Jan 1798 28		Blacksmith. Living in Lower Antietam Hundred.
Hoover Germany	John Ulrich	04 Dec 1839 35		Frederick Kimler
Hopkins	Patrick	27 May 1830 31 Mar 1834 32		Peter Ganahan Report made at Philadelphia, PA.
Horn Hesse Darmstadt	John	05 Oct 1846 30		Peter Horn Arrived as a minor.

Last Name / Place of Birth / Age	First Name / Date of Birth	Report Date / Natural. Date / Sig. Page No.	Departure Port / Arrival Port / Other	Departure Date / Arrival Date	Witness(es)
Horn Gardenheim, Hesse Darmstadt 46	Peter	17 Nov 1835 29 Mar 1839 s 6	Bremen, Germ Baltimore Arrived in Baltimore with his wife, 4 sons and 2 daughers: John - 15 yrs., Peter - 14 yrs., Frederick - 12 yrs., David - 10 yrs., Barbara - 17 yrs., Elizabeth - 6 yrs. old. Wife born in Germany.	08 Sep 1830	Philip Sicafhouse
Horn Hesse Darmstadt	Peter	16 Sep 1844 100			Peter Horn
Hose Gesbach, Hesse Castle 22	John Paul 1818	23 Mar 1840 23 Mar 1840 s 4	Bremen Baltimore	1834 1834	William Towson
Houpt	Christopher	*18 Aug 1802* *18 Aug 1802*			
Hourande Prussia	Martin	13 Nov 1848 01 Aug 1854 5	Page No. is for Natural. Date		Joseph H. Piper
Houser Setzengrice Byron, Germany 31	Andrew 8180	23 Mar 1841 16 Sep 1844 s 23	Bremen Baltimore	1838 1838	Michael Friese

Hoye	George	21 May 1853	Liverpool	1850	
Ireland		x 19	New York	09 May 1850	
33	1820				
Hoye/Hoge	Lawrence	23 Oct 1871	Liverpool	1850	James E. Hughes
Ireland		23 Oct 1871	New York	1850	Edward Stake
23	1849	s 32			
Hubberly	Godfrey	*26 Mar 1822*			
Hughes	Barnabas	09 Dec 1795			
Hughes	Henry	14 Sep 1852	Liverpool	1849	
Co. Managhon		s 5	New York	Jun 1849	
26	1826				
Hughes	James	01 Dec 1836	Dublin	1834	Charles Sweeney
Longford, Ireland		30 Sep 1839	New York	1834	
32	1804	x 40			
Hughes	James	04 Apr 1799			
Ireland		04 Apr 1799			
		16	Skin Dresser.		
Hughes	John	24 May 1877	Liverpool	1866	
Cheshire, England		s 8	New York	1866	
34	1843				

Last Name	First Name	Report Date	Departure Port	Departure Date	Witness(es)
Place of Birth		Natural. Date	Arrival Port	Arrival Date	
Age	Date of Birth	Sig. Page No.	Other		
Huhnlein	John	02 Apr 1840	Bremen	1837	
Byren, Bavaria		*07 Apr 1843*	Baltimore	1837	
31	1809	s 32			
Hunt	John	12 Jan 1798			
Germany		12 Jan 1798			
		39	Weaver. Living on Ringgold's Manor.		
Hunter	Joseph	27 Oct 1814			
Ireland					
		20			
Hunter	Samuel	17 Jan 1799			
Ireland		17 Jan 1799			
		38	Farmer. Living in Washington County.		
Hurley	James J.	25 Nov 1833	Cork	1827	
City of Cork, Ireland		20 Aug 1835	New York	May 1827	
23	1811	s 27			
Hurley	Joseph	05 Oct 1840	Cove of Cork,	1829	James Hurley
Cork, Ireland		05 Oct 1840	New York	1829	
22	1818	s 113	Departed Cove of Cork, Ireland		
Hurst	Michael	01 Mar 1804			
Germany		54			

Huslein	Michael	05 Sep 1844		Bremen	1839
Bavaria				Baltimore	1839
43	1801	s	49		
Icefeld	Meyer	01 Aug 1844			
Bavaria					
			40	Arrived as a minor.	
Ingram	Evan				Thomas Morris
		02 Apr 1844			
			13	Arrived as a minor. Owes allegiance to Great Britain & Ireland	
Innes	Peter	01 Dec 1837		Liverpool	1825
County Cavan, Ireland				New York	1825
29	1809	x	34		
Ire	Francis	09 Jan 1799			
Germany		09 Jan 1799			
			15	Miller. Living in Lower Antietam Hundred.	
Iseley	John	25 Nov 1839		Amsterdam	1836
Wirtemburgh		26 Sep 1842		Baltimore	1836
29	1811	s	17		
Isenhart	Jacob	10 Oct 1828			
		10 Oct 1828			
			IN		
Israel	Aaron	15 Sep 1855		Havre de Grace	1852
France				New York	Jun 1852
20	1835	s	20	He arrived "about the last of June 1852."	

Last Name / Place of Birth / Age	First Name / Date of Birth	Report Date / Natural. Date / Sig. Page No.	Departure Port / Arrival Port / Other	Departure Date / Arrival Date	Witness(es)
Israel / France / 32	Mark / 1821	20 Sep 1853 / / s 20	Havre de Grace / New York	1849 / Jun 1849	
James / Wales / 23	Josiah / 1817	17 Aug 1840 / 17 Aug 1840 / s 69	Liverpool / Philadelphia	1835 / 1835	David Evans
Jefferson	John	03 Oct 1838 / 03 Oct 1838			
Johnson / Ireland	John	09 Jan 1798 / 09 Jan 1798 / 30	Farmer. Living near Gilbert's Mill.		
Johnston	Arthur	08 Nov 1828 / 08 Nov 1828 / IN			
Johnston / County Louth, Ireland / 27	James / 1806	09 Jan 1834 / 29 Mar 1841 / s 56	Quebec / New York	1829 / Sep 1830	James Cox
Johnston / Ireland	John	15 Apr 1799 / 15 Apr 1799 / 53	Farmer. Living "on Antietam."		

Name	Origin	Date	Age/Other	Place	Witness/Notes
Johnston John	Gr. Brit. & Irel.	11 Apr 1844	31		Ignatius Renner
					Alpha Index says Cert. for Report but not listed in Natural. record
Johnston William	Ireland	15 Apr 1799			
		15 Apr 1799	53		Farmer. Living "on Antietam." [Antietam Creek]
Jones Thomas		16 Sep 1844	90		Robert Curtis
					Allegiance to Gr. Britain & Irel. Alpha Index says Cert. for Report
Jones Thomas D.	South Wales	27 May 1853		Liverpool	J.E. Ridenour
1819		31 Jul 1855	19	New York	William N. Fortune
Jordan Robert	County Tyrone, Ireland	27 Jun 1814			1807
25		s	16		
Kacher Conrad	Wirtemburg	04 Sep 1847			Christian Moost
		28 Sep 1849	26		
Kafity Francis		*12 Aug 1839*			
		12 Aug 1839			
Kahlbacker John	Darmstadt	10 Dec 1850		Bremen	1829
46	1804	*08 Mar 1853*		Baltimore	1829
		s	10		

Last Name Place of Birth Age	First Name Date of Birth	Report Date Natural. Date Sig. Page No.	Departure Port Arrival Port Other	Departure Date Arrival Date	Witness(es)
Kahlert Saxe Weimer, Saxony 32	Julius E. 1821	05 Jan 1853 s 24	Hamburg New York	1850 Jul 1850	
Kahn France 28	Nathan 1828	25 Oct 1856 6 s 20	Havre de Grace New York	1849 1849	
Kahoe	Michael	06 Nov 1828 06 Nov 1828 IN			
Kail Co. Mead 41	Hugh 1812	09 May 1853 x 19	Liverpool New York	1850 May 1850	
Kail Ireland 22	James 1834	30 Jul 1856 30 Jul 1856 s 4	Liverpool New York Arrived as a minor.	1849 1849	Mary Donnelly
Kail Hesse Darmstadt 41	John 1834	05 Oct 1875 s 23	Bremen New York	1855 1855	
Kaiser Hesse Cassel 39	John 1810	03 Oct 1849 06 Dec 1851 s 31	Bremen New York	1837 08 Aug 1837	Blackston Lynch

162

Kaller	Henry	12 May 1845	Bremen	1839	Hugh Murphy
Zultzomnecker, Wirtemburgh		28 Sep 1847	Baltimore	28 Jul 1839	
28		s 1817 21			
Kapp	Michael	15 Oct 1860	Bremen	1855	John Cook
Wirtemburgh		23 Oct 1866	Baltimore	24 Sep 1855	Samuel Seibert
52		- 1808 20			
Karicker	Frederick	30 Nov 1832			
		07 Apr 1835			
		IN			
Karigan	Andrew				
Karney	Patrick	27 Oct 1813			
		18 Nov 1819			
		22			
Karr	James	22 Jun 1840	Belfast	25	John Doran
County Terone, Ireland		22 Jun 1840	New York	25	
29		s 1811 56			
Kattering	Frederick	03 Oct 1838			John Frederick
		05 Oct 1840			
		112			
Katzel	Christian	24 Jul 1848	Havre de Grace	1846	Nathan McDowell
Alsace, France		30 Mar 1852	New York	24 Dec 1846	
26		s 1822 15			

Last Name	First Name	Report Date	Departure Port	Departure Date	Witness(es)
Place of Birth	Date of Birth	Natural. Date	Arrival Port	Arrival Date	
Age		Sig. Page No.	Other		
Katzel	Philip	08 Aug 1846			
		02 Oct 1848			
Keadey	George	23 Nov 1832			John H. Mann
		25 Nov 1834			
		44			
Kearney	James	03 Dec 1839			James Hughes
		32			
Keckeler	David	17 Nov 1824	Name could be Kenney. Report made in Morgan Co., VA (WV).
		04 Nov 1828			
		IN			
Keedy	Henry H.	28 Oct 1872			
		46			
Keefe	Nicholas	24 Jul 1850	Liverpool	1842	George W. Smith
Co. Killkenny, Ireland		30 Nov 1852	New York	Jan 1842	
32	1818	s 18			
Keefe	William	02 Nov 1850	Liverpool	1847	
Co. Kilkenny, Ireland			Baltimore	Mar 1847	
22	1828	s 35			

Surname	Given Name	Origin	Date	Age	Location	Notes/Sponsor
Keefhaver	John	Germany	11 Jan 1798	38		Stone mason. Living in Lower Antietam Hundred.
Keenen	Patrick		28 Oct 1872			George G. Middlekauff
			28 Sep 1875	21		James I. Hurley
						Owes allegiance to Great Britain & Ireland
Kegney	John M.	Ireland	16 Sep 1806	63		George Sharkey
Keifer	John Daniel	Bavaria	17 Oct 1819			Christan Boentl
			28 Mar 1826			
Keifer	Peter	Bavaria	06 Apr 1829		Havre de Grace	May 1828
					New York	Jun 1828
			Jan 1806	23 s		
Keifer	Theobold	Bavaria	03 Oct 1848	20		Gotlieb Trieher
				s		Arrived as a minor.
Keinen	Patrick	Ireland	28 Oct 1872		Dublin	1846
			1822	31 s	New York	1846
				50		
Kellar	Ludwig	Village of Stouger?, Baden	3 Apr 1826			
			06 Nov 1828	45		07 Aug 1819
				23 s		

Last Name / Place of Birth / Age	First Name / Date of Birth	Report Date / Natural. Date / Sig. / Page No.	Departure Port / Arrival Port / Other	Departure Date / Arrival Date	Witness(es)
Keller	Hironemus	04 Apr 1820		07 Aug 1819	
Village of Itlinger, Austria			Born in Village of Itlinger, County of Epinger, Baden, Austria.		
51		s 39			
Kelley	Patrick	19 Nov 1839	Dublin	1830	
County Kings, Ireland		22 Nov 1841	Albany, NY	1830	
27	1812	s 4			
Kelly	Bernard	16 Nov 1840			
		-- IN			
Kelly	Daniel	03 Mar 1855	Liverpool	1851	Isaac Nesbitt
Ireland			New York	Aug 1851	
22	1833	x 17	Arrived in N.Y. the "latter part of August 1851." Nov. 1854 Court		
Kelly	Michael	17 Mar 1854		1850	George Schindel
Wexford Co., England		17 Mar 1856	Baltimore	1850	
34	1820	x 6	Witness for Report was J.W. Heard.		
Kelly	Timothy	15 Apr 1829			Patrick Rodey
		08 Apr 1834			
		59	Report made at Huntingdon County, PA.		
Kelly	William L.	03 May 1803		<29 Jan 1795	
Ireland		50			

Kemman	Charles	30 Oct 1866	Bremen	1853	Jacob Craig
Hanover		30 Oct 1866	Baltimore	1853	John D. Swartz
36	1830	s 23	Honorably discharged from military service 29 Apr 1862.		
Kemps	Gregorius	13 Jan 1798			
Germany		13 Jan 1798			
		43	Clockmaker. Living in Hagerstown.		
Kendal	James	06 Apr 1797			
England		06 Apr 1797			
		19			
Kenneday	Hugh	10 Apr 1798			
Ireland		10 Apr 1798			
		25			
Kennedy	Ann	29 Mar 1824	Londonderry		
Ballydolin in Co. Londonderry			Philadelphia	12 Jun 1823	
4		- 83	Now lives in Franklin County, PA.		
Kennedy	Catharine	29 Mar 1824	Londonderry		
Ballydolin in Co. Londonderry			Philadelphia	12 Jun 1823	
7		- 83	Now lives in Franklin County, PA.		
Kennedy	Child. of James	29 Mar 1824	Londonderry		
Ballydolin in Co. Londonderry			Philadelphia	12 Jun 1823	
		s 83	All now live in Franklin County, PA.		
Kennedy	Hugh	29 Mar 1824	Londonderry		
Ballydolin in Co. Londonderry			Philadelphia	12 Jun 1823	
11		- 83	Now lives in Franklin County, PA.		

Last Name	First Name	Report Date	Departure Port	Departure Date	Witness(es)
Place of Birth	Date of Birth	Natural. Date	Arrival Port	Arrival Date	
Age		Sig. Page No.	Other		
Kennedy	John	29 Mar 1824	Londonderry		
Ballydolin in Co. Londonderry			Philadelphia	12 Jun 1823	
17		- 83	Now lives in Franklin County, PA.		
Kennedy	John	10 Jan 1799			
Ireland		10 Jan 1799	Merchant. Living in Hagerstown.		
		18			
Kennedy	Joshua	29 Mar 1824	Londonderry		
Ballydolin in Co. Londonderry			Philadelphia	12 Jun 1823	
9		- 83	Now lives in Franklin County, PA.		
Kennedy	Rachel	29 Mar 1824	Londonderry		
Ballydolin in Co. Londonderry			Philadelphia	12 Jun 1823	
18		- 83	Now lives in Franklin County, PA.		
Kennedy	Thomas	25 Aug 1802			
		39	Owes allegiance to the King of Great Britain & Ireland		
Kennedy	William	29 Mar 1824	Londonderry		
Ballydolin in Co. Londonderry			Philadelphia	12 Jun 1823	
15		- 83	Now lives in Franklin County, PA.		
Kennedy	William	03 Oct 1838			
		--	IN		

Kenney	Arthur		28 Jul 1855	Liverpool	1850
Ireland				New York	10 Oct 1850
33	1822	s	8	Now lives in Franklin County, PA.
Kenney	Arthur		28 Jul 1855	Liverpool	1850
Ireland				New York	10 Oct 1850
33	1822	s	8		
Kenney	James			See listing under Kearney, James	
Keregan	Andrew				
Kerigan	Andrew		27 Nov 1818		15 Jun 1816
County Donegal		x	40	Name could be Karigan or Keregan	
Kessel	John George		16 Sep 1844	Bremen	1839
Zultenburg, Bavaria				Baltimore	23 Jul 1839
39	1805	s	59		
Kettering	Frederick		*03 Oct 1838*		
Ketzel	Philip		08 Aug 1846		William E. Doyle
France			02 Oct 1848		
			19		

Last Name / Place of Birth / Age	First Name / Date of Birth	Report Date / Natural. Date / Sig. Page No.	Departure Port / Arrival Port / Other	Departure Date / Arrival Date	Witness(es)
Keyser Wirtemburgh 45	Louis 1813	09 Mar 1858 s 11	Rotterdam Baltimore	1845 1845	
Kickeler Wirtemburgh, Germany 30	Daniel	17 Nov 1824 s 24		1819	
Kiefer Glahn Muenchweiler, Bavaria 19	John Daniel	17 Oct 1819 s 68	Plans to live in Funkstown.		Dr. Christian Boerstler
Kilan County Meath, Ireland 40	Thomas 1794	24 Nov 1834 — Mar 1826 s 39	Dublin Albany, NY	1825 1825	
Kimerly Baden 45	Bernhard 1810	22 Mar 1855 24 Mar 1857 s 15	Manheim New York Name may be Kimberly	1848 1848	William Gassman
Kimler	Frederick	22 Nov 1837 04 Dec 1839 36			John Ulrich Hoover

Surname	Given	Date 1 / Date 2	Status	Origin / Residence	Notes
Kimmerly	John	28 Mar 1842 / 12 Feb 1844	IN		
King	Owen	04 Dec 1852		Galway / Boston	1849 / May 1849
Co. Galworthy					
27	1825	x 9			
Kinneen	Robert	17 Nov 1830		Dumore / Baltimore	Jan 1816 / Mar 1816
Dumore, County Down, Ireland					Has lived in Washington Co. for 2 yrs.
44	Feb 1786	s 28			
Kinneir	Robert	31 Mar 1840			Benjamin Bean
171					
Kinney	Thomas	03 Oct 1838	IN		
Kinsell	Patrick	08 Apr 1844			John L. Smith / James Johnson
		24		Allegiance to Gr. Britain & Ireland. Alpha Index reads "Cert."	
Kipp	John Michael	05 Nov 1850		Bremen / Baltimore	1849 / Dec 1849
Nemersdorff, Bavaria					
37	1813	s 35			
Kippart	Jacob	30 Nov 1847		Rotterdam / Baltimore	1844 / 23 Feb 1845
Creveld, Prussia					
37	1810	s 15			

Last Name First Name Place of Birth Date of Birth Age	Report Date Natural. Date Sig. Page No.	Departure Port Arrival Port Other	Departure Date Arrival Date	Witness(es)
Kirkpatrick John	16 Nov 1841 05 Oct 1846 25	Owes allegiance to Great Britain & Ireland		John D. Ridenour
Kirkpatrick Samuel Scotland	24 Sep 1806 65			Matthias Shaffner
Kisner William Hesse Cassel 22	02 Oct 1849 02 Oct 1849 x 30	Bremen Baltimore Arrived as a minor.	1837 1837	
Kleinknecht Christian Town of Edmonhauser, Wirtemb. 52 1781	03 Dec 1833 s 35	Holland Baltimore Born in the Town of Edmonhauser in Wirtemburgh, Germany.	17 May 1832 19 Jul 1832	
Klench George Wurtemburgh 26	31 Mar 1812 *01 Apr 1817* s 42	Amsterdam Name may be Klinch	27 Oct 1805	
Klenke Ferdinand Brunswick, Germany 23 1826	05 Sep 1849 05 Sep 1849 s 20	Bremen Baltimore Arrived as a minor.	1843 25 Jun 1843	George Gassman Charles Ulrick
Klinch George				

Kline	Jacob	27 Mar 1820		
Kline	John	04 Nov 1828		
		04 Nov 1828		
		IN		
Klink	Michael	30 Nov 1832		Jacob Buckwalter
		11 Apr 1836		
		31		
Kline	Golleib	27 Mar 1820	Amsterdam	
Kerchheim, Wirtemburgh, Germ.		21 Nov 1825		24 Jan 1820
37		s 3		
Klom or Kline	Jacob	27 Mar 1820	Amsterdam	
Wirtemburgh, Germany				24 Jan 1820
62		s 2		
Kloz	C.W.L. Joseph	Certificate		Michael Tricher
Wirtemburgh		16 Sep 1844		C.F. Gelwicks
		67		
Kneiream	Henry	07 Nov 1848	Bremen	1839 Thomas E. Mittag
Hesse Cassel		30 Sep 1851	Baltimore	
50	1798	s 26		
Koch	George	26 Sep 1842		
		26 Sep 1842		
		IN		

| Last Name | First Name | Report Date | Departure Port | Departure Date | Witness(es) |
| Place of Birth | Date of Birth | Natural. Date | Arrival Port | Arrival Date | |
Age		Sig. Page No.	Other		
Koch	John	18 Nov 1839	Bremen	1833	
Hesse Darmstadt		26 Sep 1842	Baltimore	1833	
28	1811	s 3			
Koch	Peter	18 Nov 1839	Bremen	1833	
Hesse Darmstadt		26 Sep 1842	Baltimore	1833	
52	1787	s 3			
Kocher	Conrad	04 Sep 1847	Rotterdam	1832	
Dezingen, Wirtemburgh		*28 Sep 1849*	Baltimore	1832	
52	1795	s 11			
Koffinberger	Peter	03 Sep 1838			
		02 Apr 1842			
Koffinberger	Peter	*03 Sep 1838*			
		02 Apr 1842			
Kohler	Jacob	03 Jan 1871	Havre de Grace	1854	
Wirtemburgh			New York	1854	
57	1813	26			
Kohn	Nathan	10 Sep 1842			
		28 Sep 1847			
		IN			

Name	Origin	Dates	Place/Notes	Other
Kolbacher John	Darmstadt	10 Dec 1850 08 Mar 1853 2		Henry Freaner
Kose Christian	Germany	09 Apr 1799 09 Apr 1799 43	Weaver. Living in Salisbury Hundred.	
Kotzenberger John		09 Oct 1838 03 Oct 1842 IN	Report column reads "Certificate"	
Kraft Conrad	Hesse Cassel 1820	25 Jul 1855 s 5	Bremen 1853 Baltimore 22 Jun 1853	
Kramer Henry		01 Oct 1857		
Kramer Leopold		29 Sep 1845 29 Sep 1845		
Krantz John P.	Wirtemburgh	25 Sep 1847 26 Sep 1849 26		Philip Smander
Kratz/Kretz Emanuel	Town of Eppinger, Baden 1786	18 Nov 1833 s 2	Bremen Jun 1833 Baltimore Aug 1833 Has lived in Maryland since his arrival in the U.S.	

Last Name	First Name	Report Date	Departure Port	Departure Date	Witness(es)
Place of Birth	Date of Birth	Natural. Date	Arrival Port	Arrival Date	
Age		Sig. Page No.	Other		
Krauss	Adolphus	05 Feb 1853	Liverpool	1851	
Warsaw, Poland			New York	Dec 1851	
22	1830	x 24			
Krautz	John P.	25 Sep 1847	Havre de Grace	1831	
Wirtemburgh			New York	12 Sep 1831	
46	1801	s 28			
Kremer	Frederick E.	29 Nov 1836	Rotterdam	Jan 1832	William Touson?
County Mark, Westphalia, Prussia		26 Mar 1839	Baltimore	1832	
42	1794	s 28			
Krokberger	Christian	15 Oct 1860			Charles Fridinger
Bavaria		17 Oct 1867			Wolfgang Brey
		11	Report column reads "Certificate."		
Kuhnler	Frederick	24 Aug 1852	London	1852	
Unterkochken, Oberant Aalerr			New York	01 Aug 1852	
28	1824	s 4	Born in Wirtemburgh.		
Kulp/Kalb	John George	04 Dec 1848	Bremen	1834	
Saxe Coburg			Baltimore	Nov 1834	
47	1801	s 6			
Kurtz-Geist	Louis	01 Dec 1838	Bremen	1832	
Frankfurt, Germany			Baltimore	1832	
40	1798	s 32			

Name	Origin	Age	Date	Port	Sponsor/Notes
Lackner Charles F.	Saxe Meiningen		01 Oct 1850		George Lackner
			31		Name may be Lockner. Arrived as a minor.
Laffertz Bernard			22 Nov 1838		
Lampas Charles	Hesse Darmstadt	40	29 Oct 1870	Bremen	Lewis Heist
		1830	21 Sep 1876	Baltimore	George Sias
			s 32		
Lampas George	Hesse Darmstadt	33	31 Oct 1859	Bremen	
		1826		New York	07 Sep 1856
			s 5		Full name is George Ferdinand Philippe Lampas.
Landen Francis	Ireland		24 Sep 1806		Matthias Shaffner
			68		
Landers Patrick	County Carey, Ireland	28	18 Nov 1834	Tralee, Ireland	1827
		1806		Philadelphia	Dec 1827
			x 4		
Landrock John C.	Hesse Cassel		27 Sep 1844		David Rush
			20 Sep 1847		
			18		
Lannan Francis K.	County Kilkenny, Ireland	22	04 Oct 1830	Ireland	02 Apr 1824 William Olhoppel
		1808	04 Oct 1830	Baltimore	06 Jun 1824 Thomas W. Vinson
			s		

Last Name Place of Birth Age	First Name Date of Birth	Report Date Natural. Date Sig. Page No.	Departure Port Arrival Port Other	Departure Date Arrival Date	Witness(es)
Lannan County Meanahan, Ireland 27	Patrick 1809	23 Nov 1836 x 14	Warean's Point, New York Departed Warean's Point, Ireland	1828 1828	
Lantz Germany	Nicholas	24 Sep 1806 67			John Miller
Lao/Lee	Patrick		See listing under Lee, Patrick		
Larkin	James	17 Nov 1841			
LaserLazer Bavaria	Anthony	29 Mar 1852 05 Dec 1854 6			Jacob Schlagel
Latta Ireland	Alexander	11 Apr 1799 11 Apr 1799 47	Living in Elizabeth Hundred.		
Lau Mecklenburg, Mecklenburg Sch. 48	Christian 1827	28 Dec 1875 13 Aug 1878 s 22	Hamburg New York Born in Mecklenburg, Mecklenburg Schweria.	1853 1853	John B. Baechtell John Hoover

Name	Origin	Date	Port	Date 2	Witness
Laughlin Allen		22 Nov 1828	Philadelphia	Aug 1807-8	John Padon
County Derry, Ireland		22 Nov 1828		Oct 1807-8	Allen Barber
	May 1783	s	3rd Witness was John Miller. Has lived in Washington Co. more than 5 yrs.		
Laughlin Michael		21 Nov 1825			
		07 Nov 1828			
		IN			
Lavely Patrick		*05 Oct 1840*			
Layten John Theodore		25 Mar 1812			
Germany		25 Mar 1812			
59		53			
Lazer Anthony		29 Mar 1852	Bremen		
Bavaria					
57	1795	s 4			
Leasey Jacob		28 Nov 1849	Bremen	1845	
Hanhika, Hesse Cassel			Baltimore	Jul 1845	
39	1810	s 2			
Leasey Michael		20 Nov 1846	Bremen	1844	William Bowers
Honneche, Hesse Cassel		01 Oct 1849	Baltimore	Aug 1844	
35	1811	x 5			
Leasure Casper		*12 Mar 1855*			Elisha Miles
Bavaria		12 Mar 1855			
		5			

Last Name Place of Birth Age	First Name Date of Birth	Report Date Natural. Date Sig. Page No.	Departure Port Arrival Port Other	Departure Date Arrival Date	Witness(es)
Lee or Lao County Limerick, Ireland 31	Patrick 1803	25 Mar 1834 s 7	Limerick New York Clerk has written Lao. His signature reads Lee.	1831 Aug 1831	
Leeger Wirtemburgh	Gotlieb	04 Sep 1845 04 Sep 1847 12			Joseph J. Merrick
Leiberlich Baden	John	19 Feb 1844 20 Sep 1847 21			Michael Freize
Leibold Wirtemburgh 47	Frederick 1820	14 Jan 1867 14 Jan 1867 s 43	Havre de Grace New York Honorably discharged from military service 08 Aug 1865.	1856 1856	Wesley Finnigan Daniel Neigh
Leight Germany	John	04 Jan 1798 04 Jan 1798 18	Tinner. Living in Hagerstown.		
Leigler Wirtemburgh	John Gotlieb	28 Sep 1847 37			Henry Kaller
Leimmerman Baden	Andrew	16 Sep 1844 20 Sep 1847 22			John G. Treiber

Name		Origin	Date	Date2	Place1	Place2	Year1	Year2	Witness
Leinchkund	Andrew		01 Oct 1849		Bremen		1846		John B. Castebbader
Haharan, Hesse Cassel			02 Feb 1852		New York		01 Sep 1846		
35		1814	s	29					
Leise	George		12 Aug 1844						Samuel Geager
Hesse Darmstadt			20 Sep 1847						
				20					
Leitz	John		30 Mar 1836						Jacob Rausler
			27 Mar 1839						
				6					
Lensbower	Peter		20 Oct 1869		Bremen		1853		Upton Rouskulp
Bavaria			20 Oct 1869		Baltimore		1853		William Smith
28		1840	s	21	3rd Witness was Sreury Creager.				
Leonard	James		09 Jun 1840		Dublin		1811		Francis Colloton
Co. Loud, Ireland			09 Jun 1840		New York		1811		
47		1793	x	49					
Lerch	Charles		cert						
			25 Jul 1853						
Letunate?	Christian H.		18 Jan 1836						
			05 Oct 1842		Report column reads "Certificate"				
				IN					
Leuxner	Philip		18 Sep 1844		Bremen		1839		
Gerotzhofen, Bavaria					Baltimore		02 Sep 1839		
36		1808	s	64					

| Last Name | First Name | Report Date | Departure Port | Departure Date | Witness(es) |
| Place of Birth | Date of Birth | Natural. Date | Arrival Port | Arrival Date | |
Age		Sig. Page No.	Other		
Leuzberg	Max	05 Apr 1860	Bremen	1854	
Prussia	1833		Baltimore	15 Jan 1855	
27		s 25			
Levy	Jacob	12 Sep 1866	Havre de Grace	1859	Gerson Levy
Bavaria	1843	12 Sep 1866	New York	1859	Jacob Joseph Loeb
23		s 18	Arrived as a minor.		
Lewis	Robert	28 Aug 1832			Peter Innes
		01 Dec 1837	Report made in Dauphin Co., PA.		
		33			
Lier	David	01 Oct 1844	Bremen	1840	
Erfurt, Prussia	1786		Baltimore	20 Jun 1840	
58		s 122			
Limbaugh	John	26 Sep 1844			Catharine Limbaugh
Murhuysen		112	Arrived as a minor.		
Limberg	Frederick	10 Aug 1847			John M. Sherman
Hesse Cassel		9			
Limerchan?	Charles	26 Nov 1832			
		IN			

Surname	Given Name	Date		Notes
Linckand Hessian	Ulrich	30 Nov 1844 20 Sep 1847	14	Henry Beitingheimer
Lindeman	Casper	*08 Aug 1857*		
Lindsay County Derry	John	18 Nov 1819		Jun 1819
		s	23 22	
Lindsey	James	16 Sep 1844	83	Joseph Fiery. Arrived as a minor. Owes allegiance to Great Britain & Ireland
Little	Patrick	16 Sep 1844	97	Michael Campbell. Alpha. Index - "Cert" in Report date. Allegiance to Gr. Brit. & Irel.
Little	Thomas	05 Oct 1840	116	John S. Pollard. Arrived as a minor. Owes allegiance to Great Britain & Ireland.
Lively	James	*22 Sep 1838*		
Lively	Michael	*22 Sep 1838*		

Last Name	First Name	Report Date	Departure Port	Departure Date	Witness(es)
Place of Birth	Date of Birth	Natural. Date	Arrival Port	Arrival Date	
Age		Sig. Page No.	Other		
Loftus	Anthony	04 Dec 1833	Slago		James Callen
Schrimeen, Ireland		23 Nov 1836	Pittsburgh	11 Aug	
31	1802	s 37			
Loftus	John	28 Mar 1837	Colerain	1828	
County Mayo, Ireland		28 Mar 1837	Niagara, NY	1828	
22	1815	s 5			
Loftus	Owen	25 Nov 1837	Belfast	1829	Anthony Loftus
County Mayo, Ireland		25 Nov 1837	New York	1829	
22	1815	s 18			
Logue	James	26 Sep 1842			
		26 Sep 1842			
		IN			
Logue	William	01 Dec 1831		04 Apr 1818	
County Londonderry, Ireland			Baltimore	Jun 1818	
45	11 Jun 1786	x 49			
Lohretz	Jacob	02 Oct 1844	Bremen	1837	David Brumbaugh, Jr.
Hesse Cassel		28 Sep 1847	Baltimore	Jul 1837	
34	1810	s 124			
Loman	Joseph	31 Oct 1842			
		IN			

Surname	Given name	Date	Age	Place	Year	Notes	Witness
Lonergan	James	26 Nov 1832	--				
Long Germany	Abraham	16 Sep 1844	89			Arrived as a minor.	Frederick Stover
Long Ireland 25	Daniel	31 Oct 1867 31 Oct 1867 s 1842	17	City of Cork New York	1848 1848		James Aherin
Long Ireland	Michael	31 Oct 1867 31 Oct 1867 x 1840	18	City of Cork New York	1848 1848		James Aherin
Longenbaugh* Lichmachswangen, Wirtemburgh 31	George	05 Dec 1837 *05 Oct 1842* s 1806	40	Bremen Baltimore	1836 1836	* Last name is Longenbaugher	
Longman Germany	John	02 Jan 1798 02 Jan 1798	9			Living in Washington County.	
Lookinsland	Boldis	*08 Sep 1845* *08 Sep 1845*					
Loudenslager Hesse Darmstadt 31	Everhart	02 Aug 1858 20 Sep 1865 s 1827	5	Bremen Baltimore	1847 09 Nov 1847		Richard H. Wise John Luft

Last Name	First Name	Report Date	Departure Port	Departure Date	Witness(es)
Place of Birth	Date of Birth	Natural. Date	Arrival Port	Arrival Date	
Age		Sig. Page No.	Other		
Louderbaugh	John	08 Apr 1799			
Germany		08 Apr 1799			
		28	Shoemaker. Living in Upper Antietam Hundred.		
Lough/Lochran	James	28 Oct 1815			John Ashberry
Ireland		?			Silas Harlan
		26	Name may be Lochran		
Louth	Peter	26 Nov 1833	Bremen	18 May 1831	
Hesse Darmstadt		28 Nov 1838	Baltimore	18 Jul 1831	
45	1788	s 28	Born in Frankisch Crumbach, Hesse Darmstadt. Has lived in Washington County since his arrival in U.S.		
Love	William	16 Sep 1845			
Lowe	George	20 Oct 1870	Havre de Grace	1865	Lewis Heist
Unterwassen, Hesse Darmstadt		29 Oct 1872	New York	1865	Adam Doanberger
26	1855	s 28	Doanberger		
Lucaphouse	Philip	29 Nov 1836			Peter Horn
		29 Nov 1839			
		10			
Ludwig	Conrad	16 Sep 1844	Bremen	1832	Jacob Retburg
Robartzheussen, Hesse Darmst.		24 Jul 1855	Baltimore	25 Nov 1832	
55	1789	s 64			

Lugensland	John George	20 Nov 1826		Jacob Myers
Montbruner?, Wurtemburg		20 Nov 1828	Aug 1817	
42		s		
Luther	John Jacob	21 Nov 1838	Bremen 1835	Jacob Butz
Cobergh, Saxony, Germany		27 Sep 1841	New York 1835	
29	1807	s 7		
Lutz	Christian	30 Nov 1842	Havre de Grace 1831	
Kircheim, Wirtemburgh			New York 1831	
29	1813	s 22		
Lynch	John	31 Oct 1867	Limerick 1851	John Beeler
Ireland		31 Oct 1867	New York 1851	William H. Grimes
36	1834	s 16		
Lynch	Patrick	17 Sep 1852	Liverpool 1851	
Co. Waterford			Boston Jun 1851	
21	1831	s 5		
Lynch	Peter	31 Mar 1837	Dublin 1826	
County Mead, Ireland			New York 1826	
36	1801	s 22		
Lytle	Peter	31 Mar 1837	Dublin 1827	
County Mead, Ireland		06 Apr 1840	Albany, NY 1827	
35	1802	s 21	Signature reads Little.	

Last Name / Place of Birth / Age	First Name / Date of Birth	Report Date / Natural. Date / Sig. Page No.	Departure Port / Arrival Port / Other	Departure Date / Arrival Date	Witness(es)
MaMachan	James	25 Aug 1802			
			Owes allegiance to Great Britain & Ireland		
Mac/May/Mey Bohemia, Austria 29	Joseph Pasheh	29 Aug 1812 s 50	Amsterdam	Dec 1804	
Machen	John	03 Oct 1838 --	IN		
Mack Backnan, Wirtumburg 28	*Godleib Fred. 22 May 1802	30 Mar 1830 *26 Nov 1833* s	Amsterdam Baltimore Has lived in Washing. Co. since arrival in U.S.	22 May 1827 Aug 1827	*Godleib Frederick Luke O'Brien
Macken	Henry	06 Apr 1835 08 Dec 1837 51			
Mackey Ireland 22	Moses	25 Nov 1817 26 Nov 1822 s 49	Londonderry	1810	Capt. John Miller
Macrander? --	Jacob	01 Oct 1840	Report was made in Frederick Co., Maryland.		Charles Gelwicks

Maesal/Maisal	William	08 Apr 1844	Bremen	1839
Co. Hoeff, Byren, Germany			Baltimore	1839
46	1798	s 27		
Magee	James	30 Nov 1844	Waterford	1839
Co. Monoghan, Ireland			New York	11 Jun 1839
35	1809	s 22		
Magee	Thomas	12 Apr 1844		James Farrell
		34	Owes allegiance to Great Britain & Ireland	
Maginnis	James	29 Mar 1819		12 Aug 1817
County London Derry				
29		48		
Mahan	John	25 Mar 1834	Limerick	1829
Limerick, Ireland			New York	Aug 1829
24	1810	s 10	Name could be Mahaine or Mahan.	
Maher	William	06 Apr 1844		Thomas Drenin
		22	Arrived as a minor. Owes allegiance to Great Britain & Ireland	
Mahler	Valentine	26 Sep 1844		Denton Oliver
Bavaria		20 Sep 1847		
		23		
Maier	Jacob	29 Jul 1857		

Last Name Place of Birth Age	First Name Date of Birth	Report Date Natural. Date Sig. Page No.	Departure Port Arrival Port Other	Departure Date Arrival Date	Witness(es)
Maisach	Jacob	30 Mar 1835 -- IN			
Malone Wexford Co., Great Britain 25	Edward 1829	11 Jul 1854 s 10	New Ross Quebec	1851 20 Oct 1851	
Malone Ireland 39	James 1834	25 Aug 1876 08 Sep 1876 s 22	Limerick New York	1852 1852	James I. Hurley F.D. Herbert
Malone	James	25 Aug 1873 7?	"James Malone makes application to be Naturalized. (See paper in Rough Bundle)." The rough bundle was lost during the courthouse fire of 1871.		
Manning	John	27 Feb 1804 44	Owes allegiance to Great Britain & Ireland		William Cromwell
Manning	Patrick		Apparently, someone sold him forged naturalization papers and this case came to court on 04 Jul 1840. There is no record of him being officially naturalized. See Appendix E.		

Name	Origin / Age	Date	Status/Age	Notes
Mark Robert	22 Sep 1819		10 Jun 1819	
County London Derry				
23		s	68	
Marko John	20 Nov 1839		Strausburgh	1833
Baden, Germany	03 Oct 1842		Baltimore	1833
45	1795	s	9	
Marlauer Samuel	04 Apr 1844			John Tedrick
			18	Arrived as a minor. Owes allegiance to Great Britain & Ireland
Marr or Man James	27 Nov 1830		Ireland	Feb 1823
County Kildare, Ireland	27 Nov 1830		Baltimore	13 Apr 1823
19	1807	x		He was 16 yrs. old when he left Ireland.
Martin Jacob	16 Sep 1844			Jacob Rettburg
Bavaria			87	
Martin James	09 Apr 1798			
Ireland	09 Apr 1798			
			22	Farmer. Living in Ringgold.
Martin James	31 Oct 1865			James E. Powell
Ireland				Col. R.E. Cook
			12	Honorably discharged from military service 29 May 1865
Martin Patrick	19 Nov 1833		Dublin	26 Jun 1828
County Gallway, Ireland			New York	Aug 1828
27		s	14	

Last Name / Place of Birth / Age	First Name / Date of Birth	Report Date / Natural. Date / Sig. Page No.	Departure Port / Arrival Port / Other	Departure Date / Arrival Date	Witness(es)
Mash/Mask Prussia	Henry	02 Dec 1840 16 Sep 1844 73			John T. Mason
Master	Conrad	29 Mar 1843 5	Alpha Index reads "Cert." in Report Column.		Abraham Newcomer
Matthews	Patrick	21 Nov 1843 --	IN		
Maughlar Allsace, France	John Christian	05 Apr 1799 05 Apr 1799 20			
Maurioch?	Leonard	21 Nov 1836 17 Aug 1840	Weaver. Living on John Shafer's mill on Antietam.		Michael Freise
Max	Joseph Pasteh	27 Aug 1812			
May Uchte, Hanover 24	*George Fred. 1820	12 Oct 1844 20 Sep 1847 s 125	Bremen Baltimore *George Frederick	1840 14 Aug 1840	Henry Spohr

Name		Date 1 / Date 2 / Age	Origin	Notes
Mayer Wurtemburgh 36	Jacob	01 Nov 1811 29 Mar 1817 s 41	Amsterdam	1804
Mayer Germany	John Daniel	26 Oct 1808 29 Oct 1811 17		
McAdams County Chanohan, Ireland	James	28 Nov 1818 s 41		02 May 1816
McAnnulty	Patrick	-- Aug 1820 01 Oct 1828 IN		
McAvoy	David	15 Aug 24 Nov 1837 14		Lawrence Schneider Report made in Huntingdon Co., PA.
McAvoy Co. Louth, Ireland 30	Patrick	13 Sep 1849 1819 x 23	Dundock Alexandria	1846 08 May 1847 Alpha Index reads "Cert." in Report column.
McAvoy	Patrick	Certificate 01 Dec 1843 IN		
McBride	Francis	02 Dec 1844 26		John M. Miller Arrived as a minor. Owes allegiance to Great Britain & Ireland

Last Name	First Name	Report Date Natural. Date	Departure Port Arrival Port	Departure Date Arrival Date	Witness(es)
Place of Birth	Date of Birth	Sig. Page No.	Other		
Age					
McCabe	John	01 Dec 1837	Liverpool	1835	
County Cavan, Ireland			New York	1835	
31	1807	s 34			
McCabe	Patrick Willia	23 Nov 1833	Liverpool	May 1824	
County Cavan, Ireland			Boston	16 Jul 1824	
29	1804	s 23			
McCann	John	02 Aug 1830			
		05 Oct 1842			
		IN	Report column reads "Certificate"		
McCarthy	John	05 Mar 1853	Liverpool	1849	John Dillehunt
Kerry Co.		09 Aug 1855	New York	1849	Thomas Harbine
58	1795	s 25	Other Witnesses: William E. Doyle, Thomas Robertson		
McCartin	Edward	08 Aug 1820		22 Aug 1818	Andrew Kershner
County Armagh, Ireland		05 Apr 1827			
22		s 51	Also made reports on 27 Nov 1820 and 30 Nov 1820.		
McCarty	John	28 Nov 1827		1825	
County Limerich, Ireland					
28		x			
McCarty	John	05 Oct 1842			
		05 Oct 1842			
		IN	Beside his name is the notation "minor"		

Name	Location	Date	Place	Other Date	Sponsor
McCarty Owen	Ireland	05 Apr 1815			John Schnebly
		50			
McCashell Peter	County Tyrone, Ireland	29 Mar 1825		1818	
		10 Oct 1828			
35		x 7			
McCleary John	Ireland	26 Oct 1813			
		21			
McCleland John	Ireland	07 Sep 1812	Londonderry	30 Aug 1810	
26		s 51			
McCloskey Peter	Drumshaver County, Ireland	01 Dec 1836	Belfast	1833	
			Baltimore	1833	
26	1810	x 38			
McClung William	County Tyrone, Ireland	28 Oct 1813			John McClain
		01 Apr 1825		1801	
32		s 31			
McCormack Bernard	County Armagh, Ireland	25 Sep 1820		25 Dec 1818	
35		s 51			
McCormack John	County Armagh, Ireland	10 Nov 1820		22 Jun 1815	
26		s 53			

Last Name Place of Birth Age	First Name Date of Birth	Report Date Natural. Date Sig. Page No.	Departure Port Arrival Port Other	Departure Date Arrival Date	Witness(es)
McCormack Co. Wisnith 39	John 1811	05 Nov 1850 15 Mar 1853 x 35	Dublin New York	1830 Jun 1830	William McCormick
			Allegiance to Great Britain & Ireland		
McCosker County Terone, Ireland 34	Hugh 1806	20 Nov 1838 22 Mar 1841 s 4	Londonderry New York	1831 1832	James McQuade
McCoskey	Michael	05 Oct 1840 104	Please note that the given age and date of birth don't match up.		James McQuade
McCoy County Londonderry 22	Francis	28 Nov 1821 s 67		23 Jul 1819	
McCoy County Down, Ireland 35	Moses	19 Nov 1827 29 Mar 1830 s		1817	John Herr
McCrary Ireland	John	25 Nov 1807 36			John Hershey Samuel McCrary
McCreery County Down, Ireland 28	Robert	22 Nov 1820 10 Oct 1828 s 30		10 Aug 1816	

Name		Date		Notes
McCullock	John	— Oct 1836		Anthony Snider
		01 Apr 1839	17	Alpha Index reads "Ally. Coty. Cert" [Allegany Co., MD?]
McCullugh	James	19 Nov 1817		Belfast
Ireland				24 Jun 1811
30		s	23	Name may be McCullough
McCusker	Hugh	19 Aug 1812		Patrick Donnelly
		28 Mar 1837	7	Report made in Lancaster County, Pennsylvania.
McDervitt	James	20 Nov 1820		
County Donnegal, Ireland				01 May 1818
29		s	22	
McDonald	Christopher	19 Nov 1833		Liverpool, Eng Mar 1829
County Langford, Ireland				New York Apr 1829
25		1827	7	Departure port was "Liverpool, England"
McFadden	John	09 Oct 1838		Report column reads "Certificate."
		05 Oct 1842	IN	
McFarland	Alexander B.	06 Dec 1833		Gleenock *Sco Jul 1807
County Perth, Scotland				New York Dec 1807
37		1795	43	*Scotland. Has lived in Washington County since arrival in the U.S.
McFarland	Samuel	30 Nov 1825		Samuel Newcomer
		07 Apr 1829		

Last Name Place of Birth Age	First Name Date of Birth	Report Date Natural Date Sig. Page No.	Departure Port Arrival Port Other	Departure Date Arrival Date	Witness(es)
McGannegle	James	*04 Dec 1820* ___ *Mar 1826*			
McGee	Samuel	23 Nov 1821 27 Aug 1840			John Newcomer
McGinnis	James	*30 Mar 1819*			
McGlaughlin	William	29 Mar 1821 45		08 Feb 1819	
McGlaughlin County Derry, Ireland 22	William	08 Feb 1819 25 Mar 1824 x 59	Baltimore	Sep 1818	
McGlenin County Down, Ireland 37	Patrick 1797	25 Mar 1834 s 11	Stangford Baltimore	1819 May 1819	Oath was made in court on 29 Mar 1821.
McGlennan Co. Down, Ireland 56	James 1788	28 Sep 1844 05 Oct 1846 x 115	Belfast Baltimore	1816 Aug 1816	John Kirkpatrick Witness for Report was Michel Treiber.

Name	Origin	Dates	Port of departure	Port of arrival / Date	Notes
McGonnagle James	County Londonderry, Ireland Feb 1807	19 Nov 1828 22 Nov 1831 s		Philadelphia 1822	Spring 1821 Has lived in Maryland since arrival in U.S.
McGonnegal Samuel		04 Dec 1820 08 Apr 1826			William McLaughlin
McGory John County Halifax, Noversection 29		23 May 1820 s 47		May 1817	Migrated from Halifax in Province of Noversection. Owes allegiance to Great Britain and Ireland.
McGrave John County Meoth 40		09 Nov 1819 s 15			
McGraw John		01 Dec 1825 24 Sep 1828 IN			
McGuigan Terrance County Tyrone, Ireland 30 1806		01 Dec 1836 s 38	Londonderry	New York	1833 1833
McGuire Felix Co. Farmana, Ireland 26 1814		05 Oct 1840 x 111	Liverpool	New York	1836 1836
McGuire Owen		27 Oct 1845 23 Sep 1851 24			B. Frank Roman Report was made in Lancaster Co., PA. Owes allegiance to Great Britain & Ireland

Last Name	First Name	Report Date	Departure Port	Witness(es)
Place of Birth	Date of Birth	Natural. Date	Arrival Port	
Age		Sig. Page No.	Other	
			Departure Date	
			Arrival Date	
McGunnell	James	04 Dec 1820		
County Deary, Ireland			Sep 1818	
30		s 63	His signature read "McGonigl".	
McGurk	Patrick	12 Mar 1835		Anthony Loftus
		22 Nov 1837		
		7	Report made in Frederick Co., Maryland.	
McIntoch?	James	25 Nov 1843		

		IN		
McKee	Samuel	23 Nov 1821		
County Derry, Ireland		27 Aug 1840	07 Jul 1820	
24		x 40		
McKegney	John	*16 Sep 1806*		
		16 Sep 1806		
McKenney	John	11 Apr 1822		
County Queen, Ireland			1817	
21		s 52		
McKierman	Francis	04 Oct 1813		
Ireland		47	Name may be McKierman	

Surname	Given	Date(s)	Age	Place	Notes
McKieman Ireland	Peter	04 Oct 1813	46		Name may be McKierman
McKierman Ireland	Michael	*03 Nov 1808* 07 Oct 1811	38	<14 Apr 1802	Name may be McKinnan
McKinney County Monahim, Ireland 1799	Hugh	28 Nov 1836 x	22	Belfast 1827 Baltimore 1827	
McKnutt Ireland 25	Thomas	01 Nov 1808 01 Nov 1811 s	31	<14 Apr 1802	Arthur Johnson
McLaughlin	Michael	21 Nov 1825 07 Nov 1828	IN		
McMachan	James	25 Aug 1802	40		Owes allegiance to Great Britain & Ireland
McMahan Manahan Co., Ireland 31 1811	Anthony	01 Dec 1842 s	23	Liverpool 1839 New York 1839	
McMahan	John	25 Aug 1802			Owes allegiance to King of Great Britain & Ireland

Last Name Place of Birth Age	First Name Date of Birth	Report Date Natural. Date Sig. Page No.	Departure Port Arrival Port Other	Departure Date Arrival Date	Witness(es)
McMullen County Tyrone, Ireland 27	Francis	15 Feb 1815 28 Feb 1824 s 52	Londonderry New York	Nov 1811	
McNamara	James	cert 20 Nov 1837			
McNamara	James	27 Aug 1830 20 Nov 1837 2	Report made in District of Columbia.		David Reagan
McNamee Ireland 24	Patrick 1832	13 Mar 1856 13 Mar 1858 x 7	Liverpool New York Witness for Report was Alexander H. Nesbitt.	1849 1849	Timothy Coin
McNulty	John	03 Apr 1820			
McPhaill Scotland	Donald	21 Apr 1794			
McQuade Londonderry, Ireland 1784	Charles	24 Nov 1828 30 Mar 1832 s	Baltimore Has lived in Maryland 8 yrs. Born in Co. Tyrone, Ireland.	Apr 1819 Jun 1819	Michael Bovey

Name / Origin	Date / Age	Place / Notes	Date	Other
McQuade James County Tyrone, Ireland 29	19 Nov 1827 x		1817	
McQuade James County Tyrone, Ireland 28	29 Mar 1825 27 Oct 1828 x 7		1818	
McQuigan Terrance	01 Dec 1836 20 Nov 1838 5			Hugh McKosker
McSherry Michael County Donegal, Ireland 4 203 1792	04 Dec 1833 03 Oct 1836 x 39	Londonderry Hallifax Arrived in Baltimore in July 1818. Born in County Donegal, Parish of Climmary, Ireland.	11 Apr 1818 May 1818	George Beard
McTighe James	12 Feb 1844 12 Feb 1844 IN			
McTighe Patrick Gr.Brit. & Irel.	16 Sep 1844 102	Alpha Index has "Cert" in Report Column.		James McTighe
Meher Patrick County Kildare, Ireland 42	04 Apr 1821 x 70		04 Apr 1812	
Mehler Valentine Northiem, Bavaria 27 1817	26 Sep 1844 s 111	Bremen Baltimore	1841 12 Sep 1841	

Last Name Place of Birth Age	First Name Date of Birth	Report Date Natural. Date Sig. Page No.	Departure Port Arrival Port Other	Departure Date Arrival Date	Witness(es)
Meisach * Itlinger, Co. of Baden, Germ.	Leonard 1805	21 Nov 1836	Bremen Baltimore * Name may be Mizer.	1835 1835	
Meister Bavaria 40	Christian	18 Nov 1824 s 25		Jul 1821	
Meister Neiderlamk, Prussia 43	Martin 1809	13 Nov 1852 22 Mar 1856 s 9	Bremen Baltimore	1850 Sep 1850	Martin Ridenour
Mellon	Neill	Certificate 07 Apr 1842 IN			
Menebrecker Prussia	John Henry	14 Feb 1846 06 Sep 1848 17			Daniel King
Menius Bumburg, Bavaria 48	John 1799	10 Jan 1848 10 May 1850 s 26	Hamburg Philadelphia	1840 08 Oct 1840	John Knieniew
Menke	Anthony	22 Oct 1842 -- IN			

Mennel Christian	17 Nov 1841			Caspar Browugart
Hesse Darmstadt	16 Sep 1844			
	66			
Mernagh Dennis	10 Jul 1850	Liverpool	1848	
Co. Wicklow, Ireland		Philadelphia	Apr 1848	
38 1812	x 18			
Mesmer Joseph	05 Oct 1847	Havre de Grace	1832	
Lohr, Baden		Baltimore	Aug 1832	
59 1787	s 38			
Messell John	04 Apr 1842			Frederick Shack
Bavaria	16 Sep 1844			
	107			
Messing Adam	19 Nov 1834	Havre de Grace	1833	
Rhinebyer, Germany		New York	Aug 1833	
25 1809	s 14	Owes allegiance to Prince Ludwig.		
Messing Magdelena	19 Nov 1834	Havre de Grace	1833	
Rhinebyer, Germany		New York	Aug 1833	
60 1774	x 15	Owes allegiance to Prince Ludwig. One of only 2 woman naturalized		
Metzer Henry	28 Nov 1842	Bremen	1839	Joseph J. Merrick
Sundraugh, Hesse Castle	29 Nov 1844	Baltimore	1839	
35 1807	s 17			
Meyer Jacob	01 Nov 1811			
	29 Mar 1817			

Last Name Place of Birth Age	First Name Date of Birth	Report Date Natural. Date Sig. Page No.	Departure Port Arrival Port Other	Departure Date Arrival Date	Witness(es)
Meyerly	Frederich	05 Apr 1838 09 Apr 1840 IN			
Michael Wirtemburg	John Christoph	01 Sep 1846 01 Sep 1846 x 40	Arrived as a minor.		
Michael Sultzamnecker, Wertemburg 46	John Gottleib 1798	10 Aug 1844 01 Sep 1846 s 42	Bremen Baltimore	1834 09 Aug 1834	Henry Heigis
Michell Co. Cornwall, England 44	James 1805	30 Nov 1849	London New York	1847 Sep 1847	
Miller	Anthony	05 Dec 1837 s 3			
Miller Wirtemburgh 25	Christian 1842	17 Sep 1867 17 Sep 1867 s 6	Havre de Grace New York Honorably discharged from military service 27 May 1867.	1863	Frederick Miller Gottleib Smith
Miller Trysa?, Hesse Cassel 43	Christian 1835	01 Jan 1878 s 12	Bremen Baltimore	1862 1862	

Surname	Given name	Date	Age	Port	Year	Sponsor
Miller	Conrad	14 Aug 1850	19			Mary Miller
Sigmaringen				Arrived as a minor.		
Miller	Frederick	12 May 1845		Bremen	1837	Henry W. Dellinger
Margaretta Lengerich, Prussia		28 Sep 1847	21	Baltimore	21 Jun 1837	
37	1808	s				
Miller	George	16 Sep 1844		Obendorff	1836	Philip Smouder
Obendorff, Wirtemburgh		05 Oct 1846	61	New York	16 Jun 1836	
35	1809	s				
Miller	Henry	15 Nov 1841				
		20 Nov 1843				
207		IN				
Miller	Jacob	17 Nov 1835		Havre de Grace	1828	
Elsis, France				Baltimore	1828	
36	1799	s	3	Owes allegiance to Philip King of France.		
Miller	Jacob					Matthias Shaffner
Denmark		02 Apr 1810	39		<14 Apr 1802	
Miller	Jacob F.	17 Nov 1835		Havre de Grace	1830	Michael Klink
Wurtemburg, Germany		23 Nov 1837		Portland, Maine	1830	
32	1803	s	4			
Miller	John	24 Sep 1806				Robert Douglass
Ireland			66			

Last Name	First Name	Report Date	Departure Port	Departure Date	Witness(es)
Place of Birth	Date of Birth	Natural. Date	Arrival Port	Arrival Date	
Age		Sig. Page No.	Other		
Miller	John	13 Jan 1798			
Germany		13 Jan 1798			
		43			
Miller	John Jacob	20 Nov 1821	Baker. Living in Hagerstown.		
Wirtemburgh, Germany				Aug 1820	
45		s 23			
Miller	Kaspar	28 Nov 1842	Bremen	1840	
Bavaria			Baltimore	1840	
26	1816	s 16	Signature reads Muller.		
Miller	Matthias	25 Nov 1839	Bremen	1833	
Wirtemburgh		22 Nov 1841	Baltimore	1833	
48	1791	x 17			
Miller	Michael	22 Nov 1830	Amsterdam	25 Apr 1827	
Ourbach, Baden		04 Apr 1833	Baltimore	31 Aug 1827	
45	1785	s			
Miller	Peter	29 Oct 1810			
France		31			
Miller	Robert	24 Sep 1806			Robert Douglass
Ireland		66			

Name	Origin	Date/Age	Port/Destination	Date
Miller	Robert			
Ireland		07 Nov 1811		
		40		
Miller	Samuel Frederi	13 Apr 1857	Havre de Grace	1854
Wirtemburgh			New York	23 Oct 1854
21	1836	s 27		
Miller	Wandalin	12 Apr 1852	Havre de Grace	1849
Staddlehafer, Baden			New York	Jul 1849
26	1826	s 17		
Miller	William	*16 Nov 1840*		
		16 Nov 1840		
Miller/Mullur	Anthony	05 Dec 1837	Bremen	1834
Darmstadt, Hesse			Baltimore	1834
26	1811	s 41		
Milligan	Patrick	30 Nov 1840		
		IN		
Milligan	William	29 Mar 1832	County Down,	May 1821
Ireland			Baltimore	Jul 1821
68	Nov 1764	s 31		
Mills	Robert	30 Mar 1825		
County Donegal, Ireland		10 Oct 1828		13 Jun 1818
29		s 8		

Last Name / Place of Birth / Age	First Name / Date of Birth	Report Date / Natural. Date / Sig. Page No.	Departure Port / Arrival Port / Other	Departure Date / Arrival Date	Witness(es)
Minahan Ireland	Timothy	04 Apr 1799 04 Apr 1799 16			
Mitchell	James M.	5 Apr 1828 -- IN	Plasterer. Living in Hagerstown.		
Mizer Itlinger, County of Baden, Germ 31	Leonard 1805	21 Nov 1836 *17 Aug 1840* s 2	Bremen Baltimore Signature reads "Meisach"	1835 1835	
Moar Bavaria 31	Henry 1816	03 Dec 1847 s 21	Bremen Baltimore	1840 06 Aug 1840	
Moffett Ireland 20	William	27 Mar 1809 30 Mar 1814 s 16	*Tyrone *Tyrone, Ireland	21 Sep 1805	
Mohn France	Nathan	10 Sep 1842 28 Sep 1847 35			Abraham Levi
Molaré Baden, Germany	Joseph Francis	02 Sep 1844 48			Jacob Gruber
Report made in Baltimore City, Maryland. No date given.					

Name		Date	Port of Departure	Port of Arrival	Date of Arrival
Monday	Francis	05 Apr 1851	Bremen	Baltimore	1848
Lengenfelt, Prussia		s			May 1848
32		1818	14		
Mong	Adam	01 Nov 1808	Maryland		Nov 1804
Germany		29 Oct 1811	Has lived in MD since his arrival		
		32			
Mong	Valentine	27 Oct 1808			
Germany		29 Oct 1811			
		20			
Monger	Sebastian	18 Oct 1847	Bremen	Baltimore	1840
Schwachearaed, Bavaria		s			Jun 1840
39		1808	40		
Monnohan	Patrick	04 Dec 1837	Dublin	New York	1830
County Cavan, Ireland		x			1830
35		1802	38		
Montgomery	Archibald	31 Mar 1826			
County Down, Ireland		1 Oct 1828			Jun 1803
55		x			
Montgomery	James Alexand	31 Oct 1867	Liverpool	New Orleans	1848
England		s			1848
29		1838	15		
Montgomery	John	31 Mar 1826			
County Down, Ireland		1 Oct 1828			Jun 1803
34		s			

| Last Name | First Name | Report Date | Departure Port | Departure Date | Witness(es) |
| Place of Birth | Date of Birth | Natural. Date | Arrival Port | Arrival Date | |
Age		Sig. Page No.	Other		
Montz	John	16 Sep 1844	Bremen	1840	Adam Nail
Wershenen, Hesse Cassel		05 Oct 1846	Baltimore	04 Aug 1841	
26	1818	s 56			
Moore	George	16 Sep 1844	Bremen	1840	Michael Freize
Reinburg, Bavaria		24 Nov 1846	Baltimore	06 Aug 1840	
48	1796	s 57			
Moore	John	06 Nov 1828			
		06 Nov 1828			
		IN			
Moore	William	24 Sep 1806			John Delzell
Ireland		66			
Moore	William	15 Aug 1832			Joel B. Cahoun
		22 Nov 1836			
		8			
Mopran	Jacob	06 Nov 1828			
		06 Nov 1828			
		IN			
Moran	Gerald	28 Mar 1829	London	Sep 1818	John Ripley
City of Dublin, Ireland		05 Apr 1831	New York	Dec. 1818	
44	1785	s	Lived in Maryland last 7 yrs.		

Surname	Given name	Date	Place	Witness / Notes
Morgan	Edward	23 Mar 1835 24 Jul 1837 60		Jacob Kausler
Morgenstern	Georg	23 Jul 1856	Havre de Grace	Lewis Heist
Michelstadt, Hesse Darmstadt		23 Nov 1858	New York	
29	1827	s 17		
Morian	John Anthony	30 Oct 1811		
Leittringhausen by Dissoldorff				
38		s 41	Owes allegiance to Prince of Berge, Palatin, Germany.	
Morris	David	22 Nov 1838	Belfast	James Atwell
County Tyrone, Ireland		22 Nov 1838	Baltimore	1824
25	1813	x 10		
Morris	John	05 Oct 1846		Samuel Fortney
		30	Arrived as a minor. Owes allegiance to Great Britain & Ireland	
Morris	William	26 Nov 1838	Liverpool	1832
Wales		30 Nov 1840	Baltimore	1832
25	1813	s 15		
Morter	Francis	19 Nov 1833	Havre de Grace	10 Jun 1829
County of Eltzsaus, Germany		*21 Nov 1837*	Baltimore	Aug 1829
30	1803	s 10	Owes allegiance to King Frederick. Has lived in Maryland since arrival in U.S.	
Morter	Thomas	24 Nov 1854	Dundalk	1847
Ireland *			Alexandria, VA	08 May 1847
24	1830	x 14		I.(?) Nesbitt
			*The words used in the Report were "Ireland, he thinks"	

Last Name Place of Birth Age	First Name Date of Birth	Report Date Natural. Date Sig. Page No.	Departure Port Arrival Port Other	Departure Date Arrival Date	Witness(es)
Mossean	Jacob	*06 Nov 1828* *06 Nov 1828*			
Most Hesse Darmstadt, Germany 39	Christian 1799	03 Dec 1838 *14 May 1841* s 36	Bremen Baltimore	1832 1832	Jacob Swope
Most Hesse Darmstadt	Christian	14 May 1841 14 May 1841 55			Jacob Swope
Motter	Francis	19 Nov 1833 21 Nov 1837 5			Lawrence Schneider
Moyer Germany	John Daniel	26 Oct 1808 26 Oct 1811 33			
Mulhall Ireland	Thomas	01 Nov 1811 41			
Mulien County Fermanegh, Ireland 25	James	04 Apr 1823 s 50		Nov 1818	

Mullar France 36	Joseph	08 Feb 1845 s 47	Havre de Grace New York Name may be Muller	1831 1831	
Mullins Limerick, Ireland 37	James	30 Oct 1868 x 297	Limerick New York	1853 1853	
Mulqueen County Limerick, Ireland 29	John	19 Nov 1834 x 17	Limerick Buffalo, NY	1831 1832	
Munday 215	Patrick	27 Mar 1828 08 Dec 1836 63			Michael Iseminger
Mung Germany	John	13 Apr 1799 13 Apr 1799 52	Millwright.		
Murphy Co. Karry, Ireland 29	Bartholamew	03 Oct 1848 23 Aug 1851 s 21	Cork New York	1838	Henry Morrison
Murphy Ireland	Christopher	23 Oct 1810 16		<14 Apr 1802	William Morrow
Murphy Balmurphey, Ireland 36	Hugh	26 Sep 1844 05 Oct 1846 s 110	New Ross Buffalo, NY	1827 1830	James Doyle

Last Name	First Name	Report Date	Departure Port	Departure Date	Witness(es)
Place of Birth		Natural. Date	Arrival Port	Arrival Date	
Age	Date of Birth	Sig. Page No.	Other		
Murphy	John	22 Mar 1824		1819	
County Down, Ireland					
31		s 78			
Murphy	Michael	26 Sep 1842			William Dodge
		26 Sep 1844			
		117			
Murphy	Patrick	24 May 1859			George G. Middlekauff
Ireland		05 Oct 1874			Cornelius Shehan
		x 21	Report made in the Northern District of California.		
Murphy	Richard H.	03 Apr 1823		1817	
City of Cork, Ireland					
28		s 51			
Murray	Joseph	22 Nov 1841			
		22 Nov 1841			
		IN			
Murray	Richard	29 Mar 1820			Arthur Blackwell
		3 Apr 1826			
Murrell	John	06 Apr 1809	Co. Derry, Irel.	02 Sep 1805	
Ireland		06 Apr 1809			
23		39			

Name	Origin	Age/Date	Date	Place	Year	Note
Murry	Daniel		05 Oct 1840	Slygo	1826	
Co. Slygo, Ireland				New York	1828	
31		1809	x 100			
Murry	John		12 Apr 1822		Jul 1819	
Scotland						
21			s 51			
Murry	Michael		05 Oct 1840	Slygo	1835	
Co. Latham, Ireland				Burlington, VT	1835	
29		1811	x 103			
Murry	Michael		05 Oct 1840	Dublin	1836	
Co. Roscommen, Ireland				New York	1836	
42		1798	s 110			
Murry	Owen		03 Apr 1840	Liverpool	1836	
County Monahan, Ireland				New York	1836	
23		1817	x 34			
Murry	Richard		29 Mar 1820		1805	
County Waterford, Ireland			6 Mar? 1826			
35			s 10			
Myerly	Frederick		05 Apr 1838			Jacob Goldsmith
			09 Apr 1840			
Myers	Alexander		17 Sep 1853	Bremen	1853	
Baden				Baltimore	Sep 1853	
43		1810	s 14			

| Last Name | First Name | Report Date | Departure Port | Departure Date | Witness(es) |
| Place of Birth | Date of Birth | Natural. Date | Arrival Port | Arrival Date | |
Age		Sig. Page No.	Other		
Myers	Baltzer	30 Mar 1850	Antwerp	1848	Joseph G. Protzman
Wirtemburgh		05 Sep 1853	New York	May 1848	
37	1813	s 3			
Myers	Caspar	30 Sep 1850	Arrived as a minor.		
Bavaria		27			
Myers	George	26 Nov 1836	Bremen	1836	
Shultz, Wirtemburg, Germany			Baltimore	1836	
24	1812	s 20			
Myers	Peter	29 Sep 1849	Bremen	1842	
Reisenbanck, Hesse Darmstadt			Baltimore	Sep 1842	
25	1824	s 28			
Myers	Peter	26 Nov 1832			Michael Fries
Bavaria		30 Sep 1839			
		37			
Myers	Vincent	30 Sep 1850	Arrived as a minor.		
Bavaria		27			
Mysoch	Michael	28 Oct 1839	Report column reads "Certificate"		
		26 Sep 1842			
		IN			

Nazarenns	Frederick	03 Oct 1848		Martin Sensil
Hesse Darmstadt		22		
Neill	John O.	26 Nov 1832	Arrived as a minor.	
		--		
		IN		
Neitzell	John	06 Jan 1798		
Germany		06 Jan 1798		
		24	Cooper. Living in Williamsport.	
Nelson	Thomas	25 Aug 1802		
			Owes allegiance to Great Britain & Ireland.	
Neverlin	Joseph	04 Mar 1862	Bremen	1856
Bavaria			Baltimore	27 May 1856
34		s 8		
Neville	Patrick	22 Jan 1852	Limerick	1849
Co. Limerick, Ireland			New York	1849
22	1830	s 18		
Nibert/Neibert	John	11 Jan 1798		
Prussia		38	Taylor. Living in Marsh Hundred.	
Nicholas	Benjamin	25 Mar 1839	*Bristol	1822
Glasmorganshire, Wales			Richmond, VA	1822
43	1795	s 2	*Bristol, England	

Last Name	First Name	Report Date	Departure Port	Departure Date	Witness(es)
Place of Birth	Date of Birth	Natural. Date	Arrival Port	Arrival Date	
Age		Sig. Page No.	Other		
Nicholas	John	22 Mar 1824			
Village of Staden, Wirtemburgh				Sep 1820	
29		s 78			
Nolan	John	05 Aug 1871	Queenstown	1865	Michael Dillon, John
County Limerick, Ireland	1848	05 Aug 1871	Castle Garden	1865	Ginaill, Thomas Hickman
23		s 25	Arrived as a minor.		
Noland	Michael	03 Nov 1851	Dublin	1847	Timothy Coin
Ireland		06 Aug 1855	New York	Apr 1847	
24	1827	x 28			
Norris	David	22 Nov 1838			
		22 Nov 1838			
Notteler	Jacob	16 Sep 1844			Michael Tricher
Wirtemburgh		72			
Null	Conrad	03 Jan 1798			
Prince of Hesse		03 Jan 1798			
		16	Living in Hagerstown.		
O'Brien	Charles	07 Apr 1834	Liverpool	1830	
Cork, Ireland			New York	Jun 1830	
28	1806	s 54			

Surname	Given Name	Date 1	Date 2	Place 1	Place 2	Witnesses / Notes
O'Brien	John	25 Mar 1834		Limerick	May 1832	
County Limerick, Ireland				Albany, NY	1832	
23	1811	x	2			
O'Brien	Luke	24 Jul 1828				
		06 Jan 1834				
		48		Report made to the Marine Court of the City of New York.		
O'Brien	Timothy	08 Jun 1872		Dublin	1859	
Tipperary Co., Ireland				New York	-	
39	1833	s	25			
O'Brien	William	15 Dec 1830				John O'Brien
		25 Mar 1834				
		3		Report was made in the District of Columbia on 15 Dec 1830.		
O'Byrne	Patrick	25 Nov 1822			Sep 1819	
County Roscommon, Ireland						
		s	39			
O'Conner	Patrick	01 Oct 1868		-	-	Joseph Hoover
County Derry, Ireland		23 Oct 1871		New York	04 Oct 1846	Hugh Malomes
42	-	s	30	Report made in Lebanon Co., Pennsylvania.		
O'Donnell	Anthony	25 Mar 1835				
		IN				
		--				
O'Donnell	Dominick A.	09 Jan 1836		Londonderry	1817	Daniel Dougherty
County Donegal, Ireland		09 Jan 1836		Boston	1817	
28	1808	s	49			

| Last Name | First Name | Report Date | Departure Port | Departure Date | Witness(es) |
| Place of Birth | Date of Birth | Natural. Date | Arrival Port | Arrival Date | |
Age		Sig. Page No.	Other		
O'Donnell	Patrick	07 Sep 1868	Waterford	1852	
Limerick, Ireland		07 Sep 1868	New York	1852	
24	1844	x 284			
O'Leary	Daniel	07 Sep 1844	Kinsale	1840	Robert Fowler
Bandon, Ireland		01 Sep 1846	Boston	Jun 1840	
24	1820	s 49			
O'Leary	Thomas	26 Aug 1850			Daniel O'Leary
		21	Owes allegiance to Great Britain & Ireland		
O'Neall	John	05 Oct 1840	New Ross, Irel.	1822	
Co. Carlo, Ireland			New York	1822	
51	1789	x 108			
O'Neil	William	12 Apr 1852			--
		12 Aug 1856			
		16			
O'Neill	John	*26 Nov 1832*	Report made - City of New York. Allegiance-Great Britain & Ireland		
O'Rourk	Barnard	25 Mar 1834	Belfast	1826	
Cooks Town, County Tyrone, Irel			Philadelphia	Aug 1827	
30	1803	x 6			

Name	Origin	Date 1	Date 2	Place 1	Place 2	Witness/Notes
O'Rourk John		21 Nov 1844		Ross	1807	
Co. Wexford, Ireland				New York	02 Jul 1807	
63	1781	x	4			
ONeill (sic) William		26 Nov 1832				
		—	IN			
Obandaffer John Leonard		30 Sep 1848				Augustus Shultz
Bavaria		01 Oct 1850				
			31			Alpha Index has "Cert." in Report column.
Oertel George		15 Jun 1841		Bremen	1839	Frederick Shack
Echersday, Bayrenth, Germany		26 Sep 1844		Baltimore	25 Sep 1839	
23	1814	s	57			Owes allegiance to King of Boyern.
Oker *John Christ.		13 Sep 1841				Andrew Leibold
Wirtemburgh		28 Sep 1847				
			31			*John Christopher. Alpha Index has "Cert." in Report column.
Oppenheimer Israel		22 Jul 1858		Havre de Grace	1852	
Ickenhausen, Bavaria				New York	Jun 1852	
27	1831	s	24			
Optan John		20 Apr 1831				John McGaughlin
		29 Mar 1836				
			31			Report filed in Mifflin County, PA.
Ore Michael						
Prussia		12 Apr 1799				Millwright. Living on Lower Antietam.

Last Name / Place of Birth / Age	First Name / Date of Birth	Report Date / Natural. Date / Sig. Page No.	Departure Port / Arrival Port / Other	Departure Date / Arrival Date	Witness(es)
Ormston / Northumberland County, England / 25	Andrew	29 Oct 1818 / 05 Nov 1828 / s 63		30 Sep 1818	
Ormston / Northumberland County, England / 23	John	29 Oct 1818 / / s 63		30 Sep 1818	
Ormston	John	29 Oct 1818 / 27 Mar 1824 / 81	Oath was made in court on 20 Nov 1818.		John Swearingen / Jacob Myers
Ormston / Great Britain	Ralph	06 Jan 1798 / 06 Jan 1798 / 24	Farmer. Living near Booth's Mill.		
Orr / Germany	Nicholas	04 Apr 1799 / 04 Apr 1799 / 16	Taylor. Living on Semple? Sand?.		
Osborn	Henry	27 Oct 1845			
Osendorf	Christian	03 Sep 1838 / -- / IN			

Surname	Given	Origin	Date	Age	Place	Notes/Sponsor
Otto	Christian	Trysa, Hesse Cassel	24 Jan 1851	s	Bremen	1849
		1830		15	Baltimore	Jun 1849
						See record of John Hirschfield.
Overmyer	John	Bavaria	24 Aug 1802	33		Owes allegience to Charles Theodore, Elector of Bavaria.
Oyer	Vendel	Germany	06 Jan 1798			
			06 Jan 1798	25		Labourer. Living in Williamsport.
Padan	John	Ireland	21 Aug 1805	23		George Nigh
Parheketiare?	Joseph	Bohemia, Austria	29 Aug 1812		Amsterdam	
		29		s 28		Dec 1804
Park	Alexander		22 Nov 1841			
			22 Nov 1841	IN		
Parsons	Thomas	Ireland	02 Nov 1808	35		Thomas Post <14 Apr 1802
Patterson	John	Ireland	04 Sep 1840		Belfast	1825
		43	24 Nov 1842		Baltimore	Samuel M. Hitt 1825
		1797	s	76		

Last Name	First Name	Report Date	Departure Port	Departure Date	Witness(es)
Place of Birth	Date of Birth	Natural. Date	Arrival Port	Arrival Date	
Age		Sig. Page No.	Other		
Patterson	Robert	21 Nov 1827			John Ripley
County Down, Ireland		05 Apr 1831	Norfolk	1816	
32		s 41			
Paulder	John	22 Nov 1820			Jacob Schnell
England		32			
Paules	Paules	16 Sep 1844	Bremen	1839	
Oberauheim, Bavaria/Hanover			Baltimore	01 Sep 1839	
28	1816	s 57	Name may also be spelled Paulus Paulus.		
Paxton	Daniel	16 Sep 1844			Philip Fitzpatrick
		77	Owes allegiance to Great Britain & Ireland		
Pea	John G.	23 Nov 1836	Bremen	1830	Jacob Barth
Stonpenburg, Germany		23 Nov 1836	Baltimore	1830	
21	1815	s 16	Owes allegiance to Prince Ludwig.		
Pearshbaugh	Henry	20 Nov 1839	Bremen	1833	
Darmstadt, Germany		23 Nov 1841	Baltimore	1833	
40	1790	x 9			
Peater	John Carl	02 Dec 1856	Bremen	1854	George H. Heigas
Saxe Altenburg		05 Nov 1864	Baltimore	04 Aug 1854	
29	1828	s 16			

Name	Origin	Age	Date	Port	Date	Witness/Notes
Peiser Lewis N.	Pason, Poland, Prussia	32	28 Jul 1845 s	Hamburg New York	1843 22 Jun 1843 23	
Petercup Conrad	Stockhousen, Germany	28	29 Mar 1834 -	Bremen Baltimore	1831 Sep 1831 28	Owes allegiance to the Prince of Hesse.
Peterpenner John	Germany		10 Dec 1799 10 Dec 1799		11	Shoemaker. Living in Boonsboro.
Peyhl Joseph	Wirtemburgh		01 Oct 1840 16 Sep 1844		79	Jacob Votteler
Pfoch Henry	Saxe Weimer		20 Sep 1847		25	John Roch
Philbin Michael			24 Sep 1832 24 Nov 1836		21	Anthony Softus. Arrived as a minor. Report made in the Western District of Pennsylvania.
Philip John	Ireland		06 Aug 1868		276	
Philip Richard			02 Sep 1844		45	Robert Forrley. Arrived as a minor. Owes allegiance to Great Britain & Ireland

Last Name Place of Birth Age	First Name Date of Birth	Report Date Natural. Date Sig. Page No.	Departure Port Arrival Port Other	Departure Date Arrival Date	Witness(es)
Philips	Thomas B.	12 Feb 1844 12 Feb 1844 IN			
Phillips	Richard	*02 Sep 1844* *02 Sep 1844*			
Plumeigarr?	Michael	24 Sep 1838 01 Oct 1840			Jacob Cline
Plumenour	Nicholas	24 Sep 1838 01 Oct 1840			Michael P____, Sen.
Plumenous, Jr.	Michael	24 Sep 1838 01 Oct 1840			Michael Plumenous, Sen.
Plummenour	Nicholas	-- Mar 1838 01 Oct 1840 IN			
Plummenour Jr	Michael	-- Mar 1838 01 Oct 1840 IN			

Surname	Given Name	Origin	Age/Year	Date	Date2	Port	Other	Sponsor/Notes
Plummenour S	Michael			-- Mar 1838	01 Oct 1840 IN			Philip Schmouder
Popp	Andrew	Ebner, Bavaria	30 / 1813	15 Apr 1844	05 Oct 1846 s 37	Bremen Baltimore	1840 1840	
Powell	Michael	near Strasburgh, France	29	01 Apr 1831	19 Nov 1833 s 29	Baltimore	10 Mar 1828 10 Apr 1828	Jacob Ripley
Powles	Benjamin	Canton Weisenburgh, France / 1800		25 Nov 1839	20 Nov 1841 x 17	Havre de Grace Baltimore	1832 1832	Born in Canton Weisenburg, State of Strasburg, France.
Powles/Powlus	Peter	Bavaria		16 Sep 1844	81			Lewis Futter
Powlus	Henry	Elsser, France	37	05 Apr 1822	22 Nov 1834 s 39		1817	Peter Bell. Signature was in German script.
Pracht	Henry	Hesse Darmstadt / 1820	27	20 Sep 1847	s 13	Bremen New York	1844 Jun 1844	
Presbaugh	Henry	Hesse Darmstadt	26	30 Sep 1850				John Masel. Arrived as a minor.

| Last Name | First Name | Report Date | Departure Port | Departure Date | Witness(es) |
| Place of Birth | Date of Birth | Natural. Date | Arrival Port | Arrival Date | |
Age		Sig. Page No.	Other		
Preungart	Caspar	07 Dec 1837	Bremen	1833	
Waltfeinsten, Germany		28 Mar 1840	Baltimore	1833	
31	1806	s 49	Signature reads Lreungart.		
Price	Rezin	30 Oct 1813			
Ireland		40			
Priday	Thomas	04 Dec 1837	Dublin	1831	
County Westmade, Ireland			New York	1831	
25	1812	x 37			
Puerschel	Adolph	12 Jan 1864	Bremen	-	John Wiles
Festenburg, Prussia		29 Oct 1867	Baltimore	21 Sep 1851	Andrew Scheidar
38	-	? 13	Report made in Washington, DC.		
Punt	George	05 Oct 1846			Christian Bickley
Wirtemburgh		31	Arrived as a minor.		
Pursall	Patrick	05 Oct 1840	New Ross, Irel	1832	
Queens Co., Ireland			Burlington, VT	1832	
28	1812	x 110			
Purtill	Thomas	28 Nov 1834			
		29 Nov 1838			

Name		Date 1 / Date 2	Place 1 / Place 2	Year 1 / Year 2	Notes
Quillen	Owen	05 Oct 1840	Dublin	1831	
Co. Langford, Ireland		05 Oct 1842	New York	1831	
30	1810	x 98			
Quin	Thomas	--			
		01 Oct 1840			
Quinley	Daniel	31 Oct 1870	Londonderry	1864	
Ireland			Baltimore	1864	
26	1844	x 35			
Quinn	Michael	27 Nov 1837	Liverpool	1829	
County Longford, Ireland		27 Nov 1837	Annapolis	1829	
2]	1817	x 20			
Quinn	Patrick	21 Nov 1836	Belfast	1822	John C. Brining
Co. Faurana, Ireland		01 Oct 1840	Baltimore	1822	
33	1807	x 93			
Quynn	Bernard	26 Mar 1840	Liverpool	1830	
Longford Co., Ireland		26 Mar 1840	Annapolis	1830	
	1818	x 13			
Rable	Frederick	06 Dec 1836	Havre de Grace	1832	George Knard?
Province Pfotza, Prussia		14 Dec 1838	Baltimore	1832	
25	1811	s 54	Signature reads Rable. Clerk has written Deble.		
Rafitz	Francis	12 Aug 1839	Havre de Grace	1832	Christian Winters
Humbers/Hussler Co. Germany		12 Aug 1839	Baltimore	1832	
23	1816	s 36			

Last Name	First Name	Report Date	Departure Port	Departure Date	Witness(es)
Place of Birth	Date of Birth	Natural. Date	Arrival Port	Arrival Date	
Age		Sig. Page No.	Other		
Ragan	David	20 Nov 1835			James McNamara
		20 Nov 1837			
		3			
Ragers	Arthur	1833			John Young
		28 Nov 1836			
		25			
Raish	Christian	19 Nov 1824	Report made in Allegheny County, Maryland.		
Wirtemburgh, Germany				1817	
43		s 26			
Rake	John Henry	16 Sep 1844			Henry Mash
Altenburg		76			
Ranahan	Michael	17 Dec 1829	Report filed in Districk of Columbia on 17 Dec 1829.		Patrick McGinley
		28 Nov 1834			
		56			
Rapp	Charles F.	14 Dec 1848	Bremen	1846	
Waldkappel, Hesse Cassel		*02 Feb 1852*	New York	May 1846	
26	1822	s 12			
Rausenberger	John	25 Jul 1859	Arrived as a minor.		John B. Costenbeder
Wirtemburgh		25 Jul 1859			
		2			

Name			Date	Place	Date of Death	Other
Rauth	George		15 Dec 1852	Antwerp	1851	
Rumbaugh, Hesse Darmstadt				New York	Jul 1851	
25		1827	s 18			
Rauth	Peter		22 Sep 1855	Bremen	1853	John B. Costenbeder
Frankish-Crumbach, Hesse Darm.			24 Nov 1858	Baltimore	23 Aug 1853	
25		1830	s 20			
Read	John George		26 Dec 1866	Havre de Grace	1842	
Heidelstein, Baden			02 Aug 1856	New York	-	
55		1811	s 42			
Reagan	David		24 Nov 1835	Cork	Apr 1829	
County Cork, Ireland				Boston	1829	
20		1805	s 26			
Reberger	Christian		15 Nov 1830	Amsterdam	Sep 1817	
Shundorf, Wirtemburg				Baltimore	Jan 1818	
42		Jul 1788	s	Has lived in Washington Co. for 10 yrs.		
Rebizer	George		05 Nov 1830			
			05 Oct 1842			
			IN			
Rechly	Everhart		04 Dec 1837	Havre de Grace	1830	
Town Eltingen, Wirtemburgh				Baltimore	1830	
30		1807	s 37			
Reckley	Sebastian		30 Nov 1832			Otho Williams
			24 Jul 1837			
			61			

Last Name / Place of Birth / Age	First Name / Date of Birth	Report Date / Natural. Date / Sig. Page No.	Departure Port / Arrival Port / Other	Departure Date / Arrival Date	Witness(es)
Rediberg Nidda, Hesse Darmstadt 28	Jacob 1816	23 Sep 1844 05 Oct 1846 s 109	Bremen Baltimore	1838 27 Sep 1838	Christian Wilt
Reibshamen Metztar, Prussia 47	John Martin 1801	02 May 1848 s 11	Antwerp New York	1845 Jul 1845	
Reichard Strausburgh, Prussia 32	Andrew 1804	06 Dec 1836 05 Oct 1840 x 55	Havre de Grace Baltimore	1832 1832	Rudolph Herr
Reigler Bavaria 44	Andrew 1803	04 Sep 1847 28 Sep 1849 s 11	Bremen Baltimore	1839 1839	Everhart Beitelspacher
Reiley Great Britain & Ireland	Peter	24 Mar 1839 26 Mar 1844 2	Report made in Morgan Co., VA (now WV).		Upton Laurence
Reiley	Thomas	05 Oct 1830 26 Mar 1834 15	Report was made in Cambria County, PA.		
Reilly Ireland 44	Patrick 1808	21 Oct 1852 s 7	Sligo *Burlington *Burlington, Maine	1839 1839	

Reilly	Patrick	02 Oct 1876	Ireland	1860	Daniel Falm
Ireland		03 Oct 1876	Washington, DC	Sep 1860	John H. Reid
28	1848	s 28			
Renner	Ignatius	21 Nov 1837	Havre de Grace	1831	Jacob Sweitzer
Baden, Germany		28 Mar 1840	Baltimore	1831	
27	1810	s 4	First name may be Augustus		
Renner	Valentine	30 Nov 1847	Bremen	1840	Henry Beitingheimer
Wertsburg, Bavaria		08 Apr 1850	Baltimore	Aug 1840	
35	1812	s 16			
Reppe	Henry	04 Nov 1848	Bremen	1844	
Wald Rappel, Hesse Cassel			Baltimore	Aug 1844	
53	1792	s 24			
Retterly	Philip	27 Mar 1821		Aug 1817	
Town of Winesburg			Born in the Town of Winesburg in the Jurisdiciton of Heilbrun in the		
38		s 25	Kingdom of Wirtemburgh.		
Rhind	John	21 Nov 1839	Greenoch	1834	
Merryshire, Scotland		01 Dec 1841	New York	1834	
29	1810	s 12			
Rhodes	Arthur	20 Nov 1838	Belfast	1827	
County Armaugh, Ireland		24 Nov 1840	Albany, NY	1827	
28	1810	s 4			

Last Name / Place of Birth / Age	First Name / Date of Birth	Report Date / Natural. Date / Sig. Page No.	Departure Port / Arrival Port / Other	Departure Date / Arrival Date	Witness(es)
Rice Ireland 38	Charles	02 Dec 1814 s 38	Stone mason. Cloth weaver. At time of report, had a wife and four children.	1807	Jacob Dellinger
Rice County Donnegal, Ireland 61	Charles 1776	27 Nov 1837 08 Apr 1840 s 21	Londonderry Baltimore	1803 1803	Jacob Dellinger
Rice Mitterode, Hesse Castle 34	Henry 1808	28 Nov 1842 28 Nov 1844 s 18	Bremen Baltimore	1839 1839	Michael Freize
Rice	Joseph	05 Oct 1846 34	Arrived as a minor. Owes allegiance to Great Britain & Ireland		Samuel Lyday
Rice	Patrick	19 Jan 1834 29 Mar 1837 12			Otho H. Stull
Rice County Caslo, Ireland 36	Patrick 1798	19 Nov 1834 x 11	Waterford Alexandria, DC	19 Apr 1825 Oct 1829	
Rice	Peter	*17 Nov 1841* *10 Aug 1847*			

Surname	First Name	Date(s)	Port/Origin	Sponsor
Richtman	George	27 Mar 1821		
Town of Werstenburg, Germany		s 30		
Rickert	Martin	20 Aug 1805		Aug 1816
Wurtemburgh		22		Christian Fechtig
Ries	Peter	17 Nov 1844		
Bavaria		10 Aug 1847		John M. Sherman
		10		
Riley	Hugh	24 Sep 1844	Liverpool	1832
Co. Longford, Ireland			Baltimore	1832
32		1812 x 110		
Riley	John	03 Dec 1839	Liverpool	1827
County Caren, Ireland		03 Dec 1839	Alexandria, DC	1827
27		1811 x 33		William Ashten
Roach	Arthur	*24 Sep 1838*		
Roan	Christopher	03 Oct 1838		
		05 Oct 1840		Lewis Futerer
		105		
Roberston	John	27 Mar 1809	*Tyrone	14 Jun 1806
Ireland		30 Mar 1814		
25		s 16	*Tyrone, Ireland	

| Last Name | First Name | Report Date | Departure Port | Departure Date | Witness(es) |
| Place of Birth | Date of Birth | Natural. Date | Arrival Port | Arrival Date | |
Age		Sig. Page No.	Other		
Robertson	William	27 Oct 1813	Tyrone, Ireland		
Ireland		18 Nov 1818		09 Jul 1810	
22		s 23			
Rock	George	29 Mar 1839	Bremen	1836	
Frankinoverbaugh			Baltimore	1836	
32	1807	s 12	Frankinoverbaugh, Hesse Darmstadt		
Roernaser	John Andrew	30 Nov 1832			
		09 Apr 1835			
		IN			
Roessner	Jacob	04 Oct 1861	Bremen	1854	George R. Bowman
Hesse Darmstadt		04 Oct 1861	Baltimore	May 1854	
23	1838	s 6	Arrived as a minor.		
Roffinberger	Peter	03 Sep 1838			
		02 Apr 1842			
		IN			
Rogan	William	28 Nov 1837	Sligo, Ireland	1826	
County Mayo, Ireland			Buffalo, NY	1826	
24	1815	s 23			
Rogers	Joseph	28 Feb 1803			
Great Britain		39			

Rogers Montreal, Canada 25	Joseph 1820	12 May 1845 28 Sep 1847 x 21	St. John's New York	1839 1839	John Stewart
Roh Wirtemburgh 30	Frederick 1820	13 Dec 1850 s 12	Havre de Grace New York	1848 02 Jan 1849	
Rohr Town of Epinger in Baden, Germ 41	Joseph	20 Nov 1820 20		05 Aug 1819	
Roke	John Henry	24 Nov 1841 16 Sep 1844 IN			
Ronch Darmstadt 239	Andrew	18 Sep 1851 29 Sep 1851 26			John Julius
Roof	John W.	25 Nov 1825 01 Oct 1828 IN			
Roof	Joseph A.	01 Oct 1828 01 Oct 1828 IN			
Rooney County Carlow, Ireland	Jeremiah	27 Nov 1818 s 39		01 Jun 1816	

Last Name Place of Birth Age	First Name Date of Birth	Report Date Natural. Date Sig. Page No.	Departure Port Arrival Port Other	Departure Date Arrival Date	Witness(es)
Ropp Hesse Cassel	Charles F.	11 Dec 1848 02 Feb 1852 20			James M. Long
Rose Westphalia, Prussia 48	Abraham 1818	09 Nov 1867 24 Oct 1870 s 19	Antwerpen* New York *Antwerpen, Belgium	1864 1864	William M. Tev? Levi Stone
Rosenberger Wittemburgh 26	Henry 1842	16 Mar 1869 23 Oct 1871 s 28	Bremen New York	1866 Sep 1866	Lewis Heist Henry Einstein
Rosenfield Bavaria	Wolf	01 Sep 1846 38			Henry Enstine
Rosenstack Hesse Cassel	Christian	16 Sep 1844 82	Arrived as a minor.		Stewart F. Herbert
Rosenstock Bavaria 56	Abraham 1799	25 Oct 1856 29 Jul 1859 s 20	Bremen Baltimore	1853 1853	Henry Einstein Peter Rauth
Rosenstock Bavaria	Shemerin	29 Jul 1859 29 Jul 1859 3	Arrived as a minor.		Henry Einstein

Surname	Given name	Date	Place	Notes
Ross	James	27 Oct 1814		
Ross	Samuel	10 Jan 1798		
Ireland		10 Jan 1798		
		31	Shoemaker. Living in Williamsport.	
Rouch/Rouck	Andrew	18 Sep 1849	Bremen	1830
Leipburg, Darmstadt			Baltimore	1830
40		s 23		
Routh	George	15 Dec 1852		Lewis Heist
Hesse Darmstadt		02 Aug 1856		
241		7		
Roux	Alfred	03 Apr 1837	Havre de Grace	1836
Geneva, Switzerland			New York	1836
26	1811	s 29		
Roux	Charles F.S.	30 Jan 1824		
		21 Sep 1837		
		67	Report made in Green County, New York.	
Rowe	Edward	03 Jan 1880	Liverpool	1851
Ireland			New York	1851
49	1830	x 19		
Ruckhart	Conrad	10 Apr 1833		

Last Name Place of Birth Age	First Name Date of Birth	Report Date Natural. Date Sig. Page No.	Departure Port Arrival Port Other	Departure Date Arrival Date	Witness(es)
Rumpf? Prussia	Ludwig	04 Oct 1813 48			
Rupp Wirtemburgh	George	02 Sep 1844 47	Alpha Index has "Cert." in Report column		George Bantz
Rupprecht Reichstadt, Bavaria 39	John 1809	10 Apr 1848 30 Aug 1850 s 8	Bremen Baltimore John Eber	1841 Dec 1841	John Masel
Russaamen Prussia	John	26 Sep 1844 120			Michael Treiber
Russe	John Jacob	23 Nov 1832 23 Nov 1842 IN	Arrived as a minor.		
Russe Bavaria	John Jacob	23 Nov 1832 7			George Shafer
Rutz Hesse Darmstadt 32	T.G. 1842	09 Sep 1874 s 19	Bremen New York	1862 1862	

Surname	Given name	Origin	Age/Year	Dates	Ports	Year	Witness/Notes
Ryan	John	County Tipperary, Ireland	22 1817	04 Apr 1839 x 26	Liverpool New York	1836 1836	
Ryan	Matthew	County Tipperary, Ireland	30 1805	19 Nov 1835 s 14	Cork Cove Boston	1833 Aug 1833	
Ryan	Matthew			19 Apr 1835 24 Sep 1838	IN		
Ryan	Michael	Limerick, Ireland	1802	12 Apr 1834 s 85	Limerick White Hall, N	1827 Jul 1827	
Ryan	Patrick	Canada	21 1828	26 Sep 1849 26 Sep 1849 x 24	Quebec New York Arrived as a minor.	1837 1837	Patrick Whitney
Ryan	Peter	Co. Longford, Ireland	45 1795	05 Oct 1840 05 Oct 1842 x 101	Dublin *White Hall *White Hall, New York	1825 1825	
Ryan	Timotheus	County Tipperary, Ireland	42	21 Nov 1827 26 Mar 1834 s 34	New York	1816	Thomas H. Williams
Ryan	William			16 Nov 1830 27 Mar 1837 2	Report made in Ohio County, Virginia.		Charles Sweeney

| Last Name | First Name | Report Date | Departure Port | Departure Date | Witness(es) |
| Place of Birth | Date of Birth | Natural. Date | Arrival Port | Arrival Date | |
Age		Sig. Page No.	Other		
Ryan	William	16 Nov 1830			Andrew Colvin
		28 Mar 1837			
		5	Report made in Mifflin County, Pennsylvania.		
Ryerack?	Arthur	24 Sep1 838			
		24 Nov 1840			
		IN			
SKuse (sic)	Isaac	19 Jul 1815			
City of Bristol, England				03 Nov 1811	
39		s 19	Clothier. At time of report, he had a wife.		
Sacks	Philip	17 Nov 1833			Charles Ulerich
		01 Apr 1836			
		13			
Sacks	John Philipp	19 Nov 1833	Amsterdam	05 Jul 1830	
Town of Weinbach, Hesse Darms.		*01 Apr 1836*	Baltimore	Sep 1830	
34	1799	s 11	Born in Town of Weinbach, Hesse Darmstadt, Austria. Has lived in Washington County since his arrival.		
Sale	Philip	22 Aug 1837	Liverpool	1828	Andrew Hogmire
Isle of Man, England		22 Aug 1837	Baltimore	1828	
22	1815	s 66			
Sallman	Augustus	*24 Nov 1827*			

Surname	Given Name	Date	Port	Arrival	Witness/Notes
Sampass	George Ferdina	31 Oct 1859	Bremen	1855	John Peter Rauth
Hesse Darmstadt		18 Aug 1866	New York	7? Sep 1856	John G. Wiles
33	1826	-	Arrived in New York the "7 or 8" of Sep 1856.		11
Samuel	John	20 Nov 1833	Liverpool	Sep 1831	
County Statford, England			New York	Nov 1831	
45	1787	s 16			
Sandman	William	*04 Apr 1799*			
			This entry is not in the Court Minutes for Apr 1799		
Sandrock	*John Chris.	27 Sep 1844	Bremen	1836	
Hesse Cassel, Germany		*20 Sep 1847*	Baltimore	18 Jul 1836	
24 35	1898	s 111	*John Christopher		
Sandys/Sands	Robert M.	03 Aug 1855	?	1833?	David Christ
Ireland		03 Aug 1855	Baltimore	1833?	
23	1832	s 15	Arrived as a minor. His spoken words were that he "emigrated at an age too young to be remembered, about the year 1833."		
Santman	William	12 Apr 1799			
Germany		12 Apr 1799	Weaver. Living in Sharpsburg.		
		49			
Sarges	Frederick	12 Mar 1851	Bremen	1842	
Prussia			Philadelphia	1842	
33	1817	s 18			
Sarkin?	James	17 Nov 1841			
		--	IN		

Last Name	First Name	Report Date	Departure Port	Departure Date	Witness(es)
Place of Birth	Date of Birth	Natural. Date	Arrival Port	Arrival Date	
Age		Sig. Page No.	Other		
Savely	Patrick	05 Oct 1840	Slaygo	1836	
Co. Slaygo, Ireland			New York	1836	
20	1820	x 114			
Savertz	Barnard	23 Nov 1838	Belfast	1825	
County Tyrone, Ireland			New York	1825	
38	1800	x 8			
Sayles	William	20 Sep 1847			Daniel G. Mumma
		27			
Scaber	John C.	01 Oct 1835	Arrived as a minor. Owes allegiance to Great Britain & Ireland		
		01 Oct 1835			
		IH			
Scallion	Anthony	05 Oct 1840	Liverpool	1839	
County Mays, Ireland			New York	1839	
29	1811	s 114			
Scally	Martin	11 Mar 1873	Liverpool	1969	Henry Waters
Ireland		20 May 1875	New York	1969	John L. Dorn
26	1847	x 9?			
Scanlin	Thomas	31 Mar 1834	Limerick	1830	
County Clare, Ireland			Albany, NY	Jul 1830	
30	1804	x 34			

Surname	Name	Dates	Places	Notes
Schab	Caspar	12 Feb 1844 12 Feb 1844 IN		
Schack	Frederick	04 Apr 1842 16 Sep 1844 IN s 64		
Schaffer Byer, Germany 28	George 1812	17 Aug 1840 17 Aug 1840	Havre de Grace Baltimore	1830 1830	Michael Freis
Schaffer Comminariet of Deuxport, Bav. 3̶2̶ 37	George Frederi 1799	26 Nov 1833 s 30	Havre, France Baltimore	15 May 1832 26 Jun 1832 Born in Comminariet of Deuxport, Bavaria. Has lived in Washington County since his arrival in U.S.
Schaffer Liveyburgh, Sweyburgh, Germany 31	Jacob 1806	03 Apr 1837 s 28	Havre de Grace Baltimore	1832 1832
Schauss Cominparish of Hamburgh, Bav. 43	Philipp 1790	26 Nov 1833 s 29	Havre, France Baltimore	09 May 1833 17 Jun 1833 Born in Cominparish of Hamburgh, Bavaria. Has lived in Washington County since his arrival in U.S.
Scheeler	John	03 Aug 1855		

| Last Name | First Name | Report Date | Departure Port | Departure Date | Witness(es) |
| Place of Birth | Date of Birth | Natural. Date | Arrival Port | Arrival Date | |
Age		Sig. Page No.	Other		
Scheffer	Justus	28 Jun 1872			Dr. H.N.? Anderdnik?
Germany		30 Sep 1876	Report made in Rochester, Monroe Co., New York.		John H. Chen?
		25			
Scheide	Henry	01 Aug 1849	Bremen	?	
Hanover		13 Oct 1864	Baltimore	18 Dec 1846	
36	?	s 2	Report made in Washington, DC.		
Scheiler	John	03 Aug 1855	Havre de Grace	1852	Margaret Eliz. Hellane
Hesse Darmstadt		25 Jul 1859	New York	03 Sep 1852	
21	1834	s 14			
Schemel	Henry	27 Mar 1813	Amsterdam		
Wurtemburgh		04 Apr 1818		30 Nov 1804	
40		s 37			
Schivoebel	Martin	*29 Aug 1857*			
Schlotterback	William	11 Aug 1866	Stuttgard	1854	Lew Heist
Wittemburgh		11 Aug 1866	New York	1854	John Costenberger
26	1840	s 4	Arrived as a minor.		
Schlotterbeck	John Jacob	27 Oct 1856	Havre de Grace	1854	
Mittelstadt, Wirtemburgh			New York	23 Oct 1854	
25	1831	s 20	See Gottlieb Schmidt.		

Schmagrow	T.S.W.	16 Jul 1852	Bremen	1849	
Berlin, Prussia			New York	Sep 1849	
35	1817	s 21			
Schmidt	Frederick	18 Apr 1870	Bremen	1860	
Hesse Cassel			Baltimore	1860	
39	1831	s 26			
Schmidt	Frederick	23 Nov 1844			
		20 Sep 1847			
Schmidt	Gottlieb	27 Oct 1856	Havre de Grace	1854	
Wirtemburgh			New York	23 Oct 1854	
22	1834	s 20	See John Jacob Schlotterbeck.		
Schmidt	William A.	08 May 1852	Antwerp	1851	
Westphalia, Prussia		05 Aug 1857	New York	1851	
23	1829	s 20			
Schmutz/Smoot	Abraham	27 Feb 1804			Jacob Shrode
		49	Owes allegiance to Great Britain & Ireland		
Schneider	Jacob	22 Nov 1830	Amsterdam	25 Apr 1827	
Giren Wettersbach, Baden			Baltimore	31 Aug 1827	
38	1792	s			
Schneider	Jacob	14 Jul 1855	Havre de Grace	1853	Lewis Heist
Pfungstadt, Hesse Darmstadt		23 Nov 1858	New York	14 Jun 1853	
30	1825	s 20			

Last Name	First Name	Report Date	Departure Port	Departure Date	Witness(es)
Place of Birth	Date of Birth	Natural. Date	Arrival Port	Arrival Date	
Age		Sig. Page No.	Other		
Schneider	Louis	28 Jul 1858	Hamburg	1853	
Mecklenburg Schweringen			Portland, ME	Jul 1854	
45	1813	s 2			
Schnider	Lawrence	08 Dec 1836	Havre de Grace	1830	Jacob Sweitzer
Wirtemburgh		23 Nov 1838	Baltimore	1830	
29	1807	s 62	Signature reads Lorenz.		
Schramyer	Henry	22 Nov 1836			Samuel I. Downey
Prussia		03 Dec 1838			
		s 35			
Schranyer	Henry	22 Nov 1836	Bremen	1833	
Cappron, Prussia		*03 Dec 1838*	Baltimore	1833	
24	1812	s 4			
Schreiber	Frederick	09 Mar 1858	Bremen	1854	
Hesse Cassel			Baltimore	12 May 1854	
23	1834	s 12			
Schreiver	Frederick W.	13 Sep 1865	Bremen	1848	Thomas E. Mittag
Frankenburg, Hesse Cassel		13 Sep 1865	Baltimore	01 Jul 1848	David H. Smith
32	1834	s 8	Honorably discharged from military service 28 Jun 1865.		
Schubert	Henry	05 Apr 1858	Bremen	1857	Samuel Zellers
Bavaria		19 Sep 1865	Baltimore	11 Jun 1857	Charles Fridinger
34	1824	s 23			

Name					Sponsor
Schuh	Hugo		04 Apr 1839		John Seitz
			03 Apr 1841		
			43		
Schuker	Hugo		04 Apr 1839	Havre de Grace	
Baden, Germany				Baltimore	
27	1812		s	1831	
			27	1831	
Schultz	John		21 Oct 1808		Christian Fechtig
Germany			07 Nov 1811	< Sep 1804	
			37		
Schuster	Robert		18 Jul 1853		Lewis Heist
Baden			01 Aug 1855		
			11		
25					
Schutz	Louis		03 Jan 1853	Bremen	
Saxe Coburg, Saxe Coburg				Baltimore	
22	1830		s	1849	
			23	Nov 1849	
Schwartz	Heyman		28 Jul 1855	Havre de Grace	
France				New York	
25	1830		s	1852	
			8	10 Aug 1852	
Schwaver.	Andrew		02 Dec 1843		
			--		
		IN		*Schwaverendam	
Schweitzer	Christopher Fr		29 Oct 1872		Lewis Heist
Wirtemburgh			31		Adam Doanberger
				Arrived as a minor.	

| Last Name | First Name | Report Date | Departure Port | Departure Date | Witness(es) |
| Place of Birth | Date of Birth | Natural. Date | Arrival Port | Arrival Date | |
Age		Sig. Page No.	Other		
Schwoeble	Martin	29 Aug 1857			George Lais
Hesse Darmstadt		18 Oct 1867			Lewis Heist
		12			
Seaber	John C.	01 Oct 1835			
		01 Oct 1835			
Seagler	William	03 Jan 1798			
Germany		03 Jan 1798			
		9	Allegiance to Prince of Hesse. Lives in Marsh Hundred [census dist.]		
Seiberlich	John	19 Feb 1844			
		20 Sep 1847			
		IN			
Seis	Anthony	05 Oct 1846	Havre de Grace	1840	
Shipheim, Switzerland			New York	Aug 1840	
40	1806	s 17			
Seis	Anthony	05 Oct 1846	See Leis, Anthony		
Seitzer	John	30 Mar 1836	Rotterdam	1826	
Wirtenburg, Germany			Baltimore	1826	
44	1792	s 8			

Surname	Given				Notes
Sellinger	Richard		20 Jun 1870	Liverpool	1866
City of Limerick, Ireland				New York	1866
26		1844	s	34	
Seltzer	Charles		03 Jan 1798		
Prince of Hess			03 Jan 1798		
			11	Living in Hagerstown.	
Semler	Jacob		04 Apr 1836	Rotterdam	1832
Town Gimerick, Wirtemburgh			03 Sep 1838	Baltimore	1832
44		1792	s	15	
Semler	Lewis		06 Nov 1848		John Fridinger
Wirtemburgh			25	Arrived as a minor.	
Sengenbaugher	George		05 Dec 1836		
			05 Oct 1842		
			IN		
Shack	Frederick		16 Sep 1844		
Bavaria			105		
Shafer	Conrod		03 Jan 1798		
Prince of Hess			03 Jan 1798		
			11	Living in Boonsboro.	
Shafer	Peter		10 Dec 1850	Amsterdam	1847	William Logan
Hesse Darmstadt			06 Sep 1853	New York	01 Jun 1847
28		1822	s	10	

Last Name Place of Birth Age	First Name Date of Birth	Report Date Natural. Date Sig. Page No.	Departure Port Arrival Port Other	Departure Date Arrival Date	Witness(es)
Shaffer Illsfeld, Wurtemburgh, Germany 35	Michael	30 Nov 1821 s 65		06 Nov 1817	
Shanbecker Shamburgh Lippyein, Germany 28	Frederick 1812	30 Mar 1840 03 Oct 1842 s 22	Bremen Baltimore	1831 1831	
Shane Germany	Conrod	13 Jan 1798 13 Jan 1798 44	Whitesmith. Living in Hagerstown.		
Shane	John	Certificate 27 Oct 1842 IN			
Shane	John	-- 27 Aug 1840	Report was made in Franklin Co., Pennsylvania.		Lawrence Schnider
Shank Baden 22	Andrew 1834	28 Jul 1856 30 Jul 1858 s 2	Liverpool New York	1853 01 Jul 1853	Charles Gross Everhart Beitelspacker

Surname	Given	Date / Age	Place	Sponsor / Notes
Shannon	Edward	16 Sep 1844 / 68		Philip Fitzpatrick
				Allegiance to Gr. Brit. & Irel. Alpha Index has "Cert" in Report col.
Sharer	Henry	18 Feb 1845	Bremen	1839
Schwalenbach, Detmold		07 Nov 1848	Baltimore	Jun 1839
40		s 49	Owes allegiance to the Prince of Lisse.	
Sharkey	George	16 Sep 1806		John M. Kegney
Ireland		62		
Shay	Thomas	24 Mar 1835		
		-- IN		
Sheehan	Edward	*30 Mar 1846*		
		30 Mar 1846		
Sheehan	Martin	31 Oct 1867	Cork, Ireland	1851
Ireland		01 Nov 1869	New York	1851
35		s 14	Samuel H. Spessard	William F. Fock
Sheehan	William	04 Oct 1870	Queenstown	1867
Ireland			New York	1867
34		s 25		
Sheld	Matthias	08 Jan 1798		
		08 Jan 1798		
		28	Taylor. Living near Antietam.	

Last Name Place of Birth Age	First Name Date of Birth	Report Date Natural. Date Sig. Page No.	Departure Port Arrival Port Other	Departure Date Arrival Date	Witness(es)
Sheppard Bavaria 53	John 1804	14 Apr 1857 s 28	Bremen Baltimore	1845 1845	
Shervin	Thomas	29 Mar 1813 10 Oct 1828 IN			
Shett	Anthony	16 Dec 1843			
Shick The Paltz in Germany 32	John (Johannes	26 Mar 1816 s 22	Owes allegience to the Emperor of France.	Nov 1804	
Shick Germany	Lawrence	26 Aug 1802 42			
Shifferer	Christian	*05 Oct 1845*			
Shika Prussia	William	03 Jan 1798 03 Jan 1798 12	Living in Hagerstown.		

Name	Origin	Dates	Port	Notes
Shilling	Frederick	31 Mar 1821		
	"near Stutgart, Wertenburgh"	10 Nov 1828		1817
38		s 57		
Shilling	Joachim	21 Nov 1836	Bremen	1834
	Town of Clat, Wirtemburgh	01 Oct 1840	Baltimore	1834 John Seitz
30	1806	s 3		
Shirdon	Patrick	26 Dec 1850	Liverpool	1847
	Ireland		New York	May 1847
35	1815	x 13		
Shober	Lawrence	12 Feb 1844		
	IN	--		
Shouse	Philip	12 Jan 1798		
	Germany	12 Jan 1798		
57		39		Shoemaker. Living in Lower Antietam Hundred.
Shrador	Henry	10 Jan 1798		
	Prussia	10 Jan 1798		
		30		
Shroy	John	*27 Mar 1816*		
		27 Mar 1816		Living in Marsh Hundred.
Shuchman	Adam	18 Nov 1833	Bremen	Jun 1833
	Town of Eppinger, Baden		Baltimore	Aug 1833
35	1798	s 3		Has lived in Maryland since his arrival in the U.S.

Last Name	First Name	Report Date	Departure Port	Departure Date	Witness(es)
Place of Birth	Date of Birth	Natural. Date	Arrival Port	Arrival Date	
Age		Sig. Page No.	Other		
Shultz	Augustus				Cornelius Phawan
Prussia		01 Oct 1850			
		32			
Shultz	John	*02 Nov 1808*	Arrived as a minor.		
		07 Nov 1811			
Shuman	John M	16 Sep 1844			Caspar Baumgart
Bavaria		106	Alpha Index has "Cert" in Report column		
Shuster	Robert	18 Jul 1853	Bremen	1849	
Neuhausen, Baden		*01 Aug 1855*	New York	Apr 1849	
28	1825	s 20			
Shutt	Anthony	16 Dec 1843			
		-- IN			
Sicaphouse	Philip	29 Nov 1836	Bremen	1832	
Ridelburgh, Hesse Darmstadt		*29 Mar 1839*	Baltimore	1832	
34	1802	s 28			
Siler	E.	02 Dec 1868	Bremen	1839	
Bavaria			Baltimore	1839	
62	1806	s 529			

258

Name	Origin	Date/Age	Location	Dates	Notes
Silver Lewis	Amsterdam, Holland	22		28 Mar 1822 s 27	06 Nov 1816
Simler Conrad	Walheim, Germany 1803	30	Havre, France Baltimore	06 Jan 1834 07 Apr 1837 s 46	May 1803 17 Jul 1803 Jacob Bolinger. Has resided in Washington Co. since his arrival.
Simon Rudolph	Canton Bern, Switzerland 1786	42	Switzerland Baltimore	04 Apr 1829 05 Apr 1832 s 47	Apr 1826 Jul 1826 Daniel Boerstler
Simpson John	Great Britain		Presbyterian	25 Feb 1804 38	John Shriver
Simpson John	Ireland			07 Apr 1800 07 Apr 1800 10	
Sippal Conrad	Hesse Cassel		Living near Burketts Mill.	03 Dec 1853 29 Nov 1858 7	Lewis Heist
Sites John	Germany	33		17 Apr 1800 17 Apr 1800 34	Cooper. Living in Jeruselem. [Funkstown] "Menonist" religion.
Sitzler George	Essing, Baden, Germany Apr 1794	37	Amsterdam Philadelphia	15 Nov 1830 *05 Oct 1842* s 25	Jul 1817 Oct 1817 Has lived in Washington Co. for 3 yrs.

Last Name Place of Birth Age	First Name Date of Birth	Report Date Natural. Date Sig. Page No.	Departure Port Arrival Port Other	Departure Date Arrival Date	Witness(es)
Sively	James	23 Sep 1838 -- IN			
Sively	Michael	22 Sep 1838 -- IN			
Sleath	Gabriel	05 Mar 1828 30 Mar 1830			Samuel M. Hill
Sleckennious Hesse Cassel 32	Godfrey 1811	10 Apr 1843 s 22	Hamburg Baltimore	1834 1834	
Small Germany	John	13 Apr 1793 13 Apr 1793 31			
Smith Germany	Caleb	30 Oct 1813 38			
Smith Wirtemburg 29	Charles 1836	20 Sep 1865 20 Sep 1865 s 9	Rotterdam, *G Baltimore	1847 -	John R. King Alexander Leeds

Honorably discharged from military service 20 Jun 1865.
*"Rotterdam, Germany"

Smith Hesse Cassel	Charles A.	19 Feb 1844 02 Oct 1848 20		John Julius
Smith Liehenau, Hanover 36	Christian 1808	31 Oct 1844 30 Mar 1847 s 126	Bremen Baltimore Signature reads Schmidt.	1839 24 Aug 1839	Lewis R. Martin
Smith Germany	Daniel	30 Oct 1813 39		
Smith Libhenan, Hanover 29	Deitrick 1815 x 60	16 Sep 1844 20 Sep 1847	Bremen Baltimore	1839 28 Oct 1839	George Shafer
Smith County Monhow, Ireland	Edward	27 Nov 1818 x 39		ca.May 1816
Smith	Ernst Willilam	05 Feb 1844 05 Feb 1844 IN		
Smith Liebernaught, Hanover 28	Frederick 1816	23 Nov 1844 20 Sep 1847 s 7	Bremen Baltimore	1839 26 Aug 1839	Lewis R. Martin
Smith Hesse Darmstadt	George	05 Oct 1846 33	Arrived as a minor.		Henry Kneaming

Last Name	First Name	Report Date	Departure Port	Departure Date	Witness(es)
Place of Birth	Date of Birth	Natural. Date	Arrival Port	Arrival Date	
Age		Sig. Page No.	Other		
Smith	Godfrey	28 Oct 1813			
Germany		28 Oct 1813			
		30			
Smith	Henry C.	01 Oct 1850			John L. Obamdaffer
Hesse Cassel		29			Joseph G. Protzman
			Arrived as a minor.		
Smith	J.C.	29 Oct 1852	Bremen	1848	
Nassau, Germany	1820	s 7	Baltimore	28 Feb 1849	
32					
Smith	John	16 Sep 1844	Bremen	1833	
Menster, Prussia	1812	s 52	Baltimore	1833	
32					
Smith	John	15 Jan 1798			
Ireland		15 Jan 1798			
		46	Bricklayer and Stone Mason. Living in Hagerstown.		
Smith	John Gottlieb	01 Feb 1847	Hamburg	1841	
Altenburg, Saxe Altenburg	1799	s 22	New York	24 Dec 1841	
48					
Smith	Michael	03 Apr 1835			Anthony Loftus
		30 Nov 1837			
		29			

Smith	Peter	01 Aug 1856	Bremen	1850	
Anspach, Bavaria			New York	20 Jan 1851	
40		1816	s 6		
Smith, Jr.	John	07 Mar 1855	Havre de Grace	1852	
Wirtemburgh			New York	03 Oct 1852	
27		1827	s 1		
Smith, Sen.	John	07 Mar 1855	Havre de Grace	1854	
Wirtemburgh			New York	23 Oct 1854	
55		1800	s 1		
Smoker	George	10 Jan 1799			
Germany		10 Jan 1799	Clergyman. Living in Hagerstown.		
		18			
Smotz	Adam	11 Jan 1798			
Germany		11 Jan 1798	Farmer. Living in Lower Antietam Hundred.		
		35			
Smoude?	George Philip	30 Nov 1840			
		12 Feb 1844			
		IN			
Sneider	Francis	16 Sep 1844	Havre de Grace	1837	
Rottenburg, Wirtemburgh			New York	24 Jul 1837	
35		1809	s 60		
Snell	George	02 Sep 1847	Bremen	1837	Richard Wise
Hesse Darmstadt		02 Oct 1849	Baltimore	Sep 1837	
34		1813	s 11		

Last Name / Place of Birth / Age	First Name / Date of Birth	Report Date / Natural. Date / Sig, Page No.	Departure Port / Arrival Port / Other	Departure Date / Arrival Date	Witness(es)
Snell	Matthias	05 Apr 1798			
Prince of Hesse		05 Apr 1798			
		8			
Sneors	John	17 Sep 1875	Bremen	1846	Frisby Doub
Hanover		25 Sep 1877	Charleston, SC	1846	George W. Miller
38	1826	s 19	Weaver. Living in Hagerstown.		
Snider	John	26 Nov 1832			

Snider	Leonard	11 Apr 1799	IN		
Germany		11 Apr 1799			
		47	Blacksmith. Living in Upper Antietam Hundred.		
Snyder	Henry	11 Jan 1798			
Germany		11 Jan 1798			
		35	Farmer. Living near Hughes' Furnace.		
Snyder	John	27 Sep 1847	Bremen	1839	
Frankfort on the Meine			Baltimore	02 Oct 1839	
30	1817	s 29	Born in Hesse Darmstadt. Signature reads Schnider.		
Snyder/Snider	Philip	24 Jul 1854	Antwerp	1848	Lewis Heist
Funkstadt, Hesse Darmstadt		05 Aug 1856	New York	1848	
27	1827	s 2			

Name		Date	Port	Sponsor
Socks	John Philipp	06 Dec 1839	Bremen	Charles Ullrich
Grosse Hartzuk, Hesse Darmst.		16 Sep 1844	Baltimore	
39	1792	s 40		
Socks	George	16 Sep 1844		Charles Ullrich
Hesse Darmstadt		95		
Socks	George Philip	12 Dec 1851		Jonathan Harbaugh
Hesse Darmstadt		13	Arrived as a minor.	John P. Ulrick
Socks	Henry	05 Oct 1846		Adam Nail
Hesse Darmstadt		34	Arrived as a minor.	
Socks	John	16 Sep 1844		Charles Ullrich
Hesse Darmstadt		94		
Soltan	Peter	16 Sep 1844	Bremen	Joseph Newcomer
Sontra, Hesse Cassel		20 Sep 1847	Baltimore	
48	1796	s 53		
Soner	Adam	06 Nov 1848		Andrew Libald
Hesse Cassel		25	Arrived as a minor.	
Spaker	Henry	06 Dec 1836	Bremen	
Westphalia, Prussia		*27 Nov 1838*	Baltimore	1832
37	1799	s 54	Signature reads Henrich Spieller.	

| Last Name | First Name | Report Date | Departure Port | Departure Date | Witness(es) |
| Place of Birth | Date of Birth | Natural. Date | Arrival Port | Arrival Date | |
Age		Sig. Page No.	Other		
Spang/Spong	Nicholas	13 Apr 1857			Frederick Hagerman
Prussia		24 Mar 1860			
		19	Report was made in Philadelphia.		
Speaker	Henry	26 Sep 1849	Bremen	1832	Samuel H. Rench
Prussia		26 Sep 1849	Baltimore	1832	
27	1822	s 25			
Speaker	Hiram	30 Nov 1844	Bremen	1837	Henry W. Dellinger
Co. Menster, Prussia		28 Sep 1847	Baltimore	1837	
28	1816	s 22	See record of Henry Wolff.		
Speaker/Spaker	Henry	06 Dec 1836			Lawrence Schnider
Prussia		28 Nov 1838			
		21			
Spor/Spohr	Henry	12 Oct 1844	Bremen	1836	Adam Wever
Landwerehagen, Hanover		20 Sep 1847	Baltimore	24 May 1836	
41	1803	x 125			
Sringer	Daniel	01 Oct 1849	London	1846	
Steinburg, Wirtemburgh			New York	Aug 1846	
42	1897	s 29			
Stark	Henry	20 May 1852	Liverpool	1850	
Kilkenny			New York	Oct 1850	
26	1826	s 20			

Starn Prussia 41	David 1815	01 Nov 1856 01 Aug 1859 s 21	Bremen Baltimore	1845 Sep 1845	Henry Enstein
Stederly Switzerland	Joseph	10 Sep 1873 27 Sep 1875 20	Report made in Westmoreland Co., Pennsylvania. Naturalization made in Franklin Co., Pennsylvania. He lived in Hempfield Township, Westmoreland Co.		Christian Himras? Jacob Knigton?
Steele County Longford, Ireland 28	John 1806	26 Mar 1834 x 19	Liverpool New York	1830 Aug 1830	
Steiger Hesse Darmstadt 29	Adam 1826	19 Dec 1855 s 20	Havre de Grace New York	1854 01 Oct 1854	
Steinback Prussia	Frederick	09 Jan 1799 09 Jan 1799 15	Shopkeeper. Living in Sharpsburg.		
Steiner Switzerland	Thomas	01 Nov 1811 42			
Steinger	Samuel	05 Oct 1835 05 Oct 1835 IN			

Last Name	First Name	Report Date	Departure Port	Departure Date	Witness(es)
Place of Birth	Date of Birth	Natural. Date	Arrival Port	Arrival Date	
Age		Sig. Page No.	Other		
Steinle	William G.	01 Aug 1855	Havre de Grace	1853	
Wirtemburgh			New York	26 Sep 1853	
18	1837	s 12			
Stemler	Constantine	30 Oct 1852	Rotterdam	1844	Jacob Butts
Unsechiem, Baden		19 Dec 1854	New York	15 Jun 1844	
45	1807	s 8			
Stemple	Christian	03 Jan 1798			
Wirtemburg		03 Jan 1798			
		16			
Stenagers?	John	Certificate	Living in Hagerstown.		
		12 Feb 1844			
		IN			
Stender	Michael	10 Nov 1847			George W. Martin
Germany		20 Sep 1850			
		24	Alpha Index has "Cert" in Report column		
Stevens	Clans	28 Sep 1849	Bremen	1839	
Basbeck, Hanover			Baltimore	Jul 1839	
48	1801	s 27			
Stewart	John	02 Apr 1839	Belfast	1828	James Johnston
County Armaugh, Ireland		06 Apr 1841	New York	1828	
34	1805	x 19			

Stine	Augustus	30 Sep 1851	Bremen	1837	David Rush
Hesse Darmstadt		30 Sep 1851	Baltimore	1837	
22	1829	s 27	Arrived as a minor.		
Stine	George	11 Jan 1798			
Germany		11 Jan 1798			
		38	Weaver. Living in Lower Antietam Hundred.		
Stine	John	04 Dec 1850	Bremen	1840	Samuel Leach
Darmstadt		04 Dec 1852	Baltimore	1840	
58	1792	s 5			
Stinemets	John W.	05 Apr 1825			John Bowles
		46	Name may be Steinmetz		
Stinemetz	George	22 Nov 1844			Henry Winder
Germany		20 Sep 1847			
		s 9			
Slinger	Samuel	*05 Oct 1835*			
		05 Oct 1835			
Stiver	Frederick	28 Nov 1838	Havre de Grace	1829	Peter Crouse
Ealsfelt, Wirtemburgh		*26 Sep 1842*	Baltimore	1829	
40	1802	s 22			
Stivers	Wenich?	28 Nov 1838			
		26 Sep 1842			
		IN			

Last Name	First Name	Report Date	Departure Port	Departure Date	Witness(es)
Place of Birth	Date of Birth	Natural. Date	Arrival Port	Arrival Date	
Age		Sig. Page No.	Other		
Stock	Frederick	21 Aug 1850			Daniel South
Wirtemburgh		20			Henry Whisner
			Arrived as a minor.		
Stock	J. C.	04 Dec 1855	Bremen	1839	Marcus Banner
Wirtemburgh	1834	04 Dec 1855	Baltimore	1839	
21		s 12	Arrived as a minor.		
Stoener	Jacob	04 Oct 1850	Bremen	1836	
Wirtemburgh	1802		Baltimore	1836	
48		s 34			
Stoll	George	28 Oct 1813			
Balderstive?, Germany		26 Mar 1819		1802	
46		x 31			
Stoll	John	17 Apr 1852	Havre de Grace	1849	
Baden	1829		New York	1849	
23		s 20			
Stone	Henry	06 Sep 1865	Liverpool	1861	William Logan
London, England	1836	06 Sep 1865	New York	25 Sep 1861	James McLaughlin
30		s 6			
Stone	Levi	05 Sep 1866	Hamburg	1856	
Poland (Czar of Russia)	1835		New York	1857	
31		s 16			

Surname	Given	Date 1	Date 2	Place 1	Place 2	Notes
Stone	Levi	05 Sep 1868	05 Sep 1868	Hamburg	Baltimore	
Poland		-	283			Born in Poland, but a native of Russia and a citizen of Poland.
31	1835					
Straub	Michael	03 Dec 1839		Bremen	Baltimore	
Slimpfhoof, Germany						
49	1790	s	31			Owes allegiance to Prince Byren of Germany.
Streker	John Michael	15 Nov 1819		Amsterdam		
Wirtemburgh, Germany						
36		s	15			28 Jul 1819
Strobal	John	14 Oct 1844	03 Oct 1848	Bremen	Baltimore	Frederick Shack
Hoff, Bavaria						
32	1812	s	126			1840 Aug 1840
Strock	Christian	15 Mar 1849	28 Jul 1853	Havre de Grace	New York	
Baknoung, Wirtemburg						
30	1819	s	21			1848 Apr 1848
Strohl	Philip	09 Apr 1799	09 Apr 1799			Hemp hacker. Ropemaker. Living near Antietam in Funkstown Hundred.
Allsace, Province of France						
			42			
Strouse	Henry	13 Jan 1798	13 Jan 1798			Stonecutter. Living in Hagerstown.
Germany						
			45			
Stull	Charles	21 Nov 1836	30 Nov 1840	Amsterdam	Philadelphia	
Contil Co. of Elvis, Germany						
30	1806	s	2			1819 1819

Last Name Place of Birth Age	First Name Date of Birth	Report Date Natural. Date Sig. Page No.	Departure Port Arrival Port Other	Departure Date Arrival Date	Witness(es)
Stump County Bollinger, Wirtemburgh 39	Anthony	24 Nov 1821 20 Nov 1827 s 68		02 Sep 1817	Gottleib Basdar
Stump	Conrod	01 Dec 1843 --	IN		
Sullivan County Limerick, Ireland 35	Jeremiah Apr 1793	17 Nov 1828 s 20	Baltimore	May 1818 Sep 1818	
Sullivan County Cork, Ireland 26	Philip	22 Nov 1821 s 39		Jul 1819	
Summer Wirtemburgh 35	John 1821	03 Nov 1856 25 Jul 1859 s 21	Havre de Grace New York	1853 05 Apr 1853	George Summers
Summers Wirtemburgh	George	23 Nov 1841 16 Sep 1844 88			Elijah Swope
Sutherland Co. Lutherland, Scotland 44	Hugh McKay 1803	09 Oct 1847 s 39	London New York	1825 1837	

Swarbrick England 41	James A. 1826	08 Oct 1867 s 8	Liverpool New York	Rudolph Herr 1852 1852
Swarbrick England	James A.	01 Aug 1870 7		George Mish Rudoph Herr
Swartz	Heyman	*28 Jul 1855*	Arrived as a minor.	
Swartz	Jacob	03 Apr 1833 03 Oct 1836	IN	
Swartz Darmstadt, Germany 33	John George 1804	31 Mar 1837 30 Sep 1839 s 20	Bremen Baltimore	Zacharius McCemas 1832 1832
Swartz France	Peter	17 Aug 1803 22		Jacob Zellar
Swartzwelder Baden, Germany 25	John G.	15 Nov 1819 -- Mar 1828 s 16	Amsterdam	29 Aug 1817
Sweeney	Charles	07 Aug 1823 25 Mar 1830	Report made in Lebanon Co., PA	John Duffey

Last Name First Name Place of Birth Date of Birth Age	Report Date Natural. Date Sig. Page No.	Departure Port Arrival Port Other	Departure Date Arrival Date	Witness(es)
Sweeney Francis Co. Farmannah, Ireland 28 1814	23 May 1843 x 27	Liverpool Baltimore	1840 1840	
Sweeney Garrett County Kilkenny, Ireland 29 1810	25 Mar 1840 26 Mar 1840 x 10	Dublin New York Arrived as a minor.	1828 1828	Joseph Doley?
Sweitzer Frederick Wirtemburgh	15 Oct 1870 26			George G. Middlekauff George Sias
Sweitzer Henry	05 Oct 1829 05 Oct 1829	Military Service - discharged 27 Mar 1868.		
Sweitzer Jacob Wirtemburgh 31 1806	01 Dec 1837 10 Aug 1840 s 30	Havre de Grace Baltimore	1830 1830	Lawrence Snider
Swinger Andrew Wirtemburgh 34 1803	31 Mar 1837 29 Mar 1839 s 19	Holland Baltimore	1831 1831	John Howard

Swinger Wirtemburgh	Daniel	01 Oct 1849 02 Feb 1852 18		Andrew Swinger
Switzen Bavaria 45	Henry ca 1784	05 Oct 1829 05 Oct 1829 x 54	Baltimore ca. 1793 Left Bavaria at the age of 9 yrs.	Christian Newcomer
Swope Frankenheim, Bavaria 36	Caspar 1808	16 Sep 1844 05 Oct 1846 s 53	Bremen 1839 Baltimore 1839	Nicholas Anhalt
Swope Germany	Christopher	03 Jan 1798 03 Jan 1798 17	Living in Hagerstown.	
Tackey Menden, Prussia 24	Christian 1820	24 Sep 1844 s 109	Bremen 1830 Baltimore Jun 1840	
Tagert County Londonderry, Ireland 40	Hugh 1791	30 Nov 1831 03 Oct 1836 s 47	Londonderry Baltimore	Charles Sweeny
Taggert Ireland 24	Thomas 1816	01 Oct 1840 01 Oct 1840 s 89	Londonderry Baltimore	Hugh Tagert
Tais Ireland	William	01 Nov 1815 s 16	Original report made in Jefferson County, Virginia (WV) in Aug. 1813	

Last Name Place of Birth Age	First Name Date of Birth	Report Date Natural. Date Sig. Page No.	Departure Port Arrival Port Other	Departure Date Arrival Date	Witness(es)
Tallman Majenfelt?, Wirtemburg 43	Augustus	21 Nov 1827 s	Amsterdam Baltimore	06 Aug 1819	
Taning/Tarring England 45	William 1815	20 Feb 1860 29 Oct 1866 - 22	Liverpool New York	1851 1851	Charles H. Harris George G. Middlekauff
Taunreuther Bavaria 22	Frederick 1826	20 Feb 1849 s 20	Bremen New York	1847 26 Apr 1847	
Ternsner	Lewis	*26 Sep 1849*			
Terry Wuff, Ireland 35	Robert 1809	16 Sep 1844 05 Oct 1846 s 62	Londonderry New York	1829 28 Jul 1829	John Aigen
Thomas England	Edward August	08 Jan 1798 08 Jan 1798 27	Surveyor. Living near Booth's Mill.		
Thomas Prussia	John Christian	06 Apr 1842 16 Sep 1844 86			Henry Rice

Thomas	William	08 Nov 1828		
		08 Nov 1828		
		IN		
Thompson	Adair C.	30 Sep 1829	Belfast	1811	William M. Marshall
City of Belfast, Ireland		30 Sep 1829	New York	1811	
21	Jul 1808	s			
Thompson	John	09 Jan 1799			
Ireland		09 Jan 1799			
		16			
Thompson	Merritt	16 Nov 1840	Weaver. Living near Antietam (not the Hundred).		
		05 Feb 1844			
		IN			
Thompson	Victor	05 Oct 1835			
		05 Oct 1835			
		IN			
Thompson	William C.	19 Sep 1827		1811	Vachel? W. Randall
City of Belfast, Ireland		05 Apr?1827			
26	1800	s	Migrated to York with parents and lived there for 4 yrs. Then to Frederick Town for 4 yrs. Then to Washington, DC for 3 yrs. Then to Hagerstown.		
Tierney	John	06 Apr 1829	Dublin	Feb 1818	
County Wichley?, Ireland			South Amboy	Jul 1818	
40	1789	s			

Last Name Place of Birth Age	First Name Date of Birth	Report Date Natural. Date Sig. Page No.	Departure Port Arrival Port Other	Departure Date Arrival Date	Witness(es)
Tietias/Tietiar Hanover	Christian	24 Sep 1806 64			William Kais
Timman	John	05 Dec 1820 -- Mar 1826 IN			
Tinkel Seckinger, Germany 25	John 1812	05 Jul 1837 05 Jul 1837 s 52	Havre de Grace New York Signature reads Fizl.	1830 1830	
Tip/Tife Hesse Castle	Henry	05 Apr 1798	Farmer.		
Toland County Donagal, Ireland circa 1807	John	29 Nov 1827 29 Nov 1827	Was 11 yrs. old upon arrival in U.S.	1818	William Fitzhugh, Jr.
Toll	Jacob	30 Nov 1821 05 Nov 1828 IN			
Toner County Donegal, Ireland 34	Daniel 1800	21 Nov 1834 x 25	Londonderry New York	1833 May 1833	

Name		Dates	Origin/Destination		Sponsor
Trainor	Owen	23 May 1843	Liverpool	1840	
Co. Monaghan, Ireland			Baltimore	1840	
22	1821	s 27			
Treehause	John Henry	26 Sep 1844			Samuel J. Downey
Prussia		118			
Treiber	Michael	10 Aug 1840	Havre de Grace		George Gossman
Hanbershous, Wirtemburgh		10 Aug 1840	Baltimore	13 Aug 1830	
21	27 Jul 1818	s 60			
Trieber	Gotleib	05 Oct 1842			
		05 Oct 1842			
		IN	Report column reads "Certificate"		
Trumpart?	John	26 Nov 1840			
		12 Feb 1844			
		IN			
Turner	George	01 Apr 1833			
		03 Oct 1836			
		IN			
Turner	William	09 Jan 1834	Liverpool	1831	
Kediminster, England			New York	Jul 1831	
29	1804	s 59			
Twichouse	John Henry	26 Sep 1842			
		26 Sep 1844			
		IN			

| Last Name | First Name | Report Date | Departure Port | Departure Date | Witness(es) |
| Place of Birth | Date of Birth | Natural. Date | Arrival Port | Arrival Date | |
Age		Sig. Page No.	Other		
Tyrell	Thomas	30 Dec 1818			
County Dublin, Ireland				08 Dec 1816	
25		s 53	$1 fee paid.		
Ullrich	Charles	29 Nov 1839	Bremen	1834	
Hesse Darmstadt		03 Oct 1842	Baltimore	1834	
25	1814	s 27			
Ulrich	John C. [Cart?]	07 Jan 1836	Bremen	1834	Andrew Swinger
Kingdom of Hesse, Germany		25 Sep 1840	Baltimore	1834	
50	1785	s 42			
Ulrich	John Peter	*20 Nov 1822*			
Unger	Frederick	01 Apr 1828			
		01 Apr 1828			
		IN			
Unger	Fritz Ernest	27 Mar 1811			
Westphalia		27 Mar 1811		1802	
32		s 23			
Unger	John F.*	24 Nov 1825			
		--			
		IN	*John Frederick		

280

Surname	Given	Origin	Date		Port	Arrival	Sponsor/Notes
Urber	Jacob	Germany	05 Jan 1798				
			05 Jan 1798	21			Labourer. Living in Hagerstown.
Urich	John Peter	County Rinefelt, Switzerland	20 Nov 1822			Oct 1817	
			s	24			
Varner	John	Wirtemburgh, Germany	22 Nov 1836		Bremen	1833	Henry Heiges
			30 Sep 1839		Baltimore	1833	
		37 1799	s	4			
Vestris	Herman	Prussia	03 Dec 1847				John D. Reamer
			11 Dec 1854	8			
Vetch	John		Certificate				Report was made in Chester Co., PA.
			12 Feb 1844				
			IN				
Voekler	Frederick		24 Sep 1838				
			24 Sep 1838				
			IN				
Vogel	J. Charles	Wodenburg, Germany	09 Jan 1855		Havre de Grace	1852	
					New York	22 Sep 1852	
		43 1812	s	16			
Votteler	Jacob	Beatlingen, Wirtemburgh	01 Oct 1840		Bremen	1839	
			16 Sep 1844		Baltimore	1839	
		25 1815	s	91			

Last Name Place of Birth Age	First Name Date of Birth	Report Date Natural. Date Sig. Page No.	Departure Port Arrival Port Other	Departure Date Arrival Date	Witness(es)
Vulwiler Baden, Germany 33	Christopher 1809	28 Nov 1842 29 Sep 1845 s 16	Bremen Baltimore	1840 1840	
Wable Bavaria 25	John 1829	09 Dec 1853 09 Dec 1853 x 7	Bremen Baltimore	1838 1838	
Waffensmith Germany 29	John 1847	03 Oct 1876 s 30	Frankfurt Newark, NJ	1870 1870	
Waggoner Welleswichn?, Prussia 24	John Christian	23 Nov 1826 04 Apr 1829 s		22 Jul 1822	David Cushwa
Waggoner France	John	02 Jan 1798 02 Jan 1798 8	Living in Washington County.		
Wagner Michel Stadt, Hesse Darmstadt 30	Leonhard 1845	05 Oct 1875 05 Oct 1877 s 23	Bremen New York	1871 1871	William Wagner Justus Heimel
Wagner Hesse Darmstadt 25	William 1843	15 Mar 1869 s 24	Havre de Grace New York	1857 1857	

Name	Origin	Year	Date	Age	Port	Year	Witnesses/Notes
Wagoner Christian	County Baitenn, Germany	1816	24 Jul 1837 03 Oct 1838	s 55	Bremen Baltimore	1833 1833	Owes allegiance to Prince Leopold.
21							
Wall Michael	Queens Co., Ireland	1808	17 Aug 1840	s 61	Liverpool New York	1827 1827	
32							
Wallace James			05 Oct 1835 05 Oct 1835 IN				
Walter/Walder George	Bavaria	1811	02 Oct 1849 03 Feb 1852	s 30	Bremen Baltimore	1839 1839	Robert Curtis Name may be Walker
38							
Waltmyer Henry			05 Nov 1828 05 Nov 1828 IN				
Ward James	Great Britian & Ireland		01 Oct 1850	33			Arrived as a minor. Alozin A. Fox
Ward James W.	Town Denegal, Ireland	1804	27 Aug 1840 27 Aug 1840	x 72	Baltimore	1816 1816	John J. Keedy Caleb Beggs
36							
Ward Michael	County Galway, Ireland	1810	06 Dec 1837	s 44	Liverpool New York	1833 1833	
27							

Last Name Place of Birth Age	First Name Date of Birth	Report Date Natural. Date Sig. Page No.	Departure Port Arrival Port Other	Departure Date Arrival Date	Witness(es)
Warner	Christian	30 Mar 1835 -- IN			
Warner Hesse Cassel 21	Robert 1829	23 Aug 1851 23 Aug 1851 s 22	Bremen Baltimore	1837 1837	William Cushwa
Warrenfeltz Germany	John	03 Oct 1876 03 Oct 1878 22	Arrived as a minor.		Lewis Futtem Hez. H. Long
Wartman Switzerland, Emperor of Germ	Lawrence	24 Sep 1806 64			Jacob D. Dietrick
Waxman Hanover, Germany 44	August 1823	04 Nov 1867 24 Oct 1871 s 37	Hanover Baltimore	1845 -	Otho J. Smith Dr. J.F Smith
Waxmout Hanover 44	August 1823	02 Nov 1867 x 18	Hanover Baltimore	1845 1845	
Weaver	Adam	15 Nov 1841 12 Dec 1844 IN			

Weaver	Ambrose		18 Nov 1833	Havre, France	Mar 1832
Kensing, Baden			24 Sep 1838	New York	Apr 1832
29	1804		s 4		
Weaver	Ferdinand		08 Apr 1839		John C. Dorsey
Baden			14 May 1841		
			56	Report made in Franklin Co., Pennsylvania.	
Weaver	William		*13 Sep 1839*		
			13 Sep 1839		
Webb	John David		03 Apr 1828		
			-- Mar 1828		
			IN		
Weigel	John		19 Mar 1858	Bremen	1850
Bavaria				Baltimore	19 Sep 1850
31	1827		s 16		
Weigel	John		11 Aug 1868		
Germany			278		
Weightman	Andrew		25 Mar 1834	*Greenoch	1817	William Rundleis
Northumberland County, England			01 Apr 1836	Boston	Aug 1817
45	1789		s 14	*Greenoch, Scotland	
Weihr	Lewis		06 Nov 1877	Bremen	1869
Berlin, Prussia				Baltimore	1869
31	1846		s 21		

Last Name Place of Birth Age	First Name Date of Birth	Report Date Natural. Date Sig. Page No.	Departure Port Arrival Port Other	Departure Date Arrival Date	Witness(es)
Weil Bavaria 27	Jacob 1842	11 Aug 1869 06 Jun 1879 s 16	Hamburg New York Witness for Report was Mark H. Fellheimer. Ref. to Rough Bundle	1865 1865	Daniel Huyett George W. Harne
Weiles Prussia 34	Jacob 1836	04 Oct 1870 s 24	Bremen New York	1864 1864	
Weische Saxony, Germany 27	Ernst William 1843	22 Oct 1870 29 Oct 1872 s 30	Hamburg New York Last name is spelled Weische or Weinsher.	1866 1866	George E. Gapman Simon S. Dinnhofer
Weise Leissic, Saxony, Germany 32	Theodore 1816	15 Mar 1849 s 21	Bremen Baltimore	1848 03 Nov 1848	
Weissman Hanover in the Kingdom of Hanover 31	William 1835	12 Sep 1865 12 Sep 1865 s 7	Baltimore Honorably discharged from military service 01 Sep 1865.	1859 01 Dec 1859	Samuel Knode, Lewis B. Nyman, Henry C. Knode
Weistenhouse	Herman	24 Sep 1838 05 Oct 1840 107	Name may be Wiesterhouse		Rudolph Herr
Welch/Welsh	Michael	22 Nov 1850 36	Arrived as a minor. Owes allegiance to Great Britain & Ireland		William Grove

Surname	Given name	Dates	Origin/Port	Sponsor/Notes
Welch	Richard	01 Feb 1829		Timothy Kelley
		19 Nov 1834		
		9	Report made in Northumberland County, PA.	
Wellar	Adam	02 Jan 1798		
Germany		02 Jan 1798		
		8	Living in Washington County	
Wellhause	George	31 Mar 1817	*Emden	
Hanover, Austria		18 Nov 1817		
26		s 46	*Emden, Holland 1806	
Wellinger	Christian	23 Oct 1871	Bremen	George P. Socks
Wirtemburgh		23 Oct 1871	Baltimore	George F.P. Lampas
2b 1850		s 28	Arrived as a minor.	
Wellinger	Jacob	11 Aug 1866	Bremen	Lewis Heist
Wittemburgh		11 Aug 1866	Baltimore	John Costenberger
25 1841		s 7	Arrived as a minor.	
Welsh	Henry	07 Sep 1849	Liverpool	Reuben Waters
Co. Kildare, Ireland		26 Sep 1851	New York	24 Apr 1842
28 1821		x 21		
Welsh	Richard	18 Feb 1805		George Nigh
Ireland		19		
Wench?	James W.	27 Aug 1840		
		27 Oct 1842		
		IN		

Last Name / Place of Birth / Age	First Name / Date of Birth	Report Date / Natural. Date / Sig. Page No.	Departure Port / Arrival Port / Other	Departure Date / Arrival Date	Witness(es)
Werner / Germany /	John Jacob	11 Jan 1798 / 11 Jan 1798 / 35			
Wever/Weaver / Bavaria /	Michael	25 Jul 1846 / 15 Sep 1848 / 18	Bookbinder. Living in Hagerstown.		Michael Freise
Wevil / Dormens, Baden, Germany / 21	William / 1818	30 Sep 1839 / 30 Sep 1839 / ? 38	Havre de Grace / Baltimore	1833 / 1833	Jacob Butz
Whalen / Co. Wecksford / 27	John / 1825	14 Sep 1852 / x 4	Liverpool / New York	1850 / Dec 1850	
Whitney / /	Patrick	03 May 1839 / 27 Sep 1841 / 60			Michael Quinn
Wickless / Bavaria /	John	04 Feb 1845 / 01 Oct 1850 / 30	Report was made in Frederick Co., Maryland.		John L. Obamdaffer
Wiesner / Wertsburg, Bavaria / 35	Valentine / 1811	09 Apr 1846 / s 13	Bremen / Baltimore	1839 / 10 Oct 1839	

Name	Origin		Date	Place	Date	Witness/Notes
Wilbrink 48	Bernard Oldenburg, Germany 1799		21 Sep 1847 s 28	Bremen Baltimore	1845 Oct 1845	
Wild	Christopher		17 Aug 1840 05 Oct 1842 IN			
Wilhelm 26	Jacob Baden, German 1808		10 Apr 1834 s 76	Havre de Grace Portland, ME	1830 1830	
Will	Henry		15 Nov 1841 20 Nov 1843 IN			
Williams 29	John Great Britain		16 Sep 1806 63			Nathaniel Rochester
Williams	William Wales, England		02 Apr 1814 41			
Williams	William Canada		31 Oct 1865 12			John W. Marnous J.W. Finnegan Honorably discharged from military service 08 Aug 1865.
Williard	Joseph France		26 Jul 1857 29 Jul 1859 4			Abraham H. Mumma Alpha Index has "Cert" in Report column

Last Name / Place of Birth / Age	First Name / Date of Birth	Report Date / Natural. Date / Sig. Page No.	Departure Port / Arrival Port / Other	Departure Date / Arrival Date	Witness(es)
Wilson / Ireland	James	04 Jan 1798 / 04 Jan 1798 / 18			
Winebrenner / Germany	Christian	08 Jan 1798 / 08 Jan 1798 / 28	Carpenter. Living in Boonsboro		
Winegardner / Shoepenburg, Bavaria / 28	Philip / 1819	11 Oct 1847 / s 39	Living in Hagerstown. Bremen / Baltimore	1844 / 1844	
Winsh / Wirtemburgh / 23	Jacob / 1832	23 Mar 1855 / s 15	Havre de Grace / New York	1852 / 1852	
Winter / Bervem, Germany / 33	Christian / 1807	10 Aug 1840 / 10 Aug 1840 / s 57	Amsterdam / Baltimore	1821 / 1821	James Maxwell
Winter	Henry	02 Dec 1843 / 02 Dec 1843 / IN	Arrived as a minor.		
Wisner	John Ulrick	22 Nov 1837 / 04 Dec 1839			

Surname	Given Name	Birth/Other Dates	Origin/Port	Notes
Witman	Frederick	24 Sep 1838		
		12 Feb 1844		
		IN		Name may be Hitman
Witt	Christopher	17 Aug 1840	Havre de Grace 1833	
Wirtemburgh			Baltimore 1833	
28	1812	s 65		
Witzenbachel	William	09 Mar 1855	London 1853	George Gassman
Michelstadt, Hesse Darmstadt		09 Mar 1859	New York Feb 1854	
29	1826	s 3		
Woesner	John Ulrich	22 Nov 1837	Bremen 1833	
Wirtemburgh, Germany			Baltimore 1833	
45	1792	s 9		Name may be Wisner
Wolff/Wolf	Henry	30 Nov 1844	Bremen 1837	Henry W. Dellinger
Co. Menster, Prussia		28 Sep 1847	Baltimore 1837	
28	1816	s 21	See record of Hiram Speaker.	
Wolfinger	Michael	11 Apr 1798		
Germany			Blacksmith. Living in Rocks Forge.	
Woods	John	27 Nov 1830		John Sayles
		25 Mar 1834		
		5	Report was made in Huntingdon County, PA.	
Woreter?	Frederick	25 Oct 1809	Alsace	
Alsace, France		*29 Mar 1815*		
		s 35		Name may be Worster

Last Name Place of Birth Age	First Name Date of Birth	Report Date Natural. Date Sig. Page No.	Departure Port Arrival Port Other	Departure Date Arrival Date	Witness(es)
Work	Robert	*30 Mar 1819*			
Wrede	John Charles	*10 Nov 1857*			
Wright England 28	John 1839	10 Sep 1867 10 Sep 1867 s 3	London New York Arrived as a minor.	1853 1853	Samuel Boger Charles Dellinger
Yelagin	John	*15 Aug 1857*			
Yetter Wirtemburgh 23	Calvin 1857	02 Mar 1874 02 Mar 1874 s 5	Bremen Baltimore Arrived as a minor.	1866 1866	Lewis Heist Christian Yetter
Yetter Sultz, Wirtemburgh 28	Christian 1825	05 Apr 1853 05 Aug 1856 s 19	Havre de Grace Philadelphia	1850 Oct 1850	David Flong Harvey Small
Young Germany	Adam	13 Jan 1798 13 Jan 1798 45	Farmer. Living in Funkstown.		

Young Andrew	26 Mar 1822	22 Jul 1819
County of Coldaburgh, Bavaria	s 8	
Young John	26 Nov 1840	
	12 Feb 1844?	
	IN	
Young John	Certificate	
	28 Nov 1843	
	IN	
Young Patrick C.	29 Mar 1810	<14 Apr 1802
Ireland	29 Mar 1810	
	21	
Young Peter A.	28 Oct 1809	Kernersloaden?
Kerarsloaden, Germany		1804
25	2 36	Owes allegiance to Napoleon, Emperor of France
Zeigler John Gottleib	24 Aug 1844	Bremen 1834
Sultz, Wirtemburgh	*28 Sep 1847*	Baltimore 1834
50 1794	s 44	
Zeise George	*12 Aug 1844*	
	20 Sep 1847	
Zelch Henry	25 Sep 1850	Henry Spohr
Hesse Cassel	25	Frederick May

Last Name Place of Birth Age	First Name Date of Birth	Report Date Natural. Date Sig. Page No.	Departure Port Arrival Port Other	Departure Date Arrival Date	Witness(es)
Zenncks Underderkheim, Wirtemburgh 34	Jacob 1820	15 May 1854 s 10	Havre de Grace New York Name may be Zernicks	1853 Apr 1853	
Zifner Eagendausen, Bavaria 35	John Adam 1810	24 Nov 1845 s 5	Bremen New York	1839 30 Nov 1839	
Zimmer City of Zwibraker, Bavaria 35	John	05 Dec 1820 28 Mar 1826 s 67		26 Aug 1820	Christian Boent
Zimmerman Woheigham, Baden 32	Andrew 1812	16 Sep 1844 *20 Sep 1847* s 63	Havre de Grace New York	1841 14 Jun 1841	
Zimmerman Province of Durrestadt, Germ. 37	John 1797	08 Apr 1836 10 Apr 1838 s 25	Bremin Baltimore Owes allegiance to Prince Ludwig.	1831 1831	
Zinckand Heroltz 38	Ulrich 1809	30 Nov 1844 *20 Sep 1847* s 21	Bremen Baltimore	1836 1836	
Zinckund	Andrew	*01 Oct 1849*	Owes allegiance to the Grand Duke of Hessian.		

Zinkund	Lorenz	14 Sep 1855	Bremen	1848
Hesse Cassel	1823	s 19	Baltimore	31 May 1848
32				
Zoll	Jacob	30 Nov 1821		26 Jul 1819
Wirtemburgh, Germany				
45		x 57		
Zopp	Andrew	15 Apr 1844		Anthony Campbell
Byren		05 Oct 1846		
		28		
Zuber/ Zaber	John	28 Apr 1856	Bremen	1855
Bavaria	1832	x 16	Baltimore	16 Oct 1855
23			Name could be Zaber.	

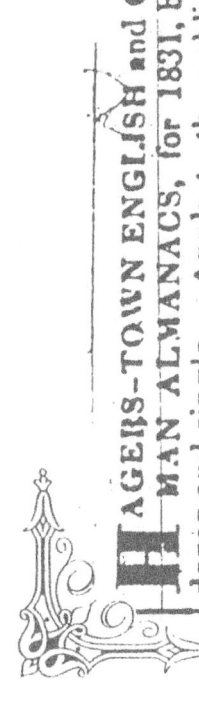

HAGERS-TOWN ENGLISH and GER-
MAN ALMANACS, for 1831, by the
dozen and single.—Apply to the publisher,
J. GRUBER.
Hagers-town, January 20   13-3w

Index

Immigrants not indexed - index is for Witness Names only. Index entries refer to name of immigrant; there may be several listings for a person.

Aherin, James....Long, Daniel
....Long, Michael
Aigen, John....Terry, Robert
Allegany County, MD....Ragers, Arthur
Allen, John....Duffy, John
Anderdnik, Dr HN....Scheffer, Justus
Anhalt, Nicholas....Swope, Caspar
Armstrong, William, Cosens, Henry
Ashberry, John....Lough, James
Ashten, William....Riley, John
Atwell, James....Morris, David
Atwell, John....Atwell, James
Baechtell, John....Lau, Christian
Baker Sr, George....Baker Jr, George
Baltimore City....Bucher, Adam
....Molare, Joseph
Baltz, John, Earhart, John
Banner, Marcus....Stock, JC
Banner, Marke....Banner, Christopher
Bantz, George....Rupp, George
Barber, Allen....Laughlin, Allen
Barnes, Owen....Conrad, John
Barry, John....Herlehy, David
Barth, Jacob....Finkbinder, Frederick
....Pea, John
Basdar, Gottleib....Stump, Anthony
Baumgart, Caspar....Shuman, John
Beall, George....Cramer, Ambrose
Bean, Benjamin....Kinnier, Robert
Beard, George....McSherry, Michael
Beeler, John....Lynch, John
Beggs, Caleb....Ward, James
Beitelspacher, Everhart....Griese, Conrad
....Reigler, Andrew
Beitelspacker, Everhart....Shank, Andrew
Beitingheimer, Henry....Linckand, Ulrich
....Renner, Valentine
Bell, Peter....Powlus, Henry
Bell, William....Davis, Richard
....Dundy, James
Beltzhoover, George....Bradley, William
Bennett, Robert.... Hinkle, John
Benshoof, David....Heihnlein, John
Berry, M.A.....Crowther, D.W.

Bickley, Christian....Christen, Zachariah
....Punt, George
Biershing, William....Gareis, George
Binkley, George....Garrett, Thomas
Blackwell, Arthur....Murray, Richard
Bodmann, William....Bodmann, Philip
Boent, Christian....Zimmer, John
Boentle, Christan....Keifer, John
Boerstler, Daniel....Simon, Rudolph
Boerstler, Dr.... Christian....Kiefer, John
Boestler, Christian....Bowser, Henry
Boger, Samuel....Wright, John
Bolinger, Jacob....Simler, Conrad
Bovey, Michael....McQuade, Charles
Bowers, William....Leasey, Michael
Bowles, John....Stinemets, John
Bowman, George....Roessner, Jacob
Breisch, John....Cummons, Caspar
....Domel, Matthias
Brey, Wolfgang....Krokberger, Christian
Briesch, John....Buser, Michael
Brining, Christian....Fleder, Andrew
Brining, John....Quinn, Patrick
Browugart, Caspar....Mennel, Christian
Brugh, P A....Breneman, Christian
Brumbaugh, David....Lohretz, Jacob
Buckwalter, Jacob....Klink, Michael
Butts, Jacob....Freise, Peter
....Stemler, Constantine
Butz, Jacob....Luther, John
....Wevil, William
Cahoun, Joel....Dermody, William
California....Murphy, Patrick
Callen, James....Loftus, Anthony
Caloun, Joel....Moore, William
Campbell, Anthony....Zopp, Andrew
Campbell, Michael....Little, Patrick
Castebbader, John...Leinchkund, Andrew
Castenbader, Baltis....Domel, Matthias
Castenbader, John....Ernst, John
Chen, John....Scheffer, Justus
Christ, Adam....Christ, John
Christ, David....Sandys, Robert
Civil War....Berger, John
....Burger, Conrad

Civil War, *cont.*
....Cameron, John
....Clement, John
....Collins, Oscar
....Dennhoefer, Simon
....Feilman, Frederick
....Kemman, Charles
....Leibold, Frederick
....Martin, James
....Miller, Christian
....Schreiver, Frederick
....Smith, Charles
....Sweitzer, Frederick
....Weissman, William
....Williams, William
Cline, Jacob....Plumeigarr, Michael
Coffee, Daniel....Coneaughton, Michael
Cohen, Timothy....Crowley, John
Coin, Timothy....McNamee, Patrick
....Noland, Michael
Colloton, Francis....Leonard, James
Colvin, Andrew....Ryan, William
Cook, John....Feilman, Frederick
....Kapp, Michael
Cook, RE....Martin, James
Copich, Augustus....Conradt, George
Costenbeder, John....Rausenberger, John
....Rauth, Peter
Costenberger, JB....Baner, Michael
Costenberger, John....Berger, John
....Clement, John; ....Doarnberger, Adam; ....Doarnberger, Henary
....Schlotterback, William
Costenberger, John....Wellinger, Jacob
Cox, James....Johnston, James
Craig, Jacob....Kemman, Charles
Creager, Sreury....Lensbower, Peter
Crist, David....Brey, John
Cromwell, William....Manning, John
Crouse, Peter....Stiver, Frederick
Curtis, Robert....Jones, Thomas
....Walter, George
Cushwa, David....Waggoner, John
Cushwa, William....Warner, Robert
Dashiell, Julius....Halm, Dr.... Reinhold
Decker, Paul....Britch, Jacob
Deitrick, Elizabeth....Deitrick, Lewis
Dellinger, Charles....Wright, John
Dellinger, Henry....Miller,Frederick
....Speaker, Hiram....Wolff, Henry

Dellinger, Jacob....Rice, Charles
Delzell, John....Moore, William
Dietrick, Jacob....Wartman, Lawrence
Dillehunt, John....McCarthy, John
Dillman, Henry....Bowser, Henry
Dillman, Henry....Garrett, James
Dillon, Michael....Can, Patrick
....Nolan, John
Dinnhofer, Simon....Weische, Ernst
District of Columbia....Ford, Franklin
....McNamara, James
....O'Brien, William
....Puerschel, Adolph
....Scheide, Henry
Doanberger, Adam....Lowe, George
....Schweitzer, Christopher
Dodge, William....Murphy, Michael
Doley, Joseph....Sweeney, Garrett
Donnelly, Edward....Dunn, Peter
Donnelly, Mary....Kail, James
Donnelly, Patrick....McCusker, Hugh
Doran, John....Karr, James
Dorn, John....Scally, Martin
Dorsey, John....Weaver, Ferdinand
Doub, Frisby....Sneors, John
Dougherty, Daniel....O'Donnell, Dominick
Douglass, Robert....Miller, John
....Miller, Robert
Downey, Samuel....Schramyer, Henry
....Treehause, John
Downs, Charles....Bassett, George
Downs, Hamilton....Gillan, Dominick
Doyle, James....Murphy, Hugh
Doyle, William....Ketzel, Philip
....McCarthy, John
Drenin, Thomas....Maher, William
Duffey, John....Sweeney, Charles
Dunn, Thomas....Dunn, Edward
....Farrell, James
Earnst, George....Briesch, Frederick
....Cestenberger, Baltzer
Eber, John....Rupprecht, John
Eberly, Dr AK....Breneman, Christian
Egan, John....Brady, John
Eichelberger, Theabold....Haggerty, John
Einstein, Henry....Rosengerger, Henry
....Rosenstock, Abraham
....Rosenstock, Shemerin
Emerich, Lodwich....Boyer, George

298

Enstein, Henry....Starn, David
Enstein, Moyer....Arnold, Julius
Enstine, Henry....Hoff, Jacob
....Rosenfield, Wolf
Evans, Daniel....Awell, David
Evans, David....James, Josiah
Falm, Daniel....Reilly, Patrick
Farrell, James....Dunn, Thomas
....Magee, Thomas
Fechtig, Christian....Dick, John
....Rickert, Martin
....Schultz, John
Fechtig, George....Cosens, Henry
....Gettle, Daniel
Fellheimer, Mark....Weil, Jacob
Fichtig, Christian....Bolinger, Christian
Fiery, Joseph....Lindsey, James
Finnegan, J W....Williams, William
Finnigan, Wesley....Leibold, Frederick
Fishach, Frederick....Baker, Daniel
....Fogel, Adam
Fitzhugh, William....Toland, John
Fitzpatrick, Philip....Campbell, Michael;
..Paxton, Daviel; ..Shannon, Edward
Flater, Andrew....Gardner, George
Flemming, Thomas....Cunningham, William
Flong, David....Yetter, Christian
Fock, William....Sheehan, Martin
Foglesong, George....Fogleson, George
Folker, Abraham....Bowers, Jacob
Forrley, Robert....Philip, Richard
Fortney, Samuel....Morris, John
Fortune, William....Jones, Thomas
Fowler, Robert....O'Leary, Daniel
Fox, Alozin....Ward, James
Foye, Michael....Bellman, Henry
Freaner, Henry....Kolbacher, John
Freaner, William....Fleming, James
Freaver, William....Breudella, William
Frederick, John....Kattering, Frederick
Frederick County, MD....Fox, Ernst
....Harvey, Henry; ....Macrander, Jacob; ....McGurk, Patrick;
....Wickless, John
Freis, Michael....Schaffer, George
Freise, Michael....Maurioch, Leonard
....Wever, Michael
Freize, Michael....Brown, Philip
....Febrey, George

....Leiberlich, John
....Moore, George; ....Rice, Henry
Fridinger, Charles....Krokberger, Christian; ....Schubert, Henry
Fridinger, John....Semler, Lewis
Fries, Michael....Myers, Peter
Friese, Michael....Dunn, Lewis
....Heiges, Henry
....Houser, Andrew
Funk, Jacob....Cost, Andrew
Futerer, Lewis....Roan, Christopher
Futtem, Lewis....Warrenfeltz, John
Futter, Lewis....Powles, Peter
Gall, John....Durney, Richard
Ganahan, Peter....Farrell, John
....Hopkins, Patrick
Gapman, George....Weische, Ernst
Garrett, James....Barr, Christopher
Gassman, George....Brinkman, Adam
....Erbb, John
....Klenke, Ferdinand
....Witzenbachel, William
Gassman, Jacob....Fridinger, Charles
Gassman, William....Kimerly, Bernhard
Geager, Samuel....Leise, Geroge
Geedy, Samuel.... Barr, Christopher
Gelwicks, C F....Kloz, C W L
Gelwicks, Charles....Macrander, Jacob
Gelwix, Charles....Hoes, Hartman
Gilleeca, Thomas....Gillespie, Anthony
Ginaill, John....Nolan, John
Gladhill, James....Fox, Ernst
Goeghagan, Ambrose....Glockner, Devault
Goldsmith, Jacob....Myerly, Frederick
Good, William....Freiderici, Ernst
Goodending, John....Goodending, Daniel
Gossman, George....Treiber, Michael
Greiner, Frederick....Greminger, John
Grimes, William....Lynch, John
Grimminger, Benedict....Greiner, Frederick
Gross, Charles....Shank, Andrew
Grove, William....Welch, Michael
Gruber, Jacob....Beydel, John
....Molare, Joseph
Hagerman, Frederick....Hagerman, Henry; ....Spang, Nicholas
Hammen, Peter....Decker, Paul

Hammerslough, Lewis....Hess, Moritz
Harbine, Thomas...McCarthy, John
Harbuagh, Jonathan....Socks, George
Harlan, Silas...Lough, James
Harne, George....Weil, Jacob
Harris, Charles....Taning, William
Hartman, George....Hartman, Michael
Hase, Hartman....Anthony, Conrad
....Faith, Adam
Hawke, Christian....Freeman, Stephen
Hawken, William....Donnelly, Edward
Hawthorn, William....Black, James
....Hawthorn, Daivd
Hays, Samuel...Flemming, John
Heigas, George....Peater, John
Heiges, Henry....Varner, John
Heigis, Gotleib....Bucher, John
Heigis, Henry....Michael, John
Heil, Albert....Happel, Martin
Heimel, Justice....Gerbig, Heinrich
Heimel, Justus....Wagner, Leonhard
Heist, Lew....Schlotterback, William
Heist, Lewis....Berger, John
....Clement, John
....Dennhoefer, Simon
....Doarnberger, Adam
....Doarnberger, Henary
....Hartman, Michael
....Heil, Adelbert
....Lampas, Charles
....Lowe, Geroge
....Morgenstern, Georg
....Morgenstern, George
....Rosenberger, Henry
....Routh, George
....Schneider, Jacob
....Schuster, Robert
....Schweitzer, Christopher
....Schwoeble, Martin
....Sippal, Conrad
....Snyder, Philip
....Wellinger, Jacob
....Yetter, Calvin
Hellane, Margaret....Scheiler, John
Heller, David...Adams, John
Helzle, Frederick....Griese, Conrad
Hemphill, Joseph....Dickey, William
Henneberger, CW....Crowther, DW
Herbert, FD....Malone, James
Herbert, Stewart....Rosenstack, Christian

Herr, Adam....Herr, Lorenz
Herr, Lorenz....Herr, Adam
Herr, Rudolph....Reichard, Andrew
....Swarbrick, James
....Weistenhouse, Herman
Hershey, John....McCrary, John
Heuyett, Peter....Geimbel, John
Heysey, James....Heartzack, Laphara
Hickman, Thomas....Nolan, John
Hill, Samuel....Sleath, Gabriel
Himras, Christian....Stederly, Joseph
Hitt, Samuel....Patterson, John
Hogmire, Andrew....Sale, Philip
Hoover, John....Kimler, Frederick
....Lau, Christian
Hoover, Joseph....O'Conner, Patrick
Hopkins, Patrick....Ganahan, Peter
Horn, Peter....Horn, John
....Horn, Peter; ...Lucaphouse, Philip
Hotz, Martin....Bowers, Peter
Houser, F.T....Earle, Thomas
Howard, Henry....Brey, John
Howard, John....Swinger, Andrew
Howard, Thomas....Curley, Patrick
Hughes, James....Ganahan, Thomas
....Gavey, Michael
....Hinds, John
....Hoye, Lawrence
....Kearney, James
Hurley, James....Coleman, John
....Eagan, Thomas
....Grady, Thomas
....Hurley, Joseph
....Keenen, Patrick
....Malone, James
Huyett, Daniel....Weil, Jacob
Innes, Peter....Lewis, Robert
Iseminger, Michael....Munday, Patrick
James, Josiah....Evans, David
Johnson, Arthur....McKnutt, Thomas
Johnson, James....Kinsell, Patrick
Johnson, Samuel....Cameron, John
Johnston, James....Stewart, John
Johnston, Samuel....Fridinger, John
Julius, John....Ronch, Andrew
....Smith, Charles A
Kahn, Nathan....Bloom, Moses
....Driefus, Raphael
Kais, William....Tietias, Christian
Kaller, Henry....Leigler, John

Kausler, Jacob....Morgan, Edward
Keedy, John....Hess, Felix
....Ward, James
Kegney, John....Sharkey, George
Kelley, Timothy....Welch, Richard
Kelly, Patrick....Brien, Henry
....Degnan, Michael
Keppler, William....Fagan, John
Kershner, Andrew....Clarkson, Edward
....McCartin, Edward
Kidwell, John....Dunn, Henry
Kiernan, Michael....Brady, John
Kimler, Frederick....Hoover, John
King, Daniel....Menebrecker, John
King, John....Brining, Christian
....Smith, Charles
Kirkpatrick, John....McGlennan, James
Klink, Michael....Miller, Jacob
Knard, George....Rable, Frederick
Kneaning, Henry....Smith, George
Kneuss, Adolph....Bayhah, John
Knieniew, John....Menius, John
Knigton, Jacob....Stederly, Joseph
Knode, Henry....Weissman, William
Knode, Samuel....Weissman, William
Kyper, Henry....Baner, Michael
Lackner, George....Lackner, Charles
Lais, George....Schwoeble, Martin
Lampas, George....Wellinger, Christian
Laurence, Upton....Reiley, Peter
Lautz, Christian....Copich, Augustus
Leach, Samuel....Stine, John
Leeds, Alexander....Smith, Charles
Leibold, Andrew....Oker, John
Leinkand, Ulrich....Clay, Francis
....Eck, John
Leis, John....Geetle, Jacob
....Gross, Jacob
Leiter, George....Cameron, John
Leitz, John....Bunner, Marks
....Earnst, John
Levi, Abraham....Mohn, Nathan
Levi, Gerson....Arnold, Joseph
Levy, Gerson....Levy, Jacob
Libald, Andrew....Soner, Adam
Lighter, Reuben....Andrews, Stephen
Limbaugh, Catharine....Limbaugh, John
Loeb, Jacob.... Levy, Jacob
Loeb, Joseph.... Levy, Jacob
Loftus, Anthony....Buckley, Dennis
....Loftus, Owen
....McGurk, Patrick
....Smith, Michael
Logan, William....Shafer, Peter
....Stone, Henry
Long, Hez....Warrenfeltz, John
Long, James....Ropp, Charles
Luft, John....Loudenslager, Everhart
Lyday, Henry....Braiesch, John
Lyday, Samuel....Rice, Joseph
Lynch, Blackston....Kaiser, John
Macgill, Charles....Hahn, Earhart
Malomes, Hugh....O'Conner, Patrick
Mann, John....Keadey, George
Markoe, John....Bestard, William
Marnous, John....Williams, William
Marshall, William....Thompson, Adair
Martin, George....Stender, Michael
Martin, John....Heckman, Christian
Martin, Lewis....Smith, Christian
....Smith, Frederick
Masel, John....Presbaugh, Henry
....Rupprecht, John
Mash, Henry....Rake, John
Mason, John....Mash, Henry
Maxwell, James....Winter, Christian
McBride, Anthony....Goodenting, John
McCemas, Zacharius....Swartz, John
McClain, John....McClung, William
McCormick, William....McCormack, John
McCrary, Samuel....McCrary, John
McDowell, Nathan....Katzel, Christian
McGaughlin, John....Optan, John
McGinley, Patrick....Ranahan, Michael
McKinnly, Bernard....Curren, Peter
McKosker, Hugh....Barry, David
....McQuigan, Terrance
....Elliott, William
McLaughlin, James....Stone, Henry
McLaughlin, William....McGonnegal, Samuel
McNamara, James....Ragan, David
McQuade, James....McCosker, Hugh
....McCoskey, Michael
McSherry, Michael....Beard, George
McTighe, James....McTighe, Patrick
Merrick, Joseph....Leeger, Gotlieb
....Metzer, Henry
Middlekauff, George....Grady, Thomas

....Keenen, Patrick
....Murphy, Patrick
....Sweitzer, Frederick
....Taning, William
Miles, Elisha....Fate, John
...Leasure, Casper
Miller, Andrew....Glanmeyer, Joseph
Miller, Frederick....Miller, Christian
Miller, George....Sneors, John
Miller, John....Boesler, Gottleib
....Lantz, Nicholas
....Laughlin, Allen
....Mackey, Moses
....McBride, Francis
Miller, Mary....Miller, Conrad
Mirt, Christian....Hoffman, Henry
Mish, George....Swarbrick, James
Missouri....Barry, David
Mittag, Thomas....Kneiream, Henry
...Schreiver, Frederick
Monath, Lewis....Dennhoefer, Simon
Mongan, F F.....Ford, Franklin
Moore, Levi....Cullen, James
Moore, Thomas....Brien, Henry
Moore, William....Delzell, John
Moost, Christian....Ebbrecht, William
....Kacher, Conrad
Morris, Thomas....Ingram, Evan
Morrison, Henry....Murphy, Bartholam.
Morrow, William....Murphy, Christopher
Mumma, Abraham....Williard, Joseph
Mumma, Daniel....Sayles, William
Murphy, Hugh....Beckelharb, Philip
....Flinn, James
....Kaller, Henry
Murphy, John....Coleman, John
Myers, Jacob....Lungensland, John
....Ormston, John
Myers, Joseph....Hassett, John
Nail, Adam....Montz, John
....Socks, Henry
Nail, Andrew....Deitlehouse, Lewis
Neigh, Daniel....Leibold, Frederick
Neill, Alexander....Heely, Thomas
Nesbitt, I....Morter, Thomas
Nesbitt, Isaac....Kelly, Daniel
New York....Brown, William
....Ganahan, Peter
....O'Brien, Luke
....O'Neil, William

....Roux, Charles
....Scheffer, Justus
Newcomer, Abraham....Master, Conrad
Newcomer, Christian....Switzen, Henry
Newcomer, John....McGee, Samuel
Newcomer, Joseph....Soltan, Peter
Newcomer, Martin....Freyfogle, John
Newcomer, Samuel....McFarland, Samuel
Nigh, George....Padan, John
....Welsh, Richard
O'Brien, John....O'Brien, William
O'Brien, Luke.... Macken, Henry
....Dorley, Joseph
O'Leary, Daniel....O'Leary, Thomas
O'Neil, William....Dunn, Peter
O'Neill, William....Clarkson, Patrick
Obamdaffer, John....Smith, Henry
....Wickless, John
Olhoppel, William....Lannan, Francis
Oliver, Denton....Mahler, Valentine
P___? Sen, Michael....Plumenour, Nicholas
Padon, John....Laughlin, Allen
Park, John....Bunce, Richard
Patterson, John.... Higgins, Patrick
Pennsylvania...Coneaughton, Michael
....Dorley, Joseph
....Duffy, John
....Dunn, Thomas
....Fagan, John
....Farrell, Edward
....Farrell, James
....Farrell, John
....Greiner, Frederick
....Greminger, John
....Guth, Rev. Michael
....Hopkins, Patrick
....Kelly, Timothy
....Lewis, Robert
....McAvoy, David
....McCusker, Hugh
....McGuire, Owen
....O'Conner, Patrick
....Philbin, Michael
....Reiley, Thomas
....Shane, John
....Spang, Nicholas
....Stederly, Joseph
....Sweeney, Charles

....Vestris, Herman
....Weaver, Ferdinand
....Welch, Richard
....Woods, John
Perry, Charles....Goodenting, John
Peters, David....Battle, Michael
Phawan, Cornelius....Shultz, Augustus
Piper, Joseph....Hourande, Martin
Plumenous, Michael....Plumenous Jr, Michael
Polch, George....Garman, Adam
Pollard, John....Evans, John
....Little, Thomas
Post, Thomas....Parsons, Thomas
Powell, James....Martin, James
Price, William....Guth, Rev.... Michael
Protzman, Joseph....Myers, Baltzer
....Smith, Henry
Quinn, Michael....Whitney, Patrick
Randall, Vachel....Thompson, William
Rausler, Jacob....Leitz, John
Rauth, John....Burger, Conrad
....Burger, John
....Sampass, George
Rauth, Peter....Rosenstock, Abraham
Reagan, David....McNamara, James
Reamer, John....Vestris, Herman
Reichard, Valentine....Baker, Henry
Reid, John....Reilly, Patrick
Reidnour, John....Basten, James
Reilly, Bernard....Duignan, James
Remley, Henry....Gillchrist, Michael
Rench, Samuel....Speaker, Henry
Renner, Ignatius....Johnston, John
Repley, Horace....Frantz, John
Repley, John....Condy, James
Retburg, Jacob....Ludwig, Conrad
Rettburg, Jacob....Martin, Jacob
Rice, Henry....Hartnack, Conrad
....Thomas, John
Ridenaur, John....Blayer, John
Ridenour, J.E....Jones, Thomas
Ridenour, John....Kirkpatrick, John
Ridenour, Martin....Meister, Martin
Rigley, Everhart....Barth, Jacob
Ripley, Jacob....Powell, Michael
Ripley, John....Moran, Gerald
....Patterson, Robert
Robertson, John....Bruck, Charles
Robertson, Thomas....McCarthy, John

Roch, John....Pfoch, Henry
Roche, Nathaniel....Williams, John
Rodey, Patrick....Kelly, Timothy
Rohrer, David....Eckstein, John
....Harman, Peter
Roke, Terrance....Dyer, Henry
Roman, B Frank....McGuire, Owen
Rosenstock, Christian....Fecher, Joseph
Rouskulp, Upton....Lensbower, Peter
Rowland, Henry....Harvey, Henry
Rundlels, William....Weightman, Andrew
Rush, David....Doyle, James
....Faik, John
....Landrock, John
....Stine, Augustus
Russaamen, John....Boadman, Godfried
Russe, John....Foster, Henry
Sayles, John....Woods, John
Scheidar, Andrew....Puerschel, Adolph
Schindel, George....Kelly, Michael
Schlagel, Jacob....Laser, Anthony
Schleigh, John....Andres, Adam
Schlottbeck, William....Happel, Martin
Schlotterbeck, William....Deitlehouse, Lewis
Schmander, George...Ahlborn, Frederick
Schmouder, Philip....Popp, Andrew
Schnebly, Daniel....Christ, Henry
Schnebly, Henry....Donnelly, Patrick
Schnebly, John....McCarty, Owen
Schneider, Lawrence....McAvoy, David
....Motter, Francis
Schnell, Jacob....Paulder, John
Schnider, Lawrence....Shane, John
....Speaker, Henry
Seibert, Samuel....Kapp, Michael
Seitz, John....Butz, Jacob
....Schuh, Hugo
....Shilling, Joachim
Sensil, Martin....Nazarenns, Frederick
Shack, Frederick....Messell, John
....Oertel, George; ....Strobal, John
Shafer, George....Russe, John
....Smith, Deitrick
Shafer, John....Fraker, George
Shaffner, Martthias....Miller, Jacob
....Kirkpatrick, Samuel
....Landen, Francis
Shank, Andrew....Gerloch, Justus

Sharkey, George....Kegney, John
Sharor, Jacob....Haupt, John
Sheckles, Richard....Holsaple, Henry
Shehan, Cornelius....Can, Patrick
....Murphy, Patrick
Sherman, John....Limberg, Frederick
....Ries, Peter
Shirp, George....Briesch, John
Shoof, Adam....Brown, William
Shriver, John....Simpson, John
Shrode, Jacob....Schmutz, Abrahm
Shultz, Augustus....Obandaffer, John
Sias, George....Eagan, Thomas
....Lampas, Charles
....Sweitzer, Frederick
Sibald, Andrew....Deitrick, George
Sicafhouse, Philip....Horn, Peter
Simler, Conrad....Danzer, William
Small, Harvey....Yetter, Christian
Smander, Philip....Krantz, John
Smith, David....Gross, John
....Schreiver, Frederick
Smith, Dr. J.F....Boswell, F C
....Waxman, August
Smith, George....Deitrick, Elizabeth
....Diederick, Francis
....Ford, Franklin
....Keefe, Nicholas
Smith, Gotleib....Miller, Christian
Smith, Henry....Baker, George
Smith, John....Beard, Robert
....Kinsell, Patrick
Smith, Joseph....Bish, Henry
Smith, Michael....Geiger, Norbert
Smith, Otho....Waxman, August
Smith, Willima....Lensbower, Peter
Smouder, Philip....Miller,George
Snider, Anthony....McCullock, John
Snider, Lawrence....Sweitzer, Jacob
Socks, George....Wellinger, Christian
Softus, Anthony....Philbin, Michael
South, Daniel....Denholdm, Charles
....Stock, Frederick
Spessard, Samuel....Sheehan, Martin
Spickler, John....Crilly, William
Spielman, Henry....Forthman, Frederick
Spohr, Henry....May, George
....Zelch, Henry
Sprecher, Nelson....Crilly, William
Spring, Peter....Hinkle, John

Stake, Edward....Hoye, Lawrence
Steffle, John....Goldsmith, Jacob
Stewart, John....Rogers, Joseph
Stover, Frederick....Long, Abraham
Stull, Otho....Rice, Patrick
Stutts, Gotleib....Ernde.... Lewis
Summers, George....Summer, John
Swartz, John....Kemman, Charles
Swearingen, John....Ormston, John
Sweeney, Charles....Brown, William
....Higgins, Patrick
....Hughes, James
....Ryan, William
Sweeney, P........Fagan, John
Sweeny, Charles....Tagert, Hugh
Sweitzer, Jacob....Burmgart, Casper
....Renner, Ignatius
....Schnider, Lawrence
Swinger, Andrew....Swinger, Daniel
....Ulrich, John
Swir, Abram....Danheiber, Isaac
Swope, Caspar....Anhalt, Nicholas
Swope, Elijah....Summers, George
Swope, Jacob....Most, Christian
Tagert, Hugh....Taggert, Thomas
Tall, Samuel.... Graffe, Jacob
Tedrick, John....Marlauer, Samuel
Terry, Robert....Agen, John
Tev, William.... Rose, Abraham
Thompson, Jesse....Gillan, Dominick
Thompson, Samuel....Hayword, William
Touson, William....Kremer, Frederick
Towson, William....Hose, John
Treiber, John....Leimmerman, Andrew
Treiber, Michael....Russaamen, John
....Kloz, C W L
Treiber, Michel....McGlennan, James
Tricher, Michael....Notteler, Jacob
Trieher, Gotlieb....Keifer, Theobold
Turner, Joshua....Cowen, Timothy
Uleis, John....Enstine, Henry
Ulerich, Charles....Sachs, Philip
Ullrich, Charles....Sochs, John
....Socks, George; ....Socks, John
Ulrich, Charles....Helena, John
Ulrick, Charles....Fridinger Jr, John
....Klenke, Ferdinand
Ulrick, John....Socks, George
Ulrick, Samuel....Adams, John
Vinson, Thomas....Lannan, Francis

Virginia....Dyer, Henry
....Frantz, John
....Gillespie, Anthony
....Kearney, James
....Reiley, Peter
....Ryan, William
....Tais, William
Vogle, Adam....Breitweiser, Geroge
Votteler, Jacob....Peyhl, Joseph
Wagner, William....Wagner, Leonard
Wagoner, Leonard....Gerbig, Heinrich
War, Civil....Berger, John
....Burger, Conrad
....Cameron, John
....Clement, John
....Collins, Oscar
....Dennhoefer, Simon
....Feilman, Frederick
....Kemman, Charles
....Leibold, Frederick
....Martin, James
....Miller, Christian
....Schreiver, Frederick
....Smith, Charles
....Sweitzer, Frederick
....Weissman, William
....Williams, William
Ward, James....Fox, Alozins
Waters, Henry....Scally, Martin
Waters, Reuben....Welsh, Henry
Ways, Charles....Gates, William
Weaver, Adam....Helena, John
Weis, John....Enstine, Henry
Weiss, Charles.... Earle, Thomas
West Virginia.... Dyer, Henry
....Frantz, John
....Gillespie, Anthony
....Kearney, James
....Reiley, Peter
....Ryan, William
....Tais, William
Westerhouse, Herman....Brill, George
Westinhouse, Herman....Feligner, Frederick
Wever, Adam....Spor, Henry
Whisner, Henry....Stock, Frederick
Whitney, Patrick....Fernsner, Lewis
....Ryan, Patrick
Wiles, David....Facksberger, Adam
Wiles, John....Burger, Conrad

....Burger, John
....Puerschel, Adolph
....Sampass, George
Williams, Otho....Reckley, Sebastian
Williams, Thomas....Ryan, Timotheus
Williamson, William....Hanly, Luke
Wilt, Christian....Redtberg, Jacob
Winder, Henry....Stinemetz, George
Winters, Christian....Rafitz, Francis
Wirt, Christian....Hoffman, Henry
Wise, Richard....Loudenslager, Everhart
....Snell, George
Yetter, Christian....Yetter, Calvin
Yingling, Allen....Crowther, D.W.
Young, John....Ragers, Arthur
Zellar, Jacob....Swartz, Peter
Zellers, Samuel....Schubert, Henry

Maryland, Washington County, to wit: m 463

At a County Court of the Fifth Judicial District of the State of Maryland, begun and holden at Hagerstown, in and for the County aforesaid, on the *fourth* Monday of *March*, being the *23d* day of the same month, in the year of our Lord, eighteen hundred and forty *six*;

PRESENT:
The Hon. *John Nesbitt* Esq. Chief Judge.
" Hon. Thomas Buchanan, } Associate Judges.
" Hon. Richard H. Marshall,

Thomas Martin, Shff.   Isaac Nesbitt, Clk.

In the record of proceedings of the same Court, amongst others is the following, to wit:

BE IT REMEMBERED, That now here on this *fifth* day of *October*, Eighteen hundred and forty *six*, *John Fridinger* in open Court, having made his application before the said Court, to become a citizen of the United States, and having at the same time made oath on the Holy Evangely of Almighty God, that it is his bona fide intention to become a citizen of the United States, and renounce forever, all allegiance and fidelity to any foreign Prince, Potentate, State or Sovereignty whatsoever, and particularly to the *King of Bavaria*. and also having made oath that he emigrated to the United States three years previous to his arriving at the age of twenty-one years; and also that it has been his intention for the last three years, to become a citizen of the United States, as required by law, establishing a uniform rule of naturalization, and prays to become a citizen of the United States; and it appearing to the satisfaction of the Court, here, on the testimony of *Samuel Johnslow* a citizen of the United States, sworn in open Court, here, that *John Fridinger* hath resided five years and upwards last past, within the limits and under the jurisdiction of the United State; and also resided one year and upwards last past, within the State of Maryland, that during that time, he has behaved as a man of good moral character, attached to the principles of the Constitution of the United States, and well disposed to the good order and happiness of the same; and the said *John Fridinger* having declared on oath, that he will support the Constitution of the United States, and that he doth absolutely and entirely renounce all allegiance and fidelity to any foreign Prince, Potentate. State or Sovereignty whatsoever, and particularly to the *King of Bavaria*; The Court thereupon admit the said *John Fridinger* to naturalization, as a citizen of the United States.

WASHINGTON COUNTY, TO WIT:

I hereby certify that the foregoing is a correct copy, taken from the record of proceedings of the County Court aforesaid

In Testimony Whereof, I hereunto subscribe my name and affix the seal of the said County Court, this *5th* day of *October* eighteen hundred and forty *six*   Isaac Nesbitt, Clk.

www.ingramcontent.com/pod-product-compliance
Lightning Source LLC
Chambersburg PA
CBHW062001220426
43662CB00010B/1190